The Encyclical Pacem in Terris And World Peace

A Muslim Perspective

Omar Sillah, Ph.D.

ISBN-13: 978-0692131480 (Omar Sillah)

ISBN-10: 0692131485

Printed in the United States of America

First printing: October, 2020

Editor: Kristen Rattanamongkhoune

Cover design: Mory Rivera

Interior design: Bintou Susso

CONTENTS

Foreword...ix

Introduction x

CHAPTER I.. 1

   1.1   Peace and War in World Politics 1

   1.2 Peace in Concept, Content and Definition....................................... 2

   1.3 War Definitions, Concepts, Content and Context 7

   1.4 The Background of *Pacem in Terris*: Historical and Contextual Analysis 12

   1.4.1 The Cuban Missile Crisis 16

   1.4.2 The Superpowers' Bipolar Equilibrium during the Cold War......... 19

   1.4.3 International Security 38

   1.4.4 Risk of Nuclear War 41

   1.4.5 Pope John XXIII's Position to Diminish the Risk of Nuclear War in the World
   47

CHAPTER II 55

   2.1 The Content of Pacem In Terris... 55

   2.2 Order and Disorder in Creation 60

   2.3 The Human Kind, Human Rights, Violence and War among the Human Kind. 66

   2.3.1 Human Rights 69

   2.3.2 The protection of Human Rights as a pre-requisite for Peace 75

   2.3.2.1 The Right to Live and Right to Life 78

   2.3.2.2 The Rights to Moral and Cultural Values.................................. 80

2.3.2.3 Right to Worship God According to one's Conscience 81

2.3.2.4 Right to choose freely one's State in Life 83

2.3.2.5 Economic Rights 85

2.3.2.6 The Right of Meeting and Association... 90

2.3.2.7 The Right to Emigrate and Immigrate... 91

2.3.2.8 Political Rights 92

2.4 Violence and War among Humankind 95

2.4.1 Realpolitik 97

2.4.2 Pacifism 98

2.4.3 Just War.. 99

2.5 Persons, Families, People and States: How to Structure New Relations to
Guarantee Peace 104

2.5.1 Persons, Families, People and States.. 104

2.5.2 How to Structure New Relations between Persons, Family, People and States
in Order to Guarantee Peace.. 108

2.6 Truth and Dialogue Guaranteed in the Quest for Justice and Peace in an
International System.. 112

2.6.1 Truth... 114

2.6.2 Dialogue 117

2.6.3 Justice 120

2.6.4 Active Solidarity.. 122

2.6.5 Interdependent Cooperation 125

2.6.6 Freedom and Liberty 132

2.6.7 Development and Democracy as the Guarantors for the International Stability
and Peace.. 137

2.6.7.1 Defining Development 137

2.6.7.2 Defining Democracy.. 140

2.7 Reduction of Arsenals as the First Step to Peace................................. 148

Chapter III 155

3.1 Responses and Reactions to *Pacem in Terris* 155

3.2 Some of the Criticisms against *Pacem in Terris*................................. 156

3.3 Some of the Eulogies for *Pacem in Terris*.. 160

3.4 The Influence of *Pacem in Terris* in Christianity............................... 166

3.5 The Influence of *Pacem in Terris* in the Muslim World 169

3.6 An Islamic Perspective on the Peace Appeal of *Pacem in Terris* 175

3.6.1 Militarist-Militant Perspective.. 189

3.6.2 Nonviolence Perspective 195

3.6.3 Defensive Perspective.. 203

3.7 An Islamic Perspective on Some of the Specific Principles of *Pacem in Terris* with Regard to the Establishment of World Peace 211

3.7.1 Human Rights.. 211

3.7.2 Right to Emigrate and Immigrate 219

3.7.3 An Islamic Perspective on Political Rights with Regard to World peace...... 224

3.7.4 An Islamic Perspective on Relations Between Individuals and Public Authorities with Regard to World Peace 226

3.7.5 An Islamic Perspective on Relations Between States with Regard to World Peace.. 231

3.7.6 An Islamic Perspective on Truth as A Principle of International Relations .. 235

3.7.7An Islamic Perspective on Justice as a Principle of International Relations .. 236

3.7.8 An Islamic Perspective on Active Solidarity as a Principle of International Relations 239

3.7.9 An Islamic Perspective on Reduction of Arsenals in International Relations 242

3.7.10 An Islamic Perspective on Freedom as a Principle of International Relations 246

3.7.11 An Islamic Perspective on the Relationship of Men and of Political Communities with the World Community 249

3.8 Role and Nature of the States in International Relations: Positions from Christianity and Islam Doctrine and Practices 253

3.8.1 Positions from Christian and Islamic Doctrine and Practices on the Role and Nature of the States 255

Conclusion 265

Bibliography and References 271

About the Author 297

Foreword

This book is about Omar Sillah's views on the world's leading religions, Islam and Christianity with regards to establishing world peace. While some people are pessimistic about religions' positive roles and contribution in establishing peace at personal, familial, societal, national and international levels, Sillah, on the contrary, is always optimistic about positive roles and contributions that religions can play in establishing peace at these levels. In this book, Sillah acknowledges the effect of the two religions on the lives of their followers and he laid perspectives from Catholicism and Islam on the realization of world peace by expounding on *Pacem in Terris*, the encyclical of one of twentieth century's short-lived and most influential Catholic Popes. Alongside the encyclical, he unearthed opinions of some Muslim jurists and Islamic scholars both divergent and convergent on the subject matter. He further included the views of some Orientalists about Islam with regards to peace.

The uniqueness of this book is that it is the single Islamic response so far to a Christian Catholic encyclical of such magnitude in the Muslim- Christian dialogue and relatedness, camaraderie and solidarity, cooperation and collaboration towards the realization of world peace on religious and moral values and principles. The book has given an insight into the harmonious relations between both religions and how they can work together for a better world in which all can live and enjoy and die in peace. This book opens the horizon and complements the understanding when it comes to religious tolerance and the role that each religion continues to play in world peace. A Must Read.

Austin S. Fallah

Minnesota, USA

Introduction

Peace and war are part and parcel of world politics. Human history, culture, experience and civilisation were formed within the tensions of peace and war to the extent that in peace time, people always tried to secure themselves from another war or prepare themselves for another war. In periods of peace, states, as legal entities, also tried to secure themselves from war or prepare for war. States need peace, security and stability, especially in their relations among one another. International transactions in trade and commerce through international networks such as communications and transportation would be hindered in times of war, instability and crisis. Hence, the main preoccupations of international relations are peace, security and stability at the international level. This is expected to be facilitated through cooperation, collaboration, coordination and interdependence among the states. For this reason, the world political community has formed a worldwide political institution with authority and legitimacy in the entity of the United Nations to facilitate and coordinate the task of establishing peace and security in the world.

Pope[1] John XXIII in Encyclical[2] *Pacem in Terris* (1963) appealed for the task of establishing world peace. The task rightly belongs to international relations and is

---

[1] Within the Roman Catholic Church, the Pope is considered the successor of Peter, Vicar of Christ.

[2] An encyclical is a solemn document that the Pope addresses to the faithful and to his public. An

expected to be manifested in and coordinated by the United Nations, the world's biggest political organisation. The main concern of *Pacem in Terris* was to address the tension existing between the two nuclear powers of the bipolar, or Cold War era (1946-1989): the USA and the USSR. Among the concerns of *Pacem in Terris* was the establishment of interstate relations on truth, justice, liberty and charity, and, through good governance, encouragement of cooperation, collaboration and active solidarity. Within this background, I will try to approach *Pacem in Terris* as a document with political concerns in international systems and try to examine it from an Islamic perspective as well. From this Islamic perspective, I will try to analyse whether and how Islam can also be a factor in enhancing international relations. I will try to investigate whether or not Islam also preoccupies itself with international peace, security and stability, cooperation, collaboration and active solidarity (dimensions of peace portrayed in *Pacem in Terris*) and whether Islam encourages world universal international relations to be based on truth, justice and freedom, or if its concern is being

---

Encyclical is not   necessarily a document *ex-cathedra* or dogmatic; neither is it a pastoral constitution nor a legislative text. Rather, it is an essential pastoral document which occupies itself ordinarily with doctrinal, moral, socioeconomic and political or any other pertinent disciplinary matters. In comparison with the dogmatic pronouncement made by the, 'extraordinary infallible *magisterium*' the encyclical has less authority. Its content is neither definitive judgment nor infallible unless clearly marked otherwise. However, Vatican II's dogmatic constitution on the church stresses obedience to the authentic teaching office of the Roman bishop "even when he is not speaking *ex-cathedra*". (Dogmatic Constitution on the Church Lumen Gentium (1964), pp. 25).

limited to Muslim inter-state relations.   About 45 states of the United Nations are Muslim majority states and Muslims form about "23.4% of the estimated 2010 world population of 6.9 billion"[3], and if current trends continue, Muslims will make up 26.4% of the world's total projected population of 8.3 billion in 2030"[4]. Against this background, Muslim's contributions to world peace, security and war are significant to the international community and international relations.

In the thesis I use the phrase "a perspective from Islam" or "an Islamic perspective", to mean a Muslim's mental vista in relation to the understanding and interpretations of the Qur'an and *Sunnah*. For Muslims, the Qur'an is the eternal word of God unbound by time, space, or geography, revealed to the universal humankind through God's universal final prophet Muhammad. However, one's understanding and interpretations of this eternal book and one's understanding and interpretations of the *Sunnah* of its universal and final prophet are neither eternal nor final, nor are they universally articulated in the same way everywhere at every place and time. As such, any understanding, interpretations and perspectives on the Qur'an and *Sunnah* are largely drawn from orientations, experiences, backgrounds, customs and cultures of the interpreters this could be referred to as the spirits of interpretation or the spirits of hermeneutic. Since the

---

[3]The Pew Forum on Religion and Public Life, The Future of the Global Muslim Population, Projections for 2010-2030. Accessed on 05-05 -13 at http://www.pewforum.org/The-Future-of-the-Global-Muslim-Population.aspx

[4] *Ibid.*

orientation, experience, background, customs and cultures of universal humankind are not universally the same, I chose the phrase 'an Islamic perspective'. There are many Islamic perspectives, and the perspective I present here may fit and may not with others' perspectives of Islam due to the spirits of interpretation and hermeneutic. My perspective is "*an* Islamic perspective" and not "*the* Islamic perspective".

CHAPTER I

1.1 Peace and War in World Politics

War and peace have always existed and still exist in world politics. It is a historical reality that relations among states are sometimes characterized by conflict orchestrated by national interest, survival and power. Some of these conflicts end up in peace treaties, while others do not. Based on the estimation of Victor Cherbulliez, from 1500 B.C.E. to 1800 C.E., about eight thousand peace treaties were signed. Each of them sought to secure permanent peace, and they lasted an average of two years[5]. Africa, for instance, in both her pre- and post-colonial era, has undergone various series of conflicts from tribal and ethnic to politics and religions, and from economic to social. From 1960 to 2006 Africa

---

[5] Stevens Bailey Henry, The Recovery of Culture, Harper and Brothers, New York, 1953, p. 221.
See also Erich Fromm, The Sane Society Routledge and Kegan Paul, London, 1956, p. 4

experienced about 40 wars, claimed over 10 million lives and caused over 10 million displaced persons[6]. In the past two decades alone, Africans have experienced human suffering on a scale unparalleled in human history[7]. Millions of Africans have been effected or killed either by deadly conflict or by conflict-related elements. The Nigerian (Biafra), Angolan, Burundian, Congolese, Liberian, Rwandan, Sudanese, Sierra Leonean, and Eretria-Ethiopian wars are well-known examples of this[8].

Peace also has existed in major epochs of world politics. Many countries in the world experience longer periods of peace than war. Intermittent wars do occur that disrupt peace, but once peace is disrupted, efforts are always made to restore it.

1.2 Peace in Concept, Content and Definition

Before making any attempt to define 'peace', I should first look at the idea of peace as a concept and content. Peace as a concept is not very paradoxical. It is universally accepted that peace does exist somewhere at some time. Every individual is expected to desire to live in peace, and it is accepted that every

---

[6] Adebajo Adekeye, "*Towards A New Pax African: Building Peace in Africa, discussion on Building Sustainable Peace*". Accessible at http://www.trustafrica.org/documents/adebajo.pdf

[7] *Levitt Jeremy, "The Law on Intervention: Africa's Path breaking Model*." In Global Dialogue Volume 7 Number 1–2, Winter/Spring 2005, http://www.worlddialogue.org/content.php.

[8] Twentieth Century Atlas: Death Tolls and Casualty Statistics for the Twentieth Century, http://users.erols.com/mwhite28/warstat3.htm. - See also *Levitt J. "The Law on Intervention: Africa's Path breaking Model"* In Global Dialogue Volume 7 Number 1–2 Winter/Spring, 2005.

human being needs peace. Peace is the culmination of all human yearnings, desires and achievements. "Peace on Earth—which man throughout the ages has so longed for and sought after" [9] can testify to this.

The content of peace is somewhat paradoxical. Peace as a concept is somewhat amorphous, thus, it comprises different things to different people and keeps evolving from one generation to another. In Cicero's time (+/- 60 B.C.E.), peace was regarded to contain salutary, liberty and tranquillity[10]. Liberty and tranquillity were the desired content of peace within the culture and the time of Cicero. His general idea was that peace can only exist in the realm of liberty. For Augustine of Hippo, peace must contain simplicity of heart, love and charity[11]. The content of Peace for Thomas Aquinas must be tranquillity of order[12]. In some African traditional religions, peace entails tranquillity, prosperity, unity, health, cordiality and fertility in human beings, animals and land[13]. Peace is seen in some African religions as fullness of life and wellbeing in the physical world. As such, any action that is capable of hindering another from attaining the fullness of life is

---

[9] John XXIII, *Pacem in Terris*, 1963, AAS 55, (1963), the preamble.

[10] See The Orations of Marcus Tullius Cicero, Volume 4, trans. By William Duncan , Sidney's press 1811 Original from the University of California Digitized Feb 26, 2008 page 653

[11] See Aquinas Thomas, "Commentary on the Gospel of John," 14, lecture 7, n.1962, http://dhspriory.org/thomas/John14.htm, (22/11/10)

[12] Aquinas Thomas, Summa Theologiae 2a-2ae, Black Friars 1975, pages 197 -199

[13] Igwebuike Onah Godfrey, "*The Meaning of peace in African Traditional Religion and Culture*". Accessible at www.afrikaworld.net/afrel/goddionah.htm (09/10/10)

considered a breach of peace[14].

The content of peace then is the striving for perfection of moral, religious, social, spiritual and material needs of the society in an undisturbed and growing blessed life in the absence of war and violence. Peace therefore involves a condition of tranquillity, security, safety and order within an individual, society or a state and among states or countries. Peace requires freedom from civil disturbance, from physical, mental and emotional torture, disquiet and oppression. It also includes harmony in personal relations, a state or period of mutual concord between governments or people, a pact or agreement for cessation of hostilities between those who have been at war, in a state of enmity or about to be so[15].

From the above mentioned understanding we can see some differences in regard to the content of peace, depending on cultures, generations and philosophies. Moreover, the content of peace may change in accordance with changing times. In our times, the link between social economic growth and peace is considered essential. Pope Paul VI gives an appropriate interpretation of peace in his time by saying: "Knowing, as we all do, that development means peace these days, what man would not want to work for it with every ounce of his

---

[14] Godfrey Igwebuike Onah, "*The Meaning of peace in African Traditional Religion and Culture*", www.afrikaworld.net/afrel/goddionah.htm (09/10/10).

[15] http://www.merriam-webster.com/dictionary/peace

strength"[16]. We will discover more of these differences as we explore the definitions of peace by the experts in peace studies.

There is a strong link between concept and definition. In fact one defines a thing according to one's concept of a thing. Hence some of the things mentioned in the concept of peace can be mentioned when defining peace. Cicero defined peace as *"tranquilla libertas,"* which one might translate as "liberty in tranquillity" or "undisturbed freedom". Augustine of Hippo defined it as "a calmness of mind, a tranquillity of soul, simplicity of heart, a bond of love and a fellowship of charity"[17]. Thomas Aquinas defined peace as *"tranquillitas ordinis"* meaning "tranquillity of order"[18]. Baruch Spinoza defined peace in these words : "Peace is not an absence of war, it is a virtue, a state of mind, a disposition for benevolence, confidence, justice"[19]. Galtung defines it as : "freedom from war and strife; freedom from conflict, disturbances, and disorder. It is a situation within a group of people in which no organized use or threat of violence takes place"[20]. For Samuel Rayan, peace is "the proper ordering of life, both personal and social. It is constituted by a web of right relationships among persons and

---

[16] Paul VI *Populorum Progressio* 1967 , AAS 59 (1967), pp. 87.

[17] Aquinas Thomas, Commentary on the Gospel of John, 14, lecture 7, n.1962, http://dhspriory.org/thomas/John14.htm, (22/11/10)

[18] Thomas Aquinas, Summa Theologiae 2a-2ae, Black Friars 1975, pages 197 -199

[19] See http://www.anvari.org.

[20] Galtung, J. Friedenforschung, 1968, p.531 as quoted by Samuel Rayan (1991). *"International models of peace making"* in Holy Land-Hollow Jubilee, God Justice and the Palestinians, (eds), Naim Ateek and Michael Prior, London, UK, 1991.

communities, and by the resultant harmony, growth, development, well-being and prosperity"[21]. For Duchrow and Liedke, peace is "the protection and liberation of creation and the realization of more justice among people"[22].

An integral and holistic peace should, more-or-less, encompass all the above definitions. It should address social, political, economic and spiritual issues, the fulfilment of which are prerequisites for peace at individual, familial, communitarian, state and interstate levels. Peace in the 21st century should be an integral and holistic peace that benefits both big and small countries, the powerful and weak, rich and poor. Peace, which is geographically complete and reaches all nations and citizens regardless of their creed, colour and sex, includes the proper ordering of life in a network of right relationships with responsibilities and duties at personal, social, political and economic levels and companied with spiritual growth, development, well-being and prosperity of people. This is enshrined in the 1948 Universal Declaration of Human Rights.

However, peace at the interstate level is different from peace at the inter-human level. At the interstate level, realists during the Cold War era assumed that, due to their nature, states could hardly live in peace in the anarchical sphere of international affairs without the overriding fear of Mutual Assured Destruction

---

[21] Rayan, Samuel, "*International models of peace making*." In Holy Land Hollow Jubilee, God Justice and the Palestinians, (eds), Naim Ateek and Michael Prior, London, UK, 1991.

[22] Duchrow, Ulrich, and G. Liedke, *Shalom – Biblical Perspectives on Creation, Justice & Peace*, WCC, Geneva World council of Churches' Press, Geneva, (1987/1989), p.112.

(MAD). Peace at the interstate level can also be realized through *pacta sunt servanda* on international treaties, laws and convention. At the inter-human level, humankind can only live in peace when inner satisfaction of individual human being is realised and this affects their external relations with one another. In the human perspective, there is human individual peace and human communal peace. The place of human individual peace is in one's self, whereas for communal peace to be maintained, the rights and dignity of others must be safeguarded as well. That is, there has to be perpetual defence and protection of others' needs and dues. Individual peace and happiness are linked with respect to the peace and happiness of others in the community. Communal peace can be established when there is active cooperation to remove ignorance, poverty, hatred, extremism and fanatical behaviour within the community.

1.3 War Definitions, Concepts, Content and Context

War can be defined as a "condition that equally permits two or more hostile groups to carry on struggle by armed force"[23].   Michael Walzer defines it as

---

[23] Wright Quincy, A Study of War, University of Chicago Press, 1964, vol.11Chapter XVII, p. 685. Also accessible at http://www.archive.org/stream/studyof warvol11001580mbp#page/n43/mode/1up). Hedley Bull defines it as "organized violence carried out by political units against each other"(Hedley Bull, The Anarchical Society. A Study of Order in World Politics, Second Edition Columbia University Press, New York, 1977, 1995, p.178). For Bull "Violence is not war unless it is carried out in the name of a political unit" *op.cit.*

follows: "War is a world apart, where life itself is at stake, where human nature is reduced to its elemental forms, where self-interest and necessity prevail. Men and women do what they must to save themselves and their communities, and morality and law have no place. *Inter arma silent leges*: in time of war the law is silent"[24]. However, this definition of war, where ethic and moral laws do not apply to warring situations ('*inter arma silent leges*'), does not suit the definition of war in the 21st century. Through the past century there have been and still are international treaties and conventions undertaken by states: that a combatant must not attack Red Cross or Red Crescent operations, prisoners must not be killed; hospitals must not be bombed, civilians must not be killed indiscriminately, etc. A war between states has rules based on *ius gentium. Ius ad bellum* justifies the decision to undertake a war, *ius in bellum* dictates the right conduct in prosecuting war, *causa iusta* gives the just cause, and *sit intention / bellantium recta* provides for a right intention in case of war.

Nevertheless, just war theory is also very difficult in practice in regard to war between states. Hence, it can also be seen as a theoretically high standard set to be realized in management of modern warfare among states, but it is not yet perfectly realized in modern warfare. Just as Ottaviani put it: "They were meant.... to cover warfare of a special kind, that [is] between mercenary armies,

---

[24] Walzer Michael, Just and Unjust Wars: A Moral Argument with Historical Illustrations, Basic Books, United States of America 1977, p. 3.

and not our mammoth warfare which sometimes entails the total downfall of the nations at grips [sic] with each other; the principles, in fact, cannot be applied in the life of modern nations without doing serious damage to the particular peoples involved"[25].

In *Pacem in Terris*, the word 'war' is seen as a "grip of constant fear", "horrific violence" and "the appalling slaughter and destruction"[26]. Some of its resources, such as "atomic weapons", "nuclear weapons" and "armaments"[27], are also mentioned therein to describe the kind of mass destruction that war can do. A war has both tactical and strategic dimensions. The tactical dimension is the conventional one with physical soldiers on the battle field using machine guns and other conventional weaponry. The strategic dimension means the use of biological weapons of mass destruction (WMD), nuclear weapons and similar tools to realise the goal. For Field-Marshal Montgomery "Strategy is the art of distributing and applying military means, such as armed forces and supplies, to fulfil the ends of policy. Tactics means the dispositions for, and control of, military forces and techniques in actual fighting. Put more shortly: strategy is the

---

[25] Ottaviani Alfredo, "*A Classic Text The future of offensive war.*" Accessible at www.oikonomia.it/pages/febb/classica.htm). Also accessible at http://www.catholicapologetics.info/morality/warfare/justwar.htm

[26] *Pacem in Terris*, 1963, AAS 55, (1963), pp.111

[27] *Ibid.*, pp.109-112

art of the conduct of war, tactics the art of fighting"[28]. Carl von Clausewitz defined military tactics and strategy by saying "Tactic is the art of using troops in battle; strategy is the art of using battles to win the war"[29]. B. H. Liddell Hart defined strategy as "the art of distributing and applying military means to fulfil the ends of policy"[30].

Although war sometimes is perceived to be a necessary condition for peace, it can also be seen as the mother of all evils. It is war that can lead to orphan-hood, widow-hood, stranger-hood, famine, enslavement, prostitution, insecurity, instability, destruction of wealth and health, and above all death. A war anywhere is a threat to peace everywhere. The consequences of war are never limited only to the culprits, they also affect the innocents[31]. "If one were to chart the percentage of combatants killed as opposed to non-combatants it would be apparent that the trend in warfare was toward the killing of more non-combatants

---

[28] Montgomery Viscount, A History of Warfare, Collins. London, 1968 as cited in (http://en.wikipedia.org/wiki/Military_strategy)

[29] As cited in "Napoleon's tactics", in Napoleon's Strategy and Tactics. Accessed at on 15-05.-13 See also "Military strategy" see http://en.wikipedia.org/wiki/Military_strategy#cite_note-5

[30] Liddell Hart, B. H. Strategy London:Faber, 1967 (2nd rev ed.) p. 321 as cited in (http://en.wikipedia.org/wiki/Military_strategy#cite_note-5)

[31] "And fear *fitna* (tumult or oppression, discord, sedition, civil war) which affected not in particular (only) those of you who do wrong: and know that God is strict in punishment " Qur'an Al-Anfaal/The Booty/ 8:25

than combatants"[32]. During World War I, civilian casualties made up fewer than 5% of all casualties. Today, about 75% or more of those killed or wounded in wars are non-combatant civilians[33]. As such, efforts should be made from familial, ethnic, communitarian, state, regional and international levels to avoid war and establish world peace. This is the approach Pope John XXIII used in *Pacem in Terris* by addressing all aspect of relations among human beings, between human beings and their societies, and between states.

War as content, its means and objectives, are succinctly worded by Carl Von Clausewitz as "war is nothing but duel on a large scale. Countless duels go to make up war, but a picture of it as a whole can be formed by imagining a pair of wrestlers. Each tries through physical force to compel the other to do his will; his immediate aim is to throw his opponent in order to make him incapable of further resistance. War is thus an act of force to compel our enemy to do our will. Force, to counter opposing force, equips itself with the invention of art and science. Attached to force are certain self-imposed, imperceptible limitations hardly worth mentioning, known as international law and custom, but they scarcely weaken it. Force- that is, physical force, for moral force has no existence save as expressed in the state and the law- is thus the means of war; to impose our will on the enemy

---

[32] Bemporad, Jack, *"Norms of War in the Jewish Tradition,"* In World Religions and Norms of War, UN Press, 2009.

[33] Benjamin, Judy A, *"Conflict, Post-Conflict, and HIV/AIDS — the Gender Connections Women, War and HIV/AIDS: West Africa and the Great Lakes"*, http://www.rhrc.org/resources/sti/benjamin.html, 21/11/10).

is its object. To secure that object we must render the enemy powerless; and that in theory, is the true aim of warfare. That aim takes the place of the object, discarding it as something not actually part of war itself"[34]. The contexts of war are usually conflicts of interests, mistrust, Paranoia and fear. For instance, an action of the culprit can be mitigated if it occurred in a context where the conflict of interest, mistrust, paranoia and fear is absent from both sides.

Although the philosophy of war has always been found in human history, its techniques differ from time to time. It is the modern nuclear war technique that frightens people all the more. "In modern sense "war" means the use of firearms, chemicals and nuclear weapons for striking and of steam, gas and electrical engines for military movement by land, sea or air"[35]. As war techniques differ so does its doctrines and theories.

1.4 The Background of *Pacem in Terris*: Historical and Contextual Analysis

Pontifical history has long been associated with the work for peace. It did not begin with *Pacem in Terris*[36]. Pope Benedict XV (1914-1922) on, August 1,

---

[34] Carl von Clausewitz On War, edited by Michael Howard and Peter Paret, Introductory Essay by Peter Paret Et al. Princeton University Press, 1976 edition, p.75.

[35] Wright, Quincy, op.cit. 1964, p. 25.

[36] Pontifical text of Pope John XXIII delivered on the April 11, 1963

1917, issued an exhortation for peace to the rulers of the belligerent powers involved in World War I and he despised war as an irrational massacre[37]. His detest for the war also manifested in his 1920 Papal text on the theme of peace and Christian reconciliation "Peace, the most beautiful task of God"[38]. According to Cardinal Peter K.A. Turkson, President of *Pontificium Consilium De Iustitia Et Pace*, "this was the first encyclical entirely devoted to the theme of peace"[39]. Following the footsteps of his predecessor, Pope Pius XI dedicated his 1922 encyclical to "the peace of Christ in the kingdom of Christ"[40]. Pope Pius XII (1939-1958), whose pontificate contemporized World War II and whose pontifical motto according to Cardinal Peter K.A. Turkson was *"Opus iustitiae pax"* (peace is the fruit or work of justice), issued and broadcast many papal addresses and messages for the promotion of "civil rights, social peace, and unity among nations"[41]. Pope Pius XII insisted that: "The calamity of a world war, with the economic and social ruin and the moral excesses and dissolution that accompany it, must not on any account be permitted to engulf the human race for

---

[37] Benedict XV's exhortation to the rulers of the belligerent powers, August 1, 1917, AAS 9 (1917) 418.

[38] See Turkson K.A Peter (Cardinal), *"Pacem in Terris* as a living document". In *Pontificium Consilium De Iustitia Et Pace*, 29 May 2012.

[39] *Ibid.*

[40] *Ibid.*

[41] *Ibid.*, See also Compendium of the Social Doctrine of the Church, 2004, pp. 93

a third time"[42]. And that: "Nothing is lost by peace; everything may be lost by war"[43].

Furthermore, Pope Pius XII issued ten encyclicals[44], on war and peace, including his post 1945 epoch: *Optatissima pax,* 18 December 1947, on prescribing public prayers for social and world peace, and *Summi maeroris,* 19 July 1950, on public prayers for peace[45], among others.

In 1956, three of them were communicated in the space of eight days: *Luctuosissimi eventus,* 28 October 1956, urged public prayers for peace and freedom for the people of Hungary; *Laetamur admodum,* 1 November 1956, renewed the exhortation for prayers for peace for Poland, Hungary and the Middle East; and *Datis nuperrime,* 5 November 1956, lamented the sorrowful events in Hungary and condemned the ruthless use of force by the Soviet Union[46].

Pope John XXIII (1958-1963), succeeded Pope Pius XII in a Cold War bipolar world. That bipolar system in 1962 produced the Cuban missile crisis. This event was not the least cause generating the conditions for *Pacem in Terris,* the ultimate Papal encyclical of Pope John XXIII. The Pope was very active in

---

[42] Pius XII's broadcast message, Christmas 1941, AAS 34 (1942) 17.

[43] *Pacem in Terris*, pp.116.

[44] Turkson K.A. Peter, *op. cit.* p. 1.

[45] Turkson, *op. cit.* p. 1-2, footnote included.

[46] *Ibid.*

contributing to defuse the Cuban missile crisis[47].

One of the architects, and an immense contributor to the encyclical *Pacem in Terris*, was the then Monsignor Pietro Pavan. His contribution to the encyclical can be deduced from the statement in Pope John XXIII's diary as quoted by Gianni Manzone: "I then dedicated the whole evening, about three hours, to the reading of the Easter encyclical in preparation, done for me by Monsignor Pavan: 'Peace among men in the order established by God and so: in truth, in justice, in love, in freedom', a typed manuscript of 111 pages. I read it all, alone, calmly, attending to the tiniest detail, and I find the work really well constructed and well done. The last part, then: the 'Pastoral exhortations' are in the fullest resonance with my spirit. I begin to pray for the impact of this document, which I hope will come out at Easter and will be reason for great edification"[48].

---

[47]*Ibid*. p. 2.

[48] The Italian version: "*Ho poi consacrato tutto il vespro, oltre tre ore, nella lettura dell'enciclica di Pasqua in preparazione, fattami da Mons. Pavan. Pace tra gli uomini nell' ordine stabilito da Dio, e cioè nella verità, nella giustizia, nell' amore e nelle libertà. Manoscritto di 111 pagine dattiloscritte. Ho letto tutto, solo con calma e piissimamente. Lo trovo un lavoro assai ben congegnato e ben fatto. L' ultima parte poi dedicata ai richiami pastorali, è in pienissima rispondenza con il mio spirito. Comincio a pregare per l'efficacia di questo documento e spero che uscirà a Pasqua e sarà motivo di grande edificazione*". See Gianni Manzone '*La pace della "Famiglia umana" nell' enciclica Pacem In Terris*' in Costruire L'unità della famiglia umana, l' orizzonte profetico del cardinale Pietro Pavan (1903- 1994). A cura di Lino Bosio e Fabio Cucculelli, edizioni Studium Roma 2004, page 76, and also Melloni Alberto, *Pacem in terris*: *Storia dell'ultima enciclica di Papa Giovanni,* Bologna: Laterza, 2010, pp. 51-52, quoting *Pater amabilis: Agende del pontefice* (1958-1963), p. 482.

1.4.1 The Cuban Missile Crisis

According to Cardinal Pietro Pavan, the 1962 Cuban missile crisis was one of the immediate events that motivated Pope John XXIII to promulgate the encyclical *Pacem in Terris*; and to encourage mediation, between John Kennedy (the first Catholic president of United States of America) and Nikita Khrushchev (the premier of the Soviet Union who was supposed to be an atheist[49]), to achieve a peaceful settlement. The Cuban missile crisis was triggered by NATO's deployment of missiles in Turkey[50], a secular state in a country with a majority Muslim population. This directly threatened the European part of the Soviet Union including Moscow. In reaction to the deployment of missiles in Turkey, Premier Khrushchev publicly expressed his resentment over NATO's public and official decision to deploy Jupiter missiles in Turkey. Then he tried to deploy the USSR's missile launchers in Cuba[51]. Afterwards, the Soviets obtained the

---

[49] Manzone Gianni, 'La pace della "famiglia umana" nell' enciclica *Pacem In Terris*' In *Costruire l'unità della famiglia umana, l' orizzonte profetico del cardinale Pietro Pavan* (1903-1994). A cura di Lino Bosio e Fabio Cucculelli, edizioni Studium Roma 2004, page 75.

[50] This was done in 1961 'by a special decision of the NATO Council'. See Jim Hershberg Anatomy of a Controversy Anatoly F. Dobrynin's Meeting With Robert F. Kennedy, Saturday, 27 October 1962 Reproduced with permission from the Cold War International History Project Bulletin issue 5, Spring 1995 Dobrynin's Cable to the Soviet Foreign Ministry, 27 October 1962. Accessed at http://www.gwu.edu/~nsarchiv/nsa/cuba_mis_cri/moment.htm

[51] http://ativor.info/usnissileturkey.html see also Hershberg Jim, "*Anatomy of a Controversy Anatoly F. Dobrynin's Meeting With Robert F. Kennedy, Saturday, 27 October 1962*". In the Cold War International History Project Bulletin issue 5, Spring 1995.

removal of NATO's missile from Turkey[52].

The missile crisis was not just a mere crisis between any other states; it had an effect on the balance of world security and international relations at the time. It was between the two principal nuclear powers, or the two superpowers at the two extreme ideological poles, both with a considerable Christian population: communist USSR and liberalist USA- both were competing to influence and lead the rest of the world.

On October 22nd, 1962, President Kennedy informed the international community about the Soviet Union's secret missile base in Cuba[53]. Kennedy called upon Khrushchev "to halt and eliminate" what he called a "clandestine, reckless and provocative threat to world peace" from Cuba and to "join an historic effort to end the perilous arm race and transform the history of man"[54]. This declaration was followed by his ordering of a naval quarantine of Cuba in order to prevent Soviet Union ships from completing the missile launchers in Cuba[55].

The United States military forces were at the peak of their readiness for an

---

[52] Jim Hershberg , *"Anatomy of a Controversy Anatoly F. Dobrynin's Meeting With Robert F. Kennedy"*, Saturday, 27 October 1962. In Cold War International History Project Bulletin issue 5, Spring 1995 Dobrynin's Cable to the Soviet Foreign Ministry, 27 October 1962. Accessed at http://www.gwu.edu/~nsarchiv/nsa/cuba_mis_cri/moment.htm

[53] Garthoff L. Raymond , Reflections on the Cuban missile crisis, the Brookings Institution Washington DC, USA, 1998, p. 55.

[54] *Ibid.*, p. 55.

[55] Garthoff Raymond, *op. cit*. 1998, p. 58.

all-out assault, "shifting from limited military preparations under wraps to open all-out build-up of the contingent air-strike and invasion forces of the U.S. Army, Navy, Air Forces and the Marines"[56] on one hand. On the other hand, Soviet Union commanders in Cuba and submarines and navy were also alerted to defend against any eventual USA invasion of the island[57].

The description by Jim Hershberg of the Cuban missile crisis shows how close the world was to nuclear war: "If the Cuban missile crisis was the most dangerous passage of the Cold War, the most dangerous moment of the Cuban missile crisis was the evening of Saturday, 27 October 1962, when the resolution of the crisis— war or peace—appeared to hang in the balance. While Soviet ships had not attempted to break the U.S naval blockade of Cuba, Soviet nuclear missile bases remained on the island and were rapidly becoming operational, and pressure on President Kennedy to order an air strike or invasion was mounting, especially after an American 'U2' reconnaissance plane was shot down over Cuba that Saturday afternoon and its pilot killed. Hopes that a satisfactory resolution to the crisis could be reached between Washington and Moscow had dimmed"[58].

Against this historical background, *Pacem in Terris* was promulgated six months after the Cuban missile crisis and two month before the death of the Pope

---

[56] *Ibid.*, p. 60.

[57] *Ibid.*

[58] Hershberg Jim, *op. Cit.*

John XXIII himself[59]. Certainly, the nuclear war was averted due to the personal decisions and actions of Khrushchev and Kennedy, influenced by the mediation of Pope John XXIII.

1.4.2 The Superpowers' Bipolar Equilibrium during the Cold War.

In *Pacem in Terris*, Pope John XXIII refers to the equilibrium (or M.A.D.) theory in international relations by stating : "There is a common belief that under modern conditions peace cannot be assured except on the basis of an equal balance of armaments and that this factor is the probable cause of this stockpiling of armaments. Thus, if one country increases its military strength, others are immediately roused by a competitive spirit to augment their own supply of armaments. And if one country is equipped with atomic weapons, others consider themselves justified in producing such weapons themselves, equal in destructive force"[60].

This bipolar system between two superpowers implied that each acknowledged the other in searching for strategic allies or alliances in economic, military, political and cultural interests, and even for ideological influence with one of the two superpowers or poles (i.e. USSR and USA) in a bid to avoid undue

---

[59] Manzone Gianni, *op. Cit.* 2004, p. 75.

[60] *Pacem in Terris*, *op. cit.*, pp. 110

domination by the other in international affairs. It also could trigger equilibrium in international relations and politics. The superpowers' bipolar equilibrium could also be seen as actively redistributing power in which the leading two states, such as USA and USSR, strived for more economic, military, and cultural influence internationally or regionally. The global political realities of the post-World War II era were mainly polarized by two states that led to the emergence of a two polar system headed by the former Soviet Union on one hand and the United States of America on the other hand, hence the phrase bipolar system. From 1947 to 1989, the security of the world from nuclear weapons was dependent on the bipolar system. The *modus operandi* of the bipolar system in international politics was neither constant nor monolithic. Depending on times, situations, circumstances and interest, it could be soft[61], hard[62] or smart (powers)[63]. Less antagonism, more governability, less anarchy, and higher rates of

---

[61] Soft power is the skill or the art of achieving one's goal through persuading and co-optioning others or the use of any intangible assets such as an attractive personality, values, institutions, and a vision that are seen as legitimate or having moral authority in achieving one's goal. See Joseph S. Nye, *"Soft Power, Hard Power and Leadership"* 10/27/06 accessed at http://www.hks.harvard.edu/netgov/files/talks/docs/11_06_06_seminar_Nye_HP_SP_Leadership. pd on 7/11/2011

[62] Hard power is the use of coercive action through military threats, economic pressure, assassination, subterfuge and hoodwink based on intimidation on others in order to achieve one's goal.

[63] Smart power, is the aptitude to combine hard and soft power in achieving one's goal. Or as Hilary Clinton put it: "the full range of tools at our disposal -- diplomatic, economic, military, political, legal, and cultural -- picking the right tool, or combination of tools, for each situation".

power hegemony and *infungibility* were the features of that bipolar system. Moreover, bipolarity could be more stable than multi-polarity[64]. Flexibility of shifting friendship did not exist in the bipolar system. Enmity fluctuation, diffusion of danger, blurring of responsibilities and obscurity in defining vital interest and many security threats are all checked in a bipolar system. A bipolar system causes great powers to mainly depend on themselves militarily. This, according to Kenneth Waltz, "is almost entirely true at the strategic nuclear level, largely true at the tactical nuclear level, and partly true at the conventional level"[65]. Since the international system is anarchic with the combination of many nuclear powers, each seeking to survive in the absence of a single super power to protect one state against the other, each has to struggle on its own for its self-preservation and survival; this sense of preservation and survival lead the states to form poles or blocs in order to join in balance against rather than to be left at the mercy of the more powerful rivals.

Polar systems can be uni-polar, bipolar, tri-polar, or multi-polar. Before World War II, the polar system in world international relations was multi-polar

---

Accessible at http://www.cbsnews.com/stories/2009/01/13/politics/main4718044.shtml accessed on 9/11/11

[64] See Walt M.Stephen, International Relations: One World, Many Theories, in Foreign Policy, No. 110, Special Edition: Frontiers of Knowledge. (Spring, 1998), pp. 29-32+34-46.

[65] Waltz Kenneth, *"The Spread of Nuclear Weapons: More May Better,"* In Adelphi Papers, Number 171 (London: International Institute for Strategic Studies, 1981). Accessed at http://www.mtholyoke.edu/acad/intrel/waltz1.htmon 21/02/2012.

system. Antagonism, aggression, anarchy, high rates of *fungibility* of power, less power hegemony and less governability were the characteristics of that multi-polar system.

At that time, the leaders of two blocks (the USA and the former USSR) were all armed with nuclear weapons. The concept of Mutually Assured Destruction (MAD) in the event of nuclear war between the two blocs was palpable, hence, the Cold War emerged. In the Cold War era, the efforts had been made by the USA to check the USSR's influence without inducing an all-out war with the USSR. For this reason, the "Containment Policy" formulated by George F. Kennan became the basis of United States strategy during the Cold War[66] to check the Soviet Union's influence in the world. This policy as described: "must be that of a long-term, patient but firm and vigilant containment of Russian expansive tendencies"[67]. And also to counteract or neutralize "Soviet pressure against the free institutions of the Western world" via "adroit and vigilant application of counter-force at a series of constantly shifting geographical and political points, corresponding to the shifts and manoeuvres of Soviet policy"[68]. 'Containment policy' was intended to "promote tendencies which must eventually find their outlet in either the break-up or the gradual mellowing of Soviet

---

[66] See 'Containment Policy. at http://history.state.gov/milestones/1945-1952/Kennan

[67] See http://history.state.gov/milestones/1945-1952/Kennan

[68] *Ibid.*

power"[69]. Economic assistance, such as the Marshall Plan, and "psychological warfare" were each intended to "roll back" the spread of Soviet influence[70]. "It is possible to say that each succeeding administration after Truman's until the collapse of communism in 1989, adopted a variation of Kennan's containment policy and made it their own"[71]. Such variations, *inter alia*, included the U.S.A. joining in a network of multilateral or bilateral alliances and organisations, such as Northern Alliance Treaty Organisation (NATO), Organization of American States (OAS), South East Asia Treaty Organization (SEATO), Central Treaty Organization (CENTO), and The Australia, New Zealand, United States Security Treaty (ANZUS), each intended to hinder the influence of the Soviet coalition.

The history of the Cold War is that the USA and the USSR strove for allies in their bids to extend, consolidate, annex and protect the network coverage of their political, economic, cultural and ideological influences, specifically from 1947 to the collapse of Berlin Wall on 9th November 1989. However, the nature and the role of economic regionalism constituted a relevant element in diminishing the successive Cold War-era tensions. Regionalism helped to impose equilibrium on the imbalances created during the Cold War. Regionalism contributed to the

---

[69] *Ibid.*

[70] This phrase was notably put forward by John Forster Dulles who "declared during the 1952 election campaign that the United States' policy should not be containment, but the "rollback" of Soviet power and the eventual "liberation" of Eastern Europe". See containment at http://history.state.gov/milestones/1945-1952/Kennan.

[71] See http://history.state.gov/milestones/1945-1952/Kennan

repair of the shattered old European power that had been present in every continent. It also worked to remedy the inability of either the hegemonic governance by states, like the UK, USA, and USSR, or 'universal governments', like the League of Nations and United Nations, to guarantee a universally accepted and balanced system[72] in the realization of world peace.

Moreover, the Non-Aligned Movement (NAM),[73] which originated in Bandung, Indonesia in 1955, was formally founded in 1961 at Belgrade, Yugoslavia, and confirmed in 1964 in Cairo, Egypt[74], blazed a trail midway between the two blocs. NAM was intended to be an alternative to the two blocs at the time, however, it could not wield significant influence on international affairs in the post-Second World War period due to the military, economic and technological edge the USA and USSR had over the NAM member countries. As such, the bipolar system remained the dominant one in the international politics at the time of Pope John XXIII. Hence, NAM failed to be an instrumentally potent force in defining the structure and content of international relations. Therefore, no effective third bloc or polar existed to match the military, economic and political powers of the USA and USSR, so international relations were left to the

---

[72] Luigi Troiani, *Regionalismi Economici e Sicurezza*, Franco Angeli, 2000, Milano, Italy, p. 18.

[73] The coining of the phrase 'Non-Alignment' itself was attributed to the Indian diplomat and statesman V.K. Krishna Menon in 1953, at the United Nations. See Muhammad Khalid Ma'aroof, *Afghanistan in World Politics (A Study in Afghan US relations),* Gian Publishing House Delhi , India 1987, P. 75.

[74] Muhammad Khalid Ma'aroof, *op. cit.* 1987 P. 13.

theory of the superpower's bipolar equilibrium and the concept of Mutually Assured Destruction.

The theory of equilibrium[75] in international politics and relations refers to the balance or equal distribution of political, military and economic powers and influences between competing superpowers. The attraction of a power equilibrium stems from the assumption that unbalanced power is dangerous. "Prudent states that are at a disadvantage in the balance of power will (or at least should) form an alliance against a potentially hegemonic state or take other measures to enhance their ability to restrain a possible aggressor. Also, one state may opt for a self-conscious balancing role, changing sides as necessary to preserve the equilibrium. A balance of power policy requires that a state moderate its independent quest for power, since too much power for one state may bring about self-defeating reactions of fear and hostility from other states"[76].

Gilpin, in dealing with equilibrium, based his model on five core propositions:

1 "An international system is stable (i.e., in a state of equilibrium) if no state believes it profitable to attempt to change the system.

---

[75] Theory of equilibrium was first used in economics and its concern is the study of demand and supply "fundamentals in an economy with multiple markets, with the objective of proving that all prices are at equilibrium. The theory analyzes the mechanism by which the choices of economic agents are coordinated across all markets". (See www.investopedia.com.)

[76] Griffiths Martin and O'Callaghan Terry, *International Relations : The Key Concepts,* Routledge, London and New York, 2002 P. 12.

2. A state will attempt to change the international system if the expected benefits exceed the expected costs (i.e. if there is an expected net gain).

3. A state will seek to change international system through territorial, political, and economic expansion until the marginal costs of further change are equal to or greater than the marginal benefits.

4. Once an equilibrium between the costs and benefits of further change and expansion is reached, the tendency is for the economic costs of maintaining the status quo to rise faster than the economic capacity to support the status quo.

5. if the disequilibrium in the international system is not resolved, then the system will be changed, and a new equilibrium reflecting the redistribution of power will be established"[77]. This statement is similar to that of Waltz who said: "The expectation is not that a balance, once achieved, will be maintained, but that a balance, once disrupted, will be restored in one way or another. Balances of power recurrently form"[78].

The philosophy of the superpowers' bipolar equilibrium itself was born out of a necessity to maintain security and peace in interstate relations. The primary aim of international relations is to avert wars and to have peace and security, and, if

---

[77] Robert Gilpin, War and Change in World Politics, Gambridge University Press, 1989, pages 10-11.

[78] Kenneth Waltz, Theory of International Politics, Addison-Wesley Company, Inc, 1979, USA, p.128. Accessed at https://www.scribd.com/doc/40007016/Kenneth-Waltz-Theory-of-International-Politics

necessary, even to wage war for the re-establishment of peace and security. For instance, the 1991 Gulf War was waged by the international community for the purpose of restoring the existence and sovereignty of a member state that had been cancelled by another member state. This is done for the purpose of establishing security, order and peace in the international spheres. Since peace is central to international relations, great efforts have been made and are still in the making to maintain international peace.

The theory supporting the superpower's bipolar equilibrium in international relations is called realism[79]. The principal challenge to realism and the concept of

---

[79] "Classical realism has usually been grounded in a pessimistic theory of human nature, either a theological version (for example, Saint Augustine and Reinhold Niebuhr) or a secular one (for example, Machiavelli, Hobbes, and Morgenthau)". See Ole R. Holsti, *op. cit.* One of the cores of a realist theory is that selfishness and egocentric conduct are not restricted to wicked individual leaders but are basic to *homo politicus.* (Ole R. Holsti, *op. cit.*). Realism perceives the anarchical international scene as a struggle for power among self-centered states and is largely pessimistic about the possibility of eradicating conflict and war among states in international relations. Realism upholds the states' persisting inclination towards conflict against each other in an anarchic system as natural. (Walt M Stephen., *International Relations: One World, Many Theories,* in Foreign Policy, No. 110, Special Edition: Frontiers of Knowledge, Spring, 1998, pp.29-32+34-46). Hence, in the absence of central authority to settle disputes among states, the principle of 'survival of the fittest' prevails. For classical realism this behavior of states is rational since states are driven by the logic of the 'national interest', manifested in survival, security, power, and relative capabilities. Differences in national interest could not affect this logic and motives among nations; hence, it becomes the base logic for national policymakers to formulate aggressive national interest policy. Thus, classical realists, "unlike 'idealists' and some 'liberal internationalists,' [...] view conflict as a natural state of affairs rather than as a consequence ... of historical circumstances, evil leaders, flawed sociopolitical systems, or inadequate international understanding and education". (Ole R. Holsti, *op. cit*).

MAD came from a broad family of liberal theories[80]. Realism seemed to be the

---

Nevertheless, classical realism has been criticized on the following basis: human nature as it is can be used as a satisfactory explanation of international relations. If human nature explains war and conflict, what then would prevent it from explaining peace and cooperation? Due to this loophole some realists have extended their theories beyond human nature to the structure of the international system to explain state behavior. (Robert Jervis, *System Effects: Complexity in Political and Social Life*. Princeton, NJ: Princeton University Press, 1997). They see inconsistencies in the classical realists interplay of concepts such as "power," "national interest," and "balance of power" (See Ole R. Holsti, *Theories of International Relations*, footnote 9) and between realism's fundamental descriptive and prescriptive elements. For instance, "on the one hand, nations and their leaders 'think and act in terms of interests defined as power,' but, on the other, statesmen are urged to exercise prudence and self-restraint, as well as to recognize the legitimate interests of other nations"(Ole R. Holsti, Theories of International Relations. Pages 4-6).

[80] Liberalism identifies several ways to pacify the conflicting tendencies in international relations: one aspect of liberalism argues that economic interdependence and cooperation would discourage states from using force against each other because warfare threatens their own prosperity. Another aspect, often associated with former President of United States of America Woodrow Wilson, assumed the spread of democracy as the key to world peace, saying that democratic states were inherently more peaceful than authoritarian states. In his Fourteen Points, world peace hinged on certain principles such as: open covenants of peace, diplomacy shall always be frank and public, all economic barriers have to be removed, fair trade conditions among all peaceful nations be established, reduction in armaments, an adjustment in colonial claims in the interests of both native peoples and colonialists, and freedom of the seas navigation, "self-determination" for those oppressed minorities, a world association of nations that would provide a system of collective security for all nations. (See President Woodrow Wilson's 14 Points (1918) at http://avalon.law.yale.edu/20th_century/wilson14.asp).

Another aspect of liberalism/idealism, more recent than the two above, claims that international institutions, such as the International Energy Agency and International Monetary Fund, could help overcome egotistic state characteristics principally by motivating states to forego immediate gains for the greater benefits of enduring cooperation. This view is associated to Robert Jervis, George Quester and Steven Van Evera. See (Stephen M. Walt, *International Relations: One World, Many Theories*. In Foreign Policy, No. 110, Special Edition: Frontiers of Knowledge,

Spring, 1998, pp. 29-32+34-46). The classical liberal theories that call for extension of domestic rule of law to international affairs *inter alia* generated The Hague Peace Conferences, International Court of Justice, League of Nations, Washington Naval Treaty, and Kellogg-Briand Pact. (see Moravcsik Andrew, *"Liberalism and International Relations Theory"* paper No.92-6, accessible at http://www.princeton.edu/~amoravcs/library/liberalism_working.pdf).

Liberalism is criticized for its support of international institutions and global society as idealist and utopian, hence unrealistic. Classical liberals are also criticized for their proposal to abolish or outlaw war and the arms race, their promotion of disarmament and implementation of collective security as proposals that lack the Machiavellian "effective truth of things" and can be refuted as "imaginary republics and monarchies that have never been seen or have been known to exist" (Machiavelli, The Prince, Ch.XV). The critics label liberalism as 'idealist', 'utopian', 'legalist', 'moralist' and 'reductionist'. Realist claimed that Equilibrium generated no World war, and branded liberalism as the caldron where Nazism, Fascism, Communism, the Spanish Civil War, Italian Ethiopian conquest and colonialism in general were generated till the explosion of World War II. Moreover, the Kantian view of a world state would be irreconcilable with diverse ethnic, national, linguistic and religious loyalties of humanity, hence, its imposition would be as bad as that of the totalitarian, autocratical, tyrannical and dictatorial state. Furthermore, the application of uniform international and universal laws regulating the affairs of humanity in both internal and external affairs would also be totalitarian inspired, because nation-states and their people do not share identical customs, cultures, or religions and have no common internal and or external constrains or values.

One challenge to these two theories comes from the Orthodox Marxist theory that assumed capitalism as the central cause for international conflicts. For the original Marxist theory, capitalist states battled each other as a consequence of their incessant struggle for profits and battled socialist states because they saw in them the seeds of their own destruction. (Stephen M. Walt, *op.cit.*). These radical traditions/Marxism called for the transformation of the entire system of state relations. Radical approaches, until the 1980s, were the main challenge to the classical realist and liberal theories. While realism and liberalism took the state system to be responsible for condition of war and peace, Marxism offered a different explanation for international conflict and a proposal for internationally transforming the existing international order. (Walt Stephen *op. cit.*) However, the existence of economic, intelligence and military cooperation among the capitalist industrial nations also discredits the assumption that capitalism is the source of international conflict and war. Furthermore, the discrepancies, divisions and bickering amongst the communist and socialist countries disprove the hypothesis that only socialism and communism are the core of peace and

dominant theoretical tradition throughout the Cold War period[81]. This domination was due to its provision of explanations for war; its provision for a helpful *cadre* in understanding the collapse of the post-World War I system. It explained the international order in the face of serial aggressions in the Far East and Europe. It was used to understand World War II and the Cold War, and also was helpful in understanding alliances, imperialisms, obstacles to cooperation, and other international phenomena. Its stress on competition between the states was

---

cordiality between states.

The works of Thomas Hobbes, Grotius, Rousseau, Clausewitz, and Kant provide bases for philosophical and intellectual theories concerning the study of contemporary international relations and its academic discipline, manifested as Realism, Liberalism and Marxism. (Williams Phil, et al, Classic Readings And Contemporary Debates in International Relations, Wadsworth Publishing Company 2005, Page 6-9.) See also Hedley Bull, *op.cit.* 1977, Chapter 2). The principal question for these theories is the causes of war and the conditions of peace. Neither Realism, nor Liberalism, nor Marxism alone has solution to world's many problems nor are they each homogeneous schools; all have their neo-versions; to indicate all of their neo-versions is beyond the scope of this thesis as such we briefly presented their traditional positions above. None of them is intrinsically and inherently bad or good, worst or best, and each has elements that can be good and bad for particular circumstances. Marshalling the best in all of them can provide opportunities to construct a productive synthesis out of them. Furthermore, all of these schools are the products of human thought and humans are limited and imperfect as such the hybrid and 'positive mapping' could be useful. By 'positive mapping' we mean taking all of the positive elements of the entire schools and beyond and using them according to the demands and necessities of the common good.

[81] Walt Stephen M., *op. cit.*. Ole R. Holsti op. cit. See also Robert O. Keohane, *"Theory of World Politics: Structural Realism and Beyond"*, in Neo Realism and its Critics, New York: Columbia University Press, 1986, page 158. As cited by Andrew Moravcsik, In *"Liberalism and International Relations Theory"* paper No.92-6

consistent with the central features of the American-Soviet rivalry[82].

Advocates of realist theories stressed the supremacy of their perspectives over liberalism/idealism in understanding the politics of deterrence, containment, alliances, crises, and wars. For them, nuclear weapons in connection to Mutually Assured Destruction (MAD) contributed to the "long peace" between major powers[83].These protagonists claim that Mutual Assured Destruction (MAD) is another way of preventing the re-occurrence of war. MAD is based on the assumption that, if the two states have equal enough weaponry to be mutually capable of destroying each other even after absorbing a first-strike attack, they will never stage war against each other because waging war on the other can lead to the destruction of the aggressor if the defender retaliates[84] equally.

Both liberalism and realism were alluded to in *Pacem in Terris*: "Everyone must sincerely co-operate in the effort to banish fear and the anxious expectation of war from men's minds. But this requires that the fundamental principles upon which peace is based in today's world be replaced by an altogether different one, namely, the realization that true and lasting peace among nations cannot consist in the possession of an equal supply of armaments but only in mutual trust. And we are confident that this can be achieved, for it is a thing which not only is dictated

---

[82] Walt M Stephen, *op. cit.*

[83] For more on this see John Lewis Gaddis, "The Long Peace: Elements of Stability in the Postwar International System," *International Security* 10 (Spring 1986): 99-142.

[84] see http://www.fact-index.com/m/mu/mutual_assured_destruction_1.html 20/11/2010

by common sense, but is in itself most desirable and most fruitful of good"[85]. And that the relationships between the states "must likewise be harmonized in accordance with the dictates of truth, justice, willing cooperation, and freedom"[86]. *Pacem in Terris* also stated that: "relations between States, as between individuals, must be regulated not by armed force, but in accordance with the principles of right reason: the principles, that is, of truth, justice and vigorous and sincere co-operation"[87]. These statements are liberal concepts.

The equilibrium or realist theory is also referred to in *Pacem in Terris* in this statement: "There is a common belief that under modern conditions peace cannot be assured except on the basis of an equal balance of armaments and that this factor is the probable cause of this stockpiling of armaments. Thus, if one country increases its military strength, others are immediately roused by a competitive spirit to augment their own supply of armaments. And if one country is equipped with atomic weapons, others consider themselves justified in producing such weapons themselves, equal in destructive force"[88]. However, this above mentioned common belief of Pope John XXIII is in agreement with some realist positions such as that of Mearsheimer. Mearsheimer assumed that: "the absence of war in Europe since 1945 has been a consequence of three factors: the bipolar

---

[85] *Pacem in Terris,* pp.113.

[86] *Ibid.,* pp. 80.

[87] *Ibid.,* pp.114.

[88] *Ibid.,* pp. 110.

distribution of military in the continent; the rough military equality between the states comprising the poles in Europe, the United States and Soviet Union; and the fact that each superpower was armed with a large nuclear arsenal. Most importantly, hyper-nationalism helped cause the two world wars, the decline of nationalism in Europe since 1954 has contributed to the peacefulness of the post war world"[89].

Nevertheless, Pope John XXIII can be in agreement with Mearsheimer on the possibility of 'hyper-nationalism' to be one of the causes of war when he said: "It is worth noting, however, that these minority groups, in reaction, perhaps, to the enforced hardships of their present situation, or to historical circumstances, frequently tend to magnify unduly characteristics proper to their own people. They even rate them above those human values which are common to all mankind, as though the good of the entire human family should subserve the interests of their own particular groups. A more reasonable attitude for such people to adopt would be to recognize the advantages, too, which accrue to them from their own special situation."[90] He asked minority groups to enter into "some kind of association with the people in whose midst they are living, and learn to share their customs and way of life." And stated that minority groups "must not sow seeds of disaffection which can only produce a harvest of evils, stifling the

---

[89] Brown E. Michael, Theories of War and Peace: An International Security Reader, MIT Press, Cambridge Mass. 1998, pages 4-5.

[90] *Pacem in Terris,* pp. 97.

political development of nations"[91].The fact remains that the resolution of international instability, negative crisis and conflicts are a dominant preoccupation of the international relation theories and Pope John XXIII also reflects this concern in *Pacem in Terris*.

Another historical era in the historical background of *Pacem in Terris* was the Cold War. The word 'cold' here indicates the existence of a high level of tension between the USA and former USSR with the threat of escalation to nuclear conflict that allegedly restrained the confrontation and prevented a 'hot' war between the two; and the word 'war' here designates the tension, arm conflict and conflict of interest, and a 'zero-sum game relationship' between the Soviet Union and United States of America[92]. "Cold War" therefore refers to an epoch in international affairs that describes the overall relationship between the United States and Soviet Union from the end of World War II to the fall of Berlin Wall[93].

---

[91] *Ibid.*, pp. 97.

[92] See Griffiths Martin and Terry O'Callaghan, *op. cit.* 2002.

[93] Three years into Pope John XXIII's pontificate, the Berlin Wall (which was a remote consequence of Yalta and Potsdam conferences 4th -11th February, 1945 and 16th July - 2nd August 1945, respectively) on 13th August 1961, was built by the USSR to mark the division between Western and Eastern influences, nominally between Washington D.C. and Moscow or between White House and Kremlin influence. The Wall physically divided Germany into two camps (World War II victors Britain, USA, and France in one camp and Union of Soviet Socialist Republics (USSR) in the other camp). It was the symbolic boundary between ideologies of democracy and Communism. It became the symbol of Cold War and remained until 9th of November 1989. Its fall then paved the way to the reunification of East and West Germany into the Federal Republic of Germany on October 3rd, 1990, and is becoming the most memorable of

The Cold War was central to contemporary international relations and major powers for peace. Although the Cold War was antagonistic, it was after the Cold War that contemporary major wars occurred such as 1991 Gulf War, Afghanistan war, Iraqi war, Balkan War of 1994. All these post-Cold War wars (unlike the wars during the Cold War such as: Russian invasion of Afghanistan, or Israeli-Arab wars) were internationalized. Despite the superpowers perpetuating the dynamic of the Cold War around the globe, the Cold War era generally witnessed a long peace between the states especially in Europe and in Sub-Saharan Africa. The Cold War generated many hypotheses about the causes, the nature, the end, and the legacy of Cold War itself in contemporary international relations from scholars of political and international relations[94].

The Cold War can be seen as a struggle between conflicting values of different states and powers: the USA's "concepts of a market economy and a multi-party democracy" and the USSR's "single party statism and a command administrative economy". It was the persisting conflict between these values and the persistence of their protagonists that sustained and dictated the Cold War. This

---

events for the Europeans. Alford Helen remarks: "For the Europeans born in the 1960's, the fall of the Berlin Wall, and all the events associated with the crumbling of the power of the Soviet Union, must rank among the most memorable events of our lifetimes." Alford Helen, Oikonomia Editoriale '*the Holy See and the Post-Communist States*' numero uno, febraio 2010). Here too the Wall sparked dispute between both Washington and Moscow.

[94] For more on these views see Martin Griffiths and Terry O'Callaghan, 2002. *op. cit.* 2002 Pages 35- 38

was manifested in the USA's policy of containment as 'defensive reactions' by forming many alliances around the world against the USSR's influence and expansion. As the USSR was incapable of enduring the longevity of rivalry with the USA, the Cold War system ended. "Nonetheless, the timing of that collapse was due in no small measure to the preparedness of the United States and its allies to match or exceed Soviet escalations of the arms race" [95].

Realist theory concludes that it was the fear of nuclear weapons triggered by Mutually Assured Destruction (MAD) that prevented the 'cold war' from exploding into a 'hot war'. "The ideological component and historical records make the Cold War an existential battle. It was waged between right and wrong, democracy and dictatorship, capitalism and socialism [liberalism and communism]. Compromise was seen as morally questionable"[96]. Conflicts of interest between the USSR and USA were inevitable during the peak of the Cold War to the collapse of the former USSR . However, due to the concept of Mutual Assured Destruction (MAD) that each polar state could mutually destroy the other, there was no direct physical war between the USA and the former USSR. They rather fought behind their bloc members who waged war either in line with their ideologies or on behalf of their ideologies[97].

---

[95] *Ibid.*, 2002 P. 36.

[96] Wallensteen Peter, Understanding, Conflict Resolution, War, Peace and Global system, *SAGE Publications Ltd*, 2007, p. 4

[97] For instance, capitalist USA's involvement in Vietnam helping anti-Communist southerners

During the Pontificate of John XXIII, the Cold War was still at its peak. Cuba's endorsement of communism as a state policy in 1959, construction of Berlin Wall in 1961, and the Cuban Missile Crisis in 1962 all escalated the tension. It was during the Cold War that bipolarity took a centre stage in international affairs. Alongside the basic immediate factors, such as the threat of nuclear war that inspired the promulgation of *Pacem in Terris*, there were the strong sense of social belonging that manifested itself in one social group perceiving itself superior and the other inferior which ended up in denying the members of other group their basic human rights, the denial of which generated conflict and disrupted co-existence. This was also a concern for Pope John XXIII[98]. Religious persecutions in some places were present, so Pope John XXIII had to call for religious freedom[99]. At the time of promulgation of *Pacem in Terris*, many countries especially in Africa were throwing off the yoke of colonialism and were giving support for Pan-African and liberation movements in the continent which then paved the way for independence. In *Pacem in Terris* John XXIII alluded to decolonization[100], the issue of population, land and

---

against pro-communist Northerners which was helped by Communist Russia is one example. During the 1979 Soviet Union's inversion of Afghanistan, USA had helped the Afghan resistance against the Soviet Union's invasion. Today USA and her allies are invading Afghanistan since 2001.

[98] *Pacem in Terris*, April 11, 1963, Pp. 44.

[99] *Ibid.*, pp. 14.

[100] *Ibid.*, pp. 42-43.

capital[101], the problem of political refugees and their rights[102]. All these factors influenced and threatened the world peace Pope John XXIII was aiming at, for this reason he addressed them in his encyclical.

1.4.3 International Security

The threat of nuclear war was the principal international security threat in 1963 and it was not ignored by Pope John XXIII in *Pacem in Terris*; today international security against global terrorism is a major concern of international relations. International security can refer to the commitments undertaken by international actors, such as states, international systems and organizations, the most encompassing of which is the United Nations, with the aim of ensuring safety against threats, disorder and instability for harmonious mutual ordering of life, mutual preservation and protection in the international sphere. These commitments can be manifested in both soft and hard powers and in international treaties and conventions of that nature. Security threats justify suspension of civil liberties, hence emergency laws are justifiable; they can even justify waging war under the pretext of a pre-emptive strike against an impending palpable security threat. Today, combating security threat absorbs a large quantity of national and international resources.

---

[101] *Ibid.,* pp. 101-102.

[102] *Ibid.,* pp. 103-106.

In the post-World War II epoch, engagement of international security studies as one of the focal points in international relations and systems increased in the academic field[103]; since that time, international security has been at the heart of international relations studies[104]. The sphere and concept of international security is not constant and it has been widening through generations. In the 21st century, the security concern is much wider and more complex than in previous times. It contains some complex and interwoven matters that threaten national and international life.

Traditional approaches concentrate on state apparatus and their military capabilities to protect state's national security concerns; their main focus is the state and they focus on the integrity of the state and its sovereignty. Their aims also include combating threats such as interstate war, nuclear proliferation, violent *coups d'état*, violent revolution and civil conflicts that can abrupt the normal functions of the state institution or the public order. In this concept, international security depends on the presupposition that the more security of the state is insured, the more the security of their citizens is insured. The states are termed as rational entities whose national interests and policies are driven by the desire for absolute power. In the traditional sense, security has been restricted to the protection of the state from external invasion.

---

[103] See Buzan, B. and L. Hansen , *The Evolution of International Security Studies*. Cambridge, Cambridge University Press, 2009.

[104] See Sheehan, M. *International Security: An Analytical Survey*. London, Lynne Rienner Publishers, 2005.

However, due to   deficiencies in the traditional concepts of state-centric notions of security, a human security or holistic approach to security has to be theorised in order to tackle what is assumed to be the basic threats to human security. This approach suggests cooperative, comprehensive and collective efforts geared to ensuring the integral safety of the individual people. The human security or holistic approach sees the individual as its main referent and thus, champions the integral integrity of the individual. The strategy of this approach is to combat ignorance, disease, poverty, hunger, natural disaster, intra- and interstate violence, landmines, human rights abuse and global warming. These are viewed by the holistic approach as security threats.

In the 21st century, the causes and prevention of war, ethnic conflict and peacekeeping, peace-making and peace building, counter terrorism and insurance of homeland security, regional and international security, arms control and weapons proliferation are core concerns of an international security system. To cope with the 21st century globalized, technological, international security needs, Nayef Al-Rodhan proposes what he refers to as a "Multi-sum security principle". Nayef's assumption is that in a globalized and technological world such as ours, "security can no longer be thought of as a zero-sum game involving states alone. Global security, instead, has five dimensions that include human, environmental, national, transnational, and transcultural security, and therefore, global security and the security of any state or culture cannot be achieved without good governance at all levels that guarantees security through justice for all individuals, states, and cultures" [105]. This "Multi-sum security principle" suggested that each of the five dimensions of security mentioned above must be necessarily taken care of in a bid to provide "just and sustainable" global security. Hence, it advocates cooperative and collaborative interactions between states and co-existence between cultural groups and civilizations[106]. In other words, it calls for an alliance of culture and civilization instead of the clash of culture and civilisation.

In the 21st century, in order to ensure that international security against potential threats, such as terrorism and organized crime, are effective and intelligent, there must be international cooperation and collaboration in collective security apparatus through transnational, regional and international policing and sharing security information across international frontiers. International security in the 21st century includes the following: economic security, food security, health security, environmental security, personal security, community security and political security[107].

1.4.4 Risk of Nuclear War

Since all-out war in the modern age equips itself with all possible art and

---

[105] See International security at http://en.wikipedia.org/wiki/International_security, and also Sustainable Global Security - Sustainable History accessible at www.sustainablehistory.com. Both cited Al-Rodhan, Nayef R.F., The Five Dimensions of Global Security: Proposal for a Multi-sum Security Principle, Berlin LIT, Verlag, 2007.

[106] *Ibid.*

[107] For more on human security see The 1994 UNDP Human Development Report (HDR).

science with the objective of achieving a strategic goal, nuclear war, the threat of which was a necessary stimulus for *Pacem in Terris*, became one of these scientific products that threatened the international security system both then and even now. Thus, it is important that we highlight the risks attached to nuclear war.

Among all the techniques of war known to human beings in this epoch, a nuclear technique is the most devastating of all. For this reason, "A nuclear war would be totally unlike any previous form of warfare in its immeasurably greater destructive power"[108]. Furthermore, the experts have suggested that: "The direct effects of a major nuclear exchange could kill hundreds of millions: the indirect effects could kill billions"[109]. It is also suggested that: "Following a major nuclear war, approximately one billion people will be left dead and millions more, probably hundreds of millions more will be injured"[110]. With such greater danger and risk attached to nuclear war, the nuclear war that was about to occur between two countries that have considerable Christian population: the United States of America and Union of Soviet Socialist Republics became a primary concern for Pope John XXIII, hence the promulgation of *Pacem in Terris*. The risk of nuclear war is not yet gone- it still exists. This being the case, it is important that we draw

---

[108] United Nations, Study on the Climatic and Other Global Effects of Nuclear War, Report A/43/351, 1988.

[109] Roback Alan , "*New Models Confirm Nuclear Winter*". In Bulletin of the Atomic Scientists September 1989.

[110] Birks W. John and Tephens L. Sherry "*Possible Toxic Environment following a Nuclear War*," In The Medical Implications of Nuclear War, National Academies Press, Page 155-166.

attention to the risk attached to every nuclear war.

Risk is a term used in numerous disciplines: military, economy, social, legal, engineering, medical etc. Thus, it is difficult to give universally one best acceptable definition of risk[111]. However, in relation to our discipline, we prefer defining risk as a status-quo that may expose to danger. It is a speculation of negative or harmful effects caused by a particular object. A particular object for our purpose is the nuclear atomic bomb.

Ever since the construction of the atomic bomb with which the risk of nuclear war has been and continues to be associated, the fear over its risk has never disappeared[112]. Dr. Helen Caldicott, an Australian physician showing her concern

---

[111] Aven Terje, Renn Ortwin, Risk Management and Governance: Concepts, Guidelines and Applications, Springer-Verlag Berlin Heidelberg,Dordrecht, London, New York 2010, p. 3.

[112] This fear was manifested in the Leo Szilard and Eugene Wigner drafted epistle endorsed, signed, dated 2nd August 1939 and sent by Albert Einstein to President Roosevelt warning him the possibility of constructing "extremely powerful bombs of a new type", and highly suspected the German government to be doing just that. (see Albert Einstein's Letters to President Franklin Delano Roosevelt dated 2nd August 1939 accessible at http://hypertextbook.com/eworld/einstein.shtm). Henceforth, in the 9th of October 1941 Roosevelt "authorized the first atomic bomb project" and in August 1942 the United States of America began to seriously engage in the nuclear project known as 'The Manhattan Project' to produce an atomic bomb. See Joseph Cirincione Bomb Scare: The History and Future of Nuclear Weapons Colombia University Press 2007, New York, U.S.A. page 3). After its first usage of an atomic bomb, the United States of America, under the presidency of Harry Truman, became the first country to initiate a proposal to the United Nations for the abandonment of the atomic bomb in November 1945: "The hope of civilization lies in international arrangements looking, if possible, to renunciation of the use and development of the atomic bomb". Joseph Cirincione Bomb Scare: The History and Future of Nuclear Weapons, Colombia University Press 2007, New York, U.S.A. p. 14). However, due to the concept of balance of power theory and the concept of

over the arms race and the risk of nuclear weapons, has stated: "We hold God's creation in the palm of our hand. This generation will either decide actively to save it, or by passive complicity to destroy it"[113]. Pope John XXIII was conscious about this risk when he said "While it is difficult to believe that anyone would dare to assume responsibility for initiating the appalling slaughter and destruction that war would bring in its wake, there is no denying that the conflagration could be started by some chance and unforeseen circumstance. Moreover, even though the monstrous power of modern weapons does indeed act as a deterrent, there is reason to fear that the very testing of nuclear devices for war purposes can, if continued, lead to serious danger for various forms of life on earth"[114].

Pope John XXIII was also conscious about the money spent on nuclear weapons that could otherwise achieve much infrastructural and societal advancement of the people. Pope John XXIII framed it this way: "This policy [nuclear program] is involving a vast outlay of intellectual and material resources, with the result that the people of these countries are saddled with a great burden, while other countries lack the help they need for their economic and social

---

Mutually Assured Destruction (MAD), some countries try to possess nuclear technology either clandestinely or openly for their own security and defense.

[113] Helen Caldicott, "Life confronting and overcoming Deat<u>h</u>". This paper was presented at the World Council of Churches, Vancouver, Canada, 1983, 24 July - 10 August, WCC 6th Assembly. See http://archives.wcc-coe.org/query/detail.aspx?ID=83116.

[114] *Pacem in Terris, op.cit.* pp. 111.

development"[115]. This statement of Pope John XXIII concurred well with the statement of Vanner Bush on the high exorbitant financial expense in manufacturing nuclear atomic bombs by saying: "to build a large stock of atomic bombs is an undertaking that will strain the resources of any highly industrialized nation"[116].

Where the resources of a nation are strained, the indicator of an internal civil strife is highly eminent. Spending gigantic amounts of public money on nuclear weapons would be to the detriment of other capacity-building projects and could slow socioeconomic development; this alone is a recipe for social strife. It is paradoxical that nuclear-power states spend enormous amounts on nuclear weapons while an unacceptably large proportion of their people are living in abject poverty. India, Pakistan and North Korea are some examples. "Even though the monstrous power of modern weapons does indeed act as a deterrent"[117] there is an awareness of the risk and cost included in their procurement. This deterrent is not the best method for peace. Hobsbawn sees it as "the cost of racking the nerves of generations": "Unfortunately, the very certainty that neither superpower would actually want to press the nuclear button tempted both sides into using nuclear gesticulation for purposes of negotiation or (in the USA) for domestic

---

[115] *Pacem in Terris*, pp. 109

[116] Thomas G. Mahnken Technology and the American Way of War Since 1945, Colombia University Press, New York USA 2008 pages 16-17.

[117] *Pacem in Terris*, pp. 111.

politics, confident that the other did not want war either. This confidence proved justified, but at the cost of racking the nerves of generations. The Cuban missile crisis of 1962, an entirely unnecessary exercise of this kind, almost plunged the world into an unnecessary war for a few days, and actually frightened even the top decision-makers into rationality for a while"[118]. On a similar tone Hosti remarks: "To say that any political value is worth national self-immolation and probably the destruction of modern civilization makes no sense. Yet, to use the weapons, even if just for deterrence, requires both sides to believe and to act as if they would be used. Thus, we see the phenomenon of American policy-makers, like the Soviet counterparts, underlining their national determination to protect vital interests through the use of nuclear weapons while almost in the same breath arguing that nuclear war would represent the height of human folly"[119].

Pope John XXIII not only condemned nuclear war and the use of force in settling conflict between the states but he went on to suggest ways and means to eliminate nuclear weapons.

---

[118] Hobsbawn Eric, The age of extremes, A History of the World, 1914-1991, 1996, Vintage books, USA pages 229-230, as cited by Cesareo Giulio, *La riflessione teologico-morale sulla pace a partire da Pacem in terris e Gaudium et spes Il contributo specifico italiano. Dissertation zur Erlangung der Doktorwürde an der Theologischen Fakultät der Universität Freiburg in der Schweiz*, 2008 p. 36.

[119] Kalevi J. Hosti, Peace and war: Armed Conflicts and International Order 1648-1989, Cambridge, University Press, 1991, p. 287

1.4.5 Pope John XXIII's Position to Diminish the Risk of Nuclear War in the World

Pope John's suggestions for reduction of nuclear weapons are multidimensional and integral or holistic. It involves psychological, spiritual, political and moral will,[120] not only that of the judicial, legislative and executive arms of governments, but also that of the whole goodwill of people by beseeching "mankind, and above all the rulers of States, to be unsparing of their labour and efforts to ensure that human affairs follow a rational and dignified course"[121]. One of Pope John XXIII's positions in reduction of the risk of nuclear war and armament is that: "Everyone must sincerely co-operate in the effort to banish fear and the anxious expectation of war from men's minds"[122]. This is important pedagogy in disarmament because, if the minds of the peoples (who include the administrators of the states) are under the grip of paranoia and fear and anxious about the impending war, their hands will not be empty of weapons for self-defence. On this line of thought, the Pope stated that: "unless this process of disarmament be thoroughgoing and complete, and reach men's very souls, it is impossible to stop the arms race or to reduce armaments"[123]. This is also in line with UNESCO Constitution which stated that: "Since wars begin in the minds of

---

[120] *Pacem in Terris*, pp.112-113

[121] *Ibid.*, pp.117.

[122] *Ibid.*, pp.113.

[123] *Ibid.*, pp.113.

men, it is in the minds of men that the defences of peace must be constructed" [124].

The UNESCO Constitution suggested in its preamble that: "Peace based exclusively upon the political and economic arrangements of governments would not be a peace which could secure the unanimous, lasting and sincere support of the peoples of the world, and that the peace must therefore be founded, if it is not to fail, upon the intellectual and moral solidarity of mankind"[125].

John XXIII's ultimate wish with regards to nuclear weapons was "to abolish them entirely"[126] and the success to this abolition rests on the constant effort to establish the order of truth, justice, charity, and liberty[127]. For Pope John XXIII, the establishment of the order of truth, justice, charity, and liberty is *sine qua non* to the establishment of durable peace, from family level through community level to the state and international levels. This order also includes respect for human dignity,[128] human rights and a responsibility to be dutiful to one another. Rights are "inextricably bound up with as many duties, all applying to one and the same person"[129]. "These rights and duties derive their origin, their sustenance, and their indestructibility from the natural law, which in conferring the one imposes the

---

[124] UNESCO Constitution, adopted in London on 16 November 1945.

[125] *Ibid.*

[126] *Pacem in Terris,* pp.113.

[127] *Ibid.,* pp. 1.

[128] *Ibid.,* pp.10.

[129] *Ibid.,* pp. 8.

other"[130]. Pope John XXIII's pedagogy is based on the assumption that, if the duties, human dignity and rights, moral solidarity, mutual collaboration and willing cooperation are observed in the order of truth, justice, charity and liberty, the paranoia of impending war could be diminished. And with it the armaments of nuclear weapons would also be diminished. If these things were guaranteed the resort to nuclear weapons for settlement of dispute would become obsolete.

Pope John XXIII suggested that the risk of nuclear war could be eliminated if relations among the states should "be harmonized in accordance with the dictates of truth, justice, willing cooperation, and freedom"[131]. Pope John XXIII proposed these to be the cornerstones on which the structures of every genuine social life and every genuine state relation for genuine and durable peace must be built. For him a "common belief that under modern conditions peace cannot be assured except on the basis of an equal balance of armaments"[132] should be replaced by truth and good neighbourliness as members of one human family[133].

Pope John XXIII suggested for moral and intellectual solidarity of humankind to eliminate nuclear weapons and their risks by recommending an impartial public authority with the world-wide sphere of activities, with the power and means co-extensive with the world problems, to take care of worldwide and

---

[130] *Ibid.*, pp. 8.

[131] *Ibid.*, pp. 80.

[132] *Ibid.*, pp. 110.

[133] *Ibid.*, pp.35.

universal common good[134]. This impartial worldwide public authority should be established not by force but rather by common consent of the people. Such a worldwide public authority endowed with such a power and means was the United Nations Organization at the time. Thus, Pope John XXIII urged the UN to occupy itself with the realization of universal common good by maintaining and strengthening peace between states through encouraging and assisting friendly relations between states by saying : "The United Nations Organization has the special aim of maintaining and strengthening peace between nations, and of encouraging and assisting friendly relations between them, based on the principles of equality, mutual respect, and extensive cooperation in every field of human endeavour"[135]. This, for Pope John XXIII could minimize the risks of an arms race.

For Pope John XXIII the elimination of the risk of nuclear war and the arms race is the demand of right reason, truth and justice. In this regard he said: "There is general agreement—or at least there should be—that relations between States, as between individuals, must be regulated not by armed force, but in accordance with the principles of right reason: the principles, that is, of truth, justice and vigorous and sincere co-operation"[136]. For him, abiding in the right reason, truth, justice and sincere cooperation can contribute a lot to minimizing the arms race

---

[134] *Ibid.*, pp. 137.

[135] *Ibid.*, pp. 142.

[136] *Ibid.*, pp.114.

and nuclear weapons and can lead to pacification in the political world. Succinctly put, one can trace in summary the concept of Pope John XXIII's position on reduction of the risk of nuclear war and arms race in the social doctrine of the Catholic Church. Because for peace and war to be the concern of a Pope, it did not commence with Pope John XXIII, Pope Benedict XV (1914-1922)[137], Pope Pius XI[138] and Pope Pius XII[139] all issued documents concerning the establishment of peace. After them came Pope John XXIII and his *Pacem in Terris*, the nucleus of which is the recognition of human relationships and human dignity in establishing world peace. From the Vatican Council II, the Church's social doctrine has deeply engaged itself with contemporary problems like peace, justice, human rights, religious liberty, environmental issues, protection of the family, the laborers, the oppressed, and the rights of minorities, the issues of the states and international relations and organizations.

The basic principles of the Church's social teaching in that regard are: human dignity, common good, solidarity and subsidiarity. The Church's principle of human dignity is based on the belief that the person has inherent God-given inalienable and inviolable rights which deserve to be promoted by the community and to be protected by governments[140]. Its principle of the common good is geared

---

[137] *Pacem, Dei munus pulcherrimum* (1920).

[138] *Ubi arcano Dei consilio* (1922).

[139] *Opus iustitiae pax, Optatissima pax,* (18.12.47).

[140] Pontifical Council for Justice and Peace, *Compendium of the Social Doctrine of the Church, pp.*

toward the promotion of "the sum total of social conditions which allow people, either as groups or as individuals, to reach their fulfilment more fully and more easily"[141].

Its principle of solidarity is viewed as an authentic moral virtue that calls for "a firm and persevering determination to commit oneself to the common good. That is to say to the good of all and of each individual, because we are all really responsible for all." For the Catholic Church, solidarity rises to the rank of fundamental social virtue since it places itself in the sphere of justice. It is a virtue directed par excellence to the common good, and is found in a commitment to the good of one's neighbour with the readiness, in the Gospel sense, to 'lose oneself' for the sake of the other instead of exploiting him, and to 'serve him' instead of oppressing him for one's own advantage (cf. Mt10:40-42, 20:25; Mk 10:42-45; Lk 22:25-27)"[142]. The Church's principle of subsidiarity promotes the dignity of the person by showing concern for the family, groups, associations, local territorial realities. In short, it promotes all the "aggregate of economic, social, cultural, sports-oriented, recreational, professional and political expressions to which people spontaneously give life" and which make it possible for them to achieve effective social growth without supplanting their initiative, freedom and

---

153

[141] *Ibid.*, pp.164.

[142] *Ibid.*, pp. 193.

responsibility [143]. The Church upholds that every aspect of social life must be related to   these principles if it is to attain its fullest meaning that stems from the dignity, unity and equality of all people. It is not surprising to see the architect of Vatican Council II, Pope John XXIII, promoting such values and deduce from them his position on world peace and disarmament. Throughout the encyclical, Pope John XXIII stressed and emphasized the pivotal role of right reason, truth, justice, liberty, charity, solidarity, human dignity and rights, and sincere co-operation for common good derived from the divine order in establishing the global peace.

---

[143] *Ibid.,* pp. 185.

CHAPTER II

2.1 The Content of Pacem In Terris

Pacem in Terris is a Catholic, and by extension a Christian, document of social teachings on world peace. Promulgated by Pope John XXIII in 1963, it was addressed to the members of the Catholic Church at various levels and to non-Catholic "goodwill people". Thus, a document like *Pacem in Terris* can be analysed from dialogical, doctrinal, moral, philosophical, social and political perspectives. Our analysis is neither densely dialogical nor doctrinal, neither moral nor philosophical nor social; it is meant to be examined from a political perspective rooted in international relations.

Pope John XXIII began this encyclical by considering 'order in the universe' and 'order in human beings'. The content of *Pacem in Terris* can be divided into five sections. The first section concerns 'order between Men'. Pope John XXIII

embedded this 'order between men' in the universal and inviolable human rights

and dignity of humankind. From paragraphs 11 to 27, more than 20 distinct rights

are listed. These rights include: the right to live, the right to bodily integrity, the

right to the means necessary for the proper development of life, the right to be

looked after in the event of circumstances beyond one's control[144], the right to a

good name, the right to freedom in investigating the truth, the right to freedom of

speech and publication, the right to freedom in pursuing whatever profession one

may choose, the right to be accurately informed about public events[145], the right

to share in the benefits of culture, the right to receive a good general education,

the right to technical or professional training consistent with the degree of

educational development in ones own country[146], the right to worship God in

accordance with one's conscience[147], the right to choose freely one's status in

life[148] and the prior right of parents to support and educate their children[149]. In

addition to this list of rights are the economic rights that include the right to work,

the right to suitable working conditions with regard to physical and moral

---

[144] *Pacem in Terris*, pp.11.

[145] *Ibid.*, pp.12.

[146] *Ibid* pp.13.

[147] *Ibid* pp.14.

[148] *Ibid* pp. 15.

[149] *Ibid.*, pp.17.

conditions, the right to economic activities suited to the degree of one's responsibility, the right to a wage consistent with one's standard of living and human dignity, and the right to own private property. The right of meeting and association, the right to emigrate and immigrate, and political rights are also included. All of these rights are hinged on reciprocal responsibility and duties between humankind[150]. For Pope John XXIII, "when society is formed on a basis of rights[151] and duties, men have an immediate grasp of spiritual and intellectual

---

[150] *Ibid.*, pp. 28-30.

[151] On these rights, Pope John XXIII's citations are largely from St. Paul, the Church fathers, Thomas Aquinas, and from encyclicals of some previous Pontifs. Hence, the only novelty if any in the encyclical with regards to the Church's social teaching is the right of religious freedom and freedom of conscience and rights of women in the contemporary world. (Russell Hittinger, *Quinquagesimo Ante*: Reflections on *Pacem in Terris* Fifty Years Later, the Global Quest for *Tranquillitas Ordinis*. Pacem in Terris, Fifty Years Later Pontifical Academy of Social Sciences, Acta 18, 2013, Page 45. Accessible at www.pass.va/content/dam/scienzesociali/pdf/acta18/acta18-hittinger.pdf). His extensive use of Augustinian teaching is noticed by Pope John Paul II in his World Day of Peace Address marking the fortieth anniversary of *Pacem in Terris*, by saying: "Boldly, but with all humility, I would like to suggest that the Church's fifteen-hundred-year-old teaching on peace as *"tranquillitas ordinis* – the tranquility of order" as Saint Augustine called it (De Civitate Dei, 19, 13), which was brought to a new level of development forty years ago by *Pacem in Terris*, has a deep relevance for the world today, for the leaders of nations as well as for individuals." (World Day of Peace Address marking the fortieth anniversary of *Pacem in Terris*, pp.6.) See also Russell Hittinger, *Quinquagesimo Ante*: Reflections on *Pacem in Terris* Fifty Years Later, the Global Quest for *Tranquillitas Ordinis*. *Pacem in Terris*, Fifty Years Later Pontifical Academy of Social Sciences, Acta 18, 2013. P. 45. Accessible at www.pass.va/content/dam/scienzesociali/pdf/acta18/acta18-hittinger.pdf)

values, and have no difficulty in understanding what is meant by truth, justice, charity and freedom"[152], and are able to recognize equality of men.

The second section addresses the "relations between individuals and the public authorities". Here Pope John XXIII stressed the importance and the origin of authority by noting: "every civilized community must have a ruling authority, and this authority, no less than society itself"[153]. For Pope John XXIII, "governmental authority, therefore, is a postulate of the moral order and derives from God"[154]; that governmental authority should appeal to the conscience of the ruled, and its purpose should be the attainment of the common good. The essential of the common good[155] was also stressed in *Pacem in Terris*. In this section, Pope John XXIII outlined the responsibilities of the public authority, the rights and duties of individuals, the structure and operation of the public authority, Citizens' Participation in Public Life. He concluded this section with the characteristics of the era[156].

The third section deals with relations between states, and the imperative of the common good in such relations. According to Pope John XXIII, such relations

---

[152] *Pacem in Terris*, pp.45.

[153] *Pacem in Terris*, pp. 46.

[154]*Ibid.*, pp.51.

[155] *Ibid.*, Pp.55.

[156] *Ibid.,* pp. 60-75.

should be based on truth, justice, and active solidarity. The problem of political refugees, refugees' rights, the causes of the arms race, the need for disarmament and an appeal for the resolution of conflict through negotiation in liberty are highlighted in this section. The signs of the times that should be considered in relations between states[157] are also found here.

The fourth section addresses the "relationship of men and of political communities with the world community". This relationship is considered to be due largely to "modern developments" and the "inadequacy of modern states to ensure universal common good". The connection between the common good and world political authority in such a relationship is also stressed, as is the idea that this world public authority should be instituted by common consent and not imposed by force. In this section, Pope John XXIII stated that the universal common good and personal rights are to be recognized, respected, safeguarded and promoted by such a world wide political community. In addition, it is in this section that he calls for the principle of subsidiarity in this world community, and in the relations between the states[158].

The fifth section is dedicated to pastoral exhortations that urge full engagement of Catholics in public life. Lay initiatives are praised and co-

---

[157] *Ibid.*, pp.80 -129.

[158] *Ibid.*, pp.130- 145.

operation of Catholics with non-Catholics in social, political and economic affairs is endorsed. However, this has to be done through "little by little" steps, not through "hotheadedness" that "was never constructive …[and] has always destroyed everything"[159]. In this section, integration of faith and action is encouraged. It is also stated that the "error" and the "errant" should be distinguished in philosophies and historical movements of the world.   It is here that the Prince of Peace figure is depicted as a model for peacemakers to follow[160].

Since Pope John XXIII began his encyclical with 'order in the universe', we will also begin our analysis and comments on order and disorder in creation and its relevance to the establishment of world peace.

2.2 Order and Disorder in Creation

The first step towards world peace is the maintenance of 'order' in creation. Order exists in the universe as well as in humankind. Order has many multiple dimensions: internal and external order[161] and national and international order.

---

[159] *Ibid.*,pp.162.

[160] *Ibid.*, pp.146 -172.

[161] Internal order lays in man's innermost being: "World's Creator has stamped man's inmost being with an order revealed to man by his conscience" (*Pacem in Terris* pp.5) and his conscience

Order in human beings refers to internal order, while order between humankind refers to external order. National order prevails within a nation or a state; international order prevails among nations in their relations. Order is needed in all of these aspects for stability and coexistence in societies. It is one of the pillars on which societal peace rests. This is where the primary recipes for peace begin at the level of social relationships. The primary steps towards world peace could come from the observance, respect and maintenance of conditions for peace. 'Order' is one of these conditions. Since order is the offshoot of peace, therefore, orderliness is one of the conditions for peacefulness[162].

Order can refer to the operation of a system, an arrangement of social life, or a pattern that leads to realization of a certain goal, values or result. According to Bull Hedley, all societies seek to ensure three primary, universal, overlapping societal goals: that life will be in some measure secure against violence resulting in death or bodily harm; that promises, pacts, treaties or agreements, once undertaken, will be fulfilled; and that ownership of things will remain stable to some degree, and will not be subject to changes that are constantly unlimited. These goals are primary because they establish the foundation of a civilised society. They are primary because other goals presuppose their realization. They

---

insists on preserving it. This is the internal order that can bring the internal peace which has a connection to external peace.

[162] In fact for some thinkers like Thomas Aquinas, peace is *"tranquillitas ordinis"* meaning "tranquillity of order". Thomas Aquinas, Summa Theologiae 2a-2ae, Black Friars 1975, pages 197 -199.

are universal because all civilised societies take account of them[163]. Therefore, order is a pre-requisite for peace and stability.

Disorder is the malfunctioning of the members or organs of a system, a society, an institution or an organisation. Hence, in a disordered society the societal goals can hardly be realised because it is in the orderly functions of its members that its goals can be realised. Disorder can cause conflict which can lead to the obstruction of the whole societal system, ending up in war.

Pacem in Terris began with the 'order in the universe'[164]: "That a marvellous order predominates in the world of living beings and in the forces of nature, is the plain lesson which the progress of modern research and the discoveries of

---

[163] Bull Hedley, The Anarchical Society A Study of Order in World Politics, Second Edition Columbia University Press, New York, 1977. See chapter 1.

[164] Perhaps knowing the strong connection between cosmology and social ethics from reading ancient philosophy, the Pope has to begin his world peace encyclical with 'order in the universe'. In the contemporary period, political thought, social and economic theories, as well as their proposals and implementation of governmental and societal reforms, are consumed and evaluated within the cadre of history of ideological movements of a particular society at the time. In the mediaeval epoch, "the *terminus a quo* of political thought was metaphysical, whereas the point of arrival was *ethical*" and for governance of society to reflect the governance of the heavens and to imitate hierarchical structure of society from the hierarchical structure of the heavens was imperative. (*Joseph Ellul, The Notion of Good Governance in the Political Thought of Al-Farabi. In Oikonmia Rivista di etica e scienze sociali* / Journal of Ethics & Social Sciences Anno 12 Numero 1 Febbraio 2013, ISSN 1720-1691. Copyright 2012 by Angelicum University Press Rome, Italy). All Rights Reserved. Accessed at http://www.oikonomia.it/ on 16-05-13

technology teach us"[165]. What Pope John XXIII implied by this, is that 'order' is the source of peace and tranquility and that the best form of that 'order' can be found in the universe. However, we should not think that a carbon copy of this order in the universe must be implemented in human relations with a state or states: "Many people think that the laws which govern man's relations with the State are the same as those which regulate the blind, elemental forces of the universe"[166]. That is to say, human beings and their political and social institutions must not be governed by blind, elemental forces as the universe does. The universe operates in a way different from that of human society and each must take its natural course. The forces of the universe are "blind, elemental forces", while a human is endowed with choice, dignity, freedom and intelligence, hence he/she is responsible and accountable for his/her actions. Once blind force is used in international and inter-social relationships, then humanity's choice, dignity, freedom and intelligence are being denied and abandoned for inhuman, irrational and destructive forces. Hence, treating human beings like the objects of the universe and expecting them to obey and act like the forces of the universe is in itself unjust and can lead to a breach of peace.

Human nature is different from the nature of the universe; the latter has neither choice nor freewill, but must obey the divine order, while human beings

---

[165] *Pacem in Terris*, pp. 2.

[166] *Ibid.*, pp. 6.

have a choice and freewill. For this reason, humans will be held accountable for their actions. Therefore, dictators and totalitarian rulers operating under the cover of the states, should not use force to impose on the people laws that are unacceptable to their nature and conscience. This will not help the establishment of durable world peace.

Pacem in Terris examined the "disunity among individuals and among nations which is "in striking contrast to this perfect order in the universe"[167]. Therefore, for there to be peace among humankind, their relations should be based on orders or laws. These laws should "clearly indicate how a man must behave toward his fellows in society, and how the mutual relationships between the members of a State and its officials are to be conducted"[168]. These laws, or order, should also outline "what principles must govern the relations between States; and finally, what should be the relations between individuals or States on the one hand, and the world-wide community of nations on the other. Men's common interests make it imperative that at long last a world-wide community of nations be established"[169].

---

[167] *Ibid.*, pp. 4.

[168] *Ibid.*, pp.7.

[169] *Pacem in Terris*, pp.7. *Gaudium et Spes* also relates 'order in human society' to the attainment of peace as it stated: "Peace results from that order structured into human society by its divine Founder, and actualized by men as they thirst after ever greater justice. The common good of humanity finds its ultimate meaning in the eternal law. But since the concrete demands of this

Pacem in Terris teaches that it is the "moral order" that affirms the indispensability of human society with authority. And the basis of this authority is the moral order itself. Any social setup needs authority and any authority needs order. Being deprived of this moral order which is the *raison d'être* of social setup and its authority, the society itself will descend into chaos and disorder which is a recipe for conflict and war[170]. In the view of Pope John XXIII, this moral order that is universal, "absolute and immutable in its principles finds its source in the true, personal and transcendent God"[171]. This moral order which is universal, absolute and immutable in its principles is the true law of right reason[172]. In establishing civilization this is the kind of law necessary to sustain the pillars of durable world peace. As order is a factor in harmonious human

---

common good are constantly changing as time goes on, peace is never attained once and for all, but must be built up ceaselessly" Gaudium et Spes Pastoral Constitution on the Church in the Modern World 1965, pp.78 accessed at http://www.vatican.va on 18/02/2012.

[170] *Pacem in Terris*, pp.83.

[171] *Ibid.*, pp.37.

[172] Here one can infer to the kind of law described by Cicero as a law that is: "harmonious with nature, diffused among all, constant, eternal; a law which calls to duty by its commands and restrains from evil by its prohibitions....It is a sacred obligation not to attempt to legislate in contradiction to this law; nor may it be derogated from nor abrogated. Indeed, by neither the Senate nor the people can we be released from this law; nor does it require any but ourselves to be its expositor or interpreter. Nor is it one law at Rome and another at Athens; one now and another at a later time; but one eternal and unchangeable law binding all nations through all time". Cicero as Quoted in Understanding the Law, by Donald L. Carper. John A. McKinsey. Bill W. West – 2007 p.50, on footnote, also by Peter Riga, Peace on Earth, A commentary on Pope John's encyclical, N.Y: Herder and Herder, 1964 p.33.

relations in the attainment of peace in society, disorder serves as a source of conflict, discord, instability and war.

Pope John XXIII in *Pacem in Terris* viewed the establishment of 'order in human beings' and 'order between humankind as a pre-requisite for peace'[173]. In fact, for John Courtney Murray "the, whole burden of the encyclical [*Pacem in Terris*] is that the order for which the postmodern world is looking cannot be an order that is imposed by force, or sustained by coercion, or based on fear"[174].

As stated above, order is vital in every human institution. Therefore, its relations to humankind, the maintenance of human rights, and the consequences of their denial that can lead to violence and war will be analysed in the segment below.

2.3 The Human Kind, Human Rights, Violence and War among the Human Kind

Humankind cannot be defined by any precise set of speculations, postulations and assumptions. The complex nature of humankind influences the actions of its institutions, such as communities, states, international relations and international systems. It is also human nature that can generate violence and war. Therefore,

---

[173] See *Pacem in Terris* pp. 2 – 45.

[174] John Courtney Murray, S.J. America (27 April 1963) 613. Accessed at http://www.shc.edu/theolibrary/resources/comments_pacem.htm.

communities, states, international relations and systems, violence and war are all determined by the nature of humankind. The nature of humankind in international relations is between a theological account of 'original sin' and a secular assumption of 'egoistic passion'. For instance, for Hobbes, the life of man is "solitary, poor, nasty, brutish, and short. ... The condition of man ... is a condition of war of everyone against everyone"[175]. Based on the concept of original sin, Carl Schmitt and John Gay assume the savage nature of humankind as *homo rapiens, rapacious hominidis*[176]. Reinhold Neibuhr postulates the Christian concept of original sin[177]on, human nature and also transfers it to the nature of the state. His antecedents, such as Machiavelli, assumed that "all men are wicked and that they will always give vent to the malignity that is in their minds when the opportunity offers"[178]. Morgenthau maintains the existence of 'egoistic passion' and "the tragic presence of evil in all political action"[179]. "Humankind cannot

---

[175] See Hobbes, Leviathan.

[176] "That nature of humanind is to plunder, destroy and desecrate, this has always been the case and will be the case: they cannot be redeemed, because there is nothing to redeem them, they are just well organized apes". See Michael Payne, Jessica Rae Barbera, A Dictionary of Cultural and Critical Theory, 2nd edition, BlackWell 2010, USA, P. 549. See also Simon Critchley, *'Politics and Original Sin'* in The ends of history 89.09 From hope to fear: the long two decades Of democracy and illiberalism Of capitalism and crises, Aspenia, an Aspen Istitute Italia Review Year 14-n.45-46 2009, p. 118.

[177] Donnelly Jack, *op.cit.* 2000 UK, p. 7

[178] *Ibid.*

[179] *Ibid.*

transcend conflicts through the progressive power of reason to discover a science of peace"[180]. This reasoning is basic to *homo politicus* and it shapes the nature of the states and their international relations. If this is the constant nature of humankind, then decision-makers are therefore very rational in calculating the states' self-interest and searching for their protection and aggrandizement. Human nature determines inter-state operations, and hence world politics, in its anarchic structure[181].

When this becomes the nature of humankind then aggression among them and their institutions is inevitable, and hence the existence of conflict, violence and wars. To check the nature of humankind with its egoism, jealousy, prejudice and hatred that engender violence and war, 'order' has to be established in both social and inter-state relations. The numerous and overlapping 'orders' stated in *Pacem in Terris* in the quest for peace should therefore be strengthened. These orders include: order in humankind (pp.4-7); order among humankind (pp.45); order between members of a political community and its authorities (pp.46-79); order between political communities (pp.80-129); and order in "relationship of men and of political communities with the world wide community" (pp.130-145).

Pacem in Terris teaches that 'order between men' should be based on certain conditions. These conditions include respecting all basic human rights which are

---

[180] Morgenthau, 1946 , pp. 90-5 as cited by Randal L. Schweller in American Political Science Review Vol. 91,N0. 4, December 1997. Page 927. Accessible at http://www.cas.buffalo.edu/classes/psc/fczagare/PSC%20504/SchwellerRealistResearch.pdf

[181] The realists theory.

sine qua non to the uplifting of the human person to a high degree and are not lessened in the establishment of a universal peace[182]. If these rights are not guaranteed between humankind, our weeping for universal peace will be like putting the wood in the fire and crying to see it burnt. These rights are echoed in the thought of David P. Forsythe as pre-requisites for international peace, when he said: "three factors may be reducing the probability of the overt international war among the major states: attention to civil and political rights, attention to economic and social rights and modern (post 1945) development"[183].

2.3.1 Human Rights

Rights used to mean a "claim or a possession that a person or a subject is morally empowered to make"[184] over some thing. Today, rights can mean any issue that a person or a subject is morally, ethically or legally empowered to possess. Thus, human rights are those issues that human beings are morally and

---

[182] *Pacem in Terris*, Pp. 8-27.

[183] Forsythe P. David, Human Rights and Peace International and National Dimensions, The University of Nebraska Press, 1993, page VII- VIII.

[184] Williams Bruce, "Human Rights: A 'Bilingual' Dialogue" presented at the inter disciplinary Symposium: '*Dritti Umani: Problema nodale nel mondo contemporaneo*' In Justice and Allied Virtues Based on the Summa Theologiae of St. Thomas Aquinas-treaties on Justice, II-II,qq.57-122-supplemented with modern sources, Pontifical University of St. Thomas Aquinas, Angelicum Rome, Italy 2009 third edition appendex page 39.

ethically or legally[185] empowered to claim and possess. However, rights can mean different things to different people. This is why when Thomas Aquinas talked about right, or *ius,* as the object of justice in the medieval period, he did not mean the qualification of one's claim or possession to some issues or things. But what he meant was "*id quod est iustum,* [meaning] that which is just, that which is objectively due in a given interaction within the community of persons"[186].

Further, there are two conceptions of human rights: the subjective, internal or liberal, and the objective, external or communitarian conceptions. In other words, the doctrine of human rights is bi-dimensional; it has both interior and exterior texture. Human rights are at the same time personal as well as social. That is to say, a human being is both an individual and a social being simultaneously. These bi-dimensional concepts have been in existence throughout history. If human rights are inalienable and inviolable as claimed, then they are older than any historic written declaration. They are as old as humanity itself. From this angle, we do not see them as rights that are conferred on human beings by the state. Rather we see them as ontological human attributes that owe their existence to the

---

[185] I include 'legally' because same-sex marriage, polygamy, polyandry and polygyny are not recognized as rights in some countries but they will become rights if they are legally approved by law or constitution of that particular land. Or they will be recognized as forms of marriages through the legal redefinition of marriage so as to expand the institution of marriage to include them. In this situation, they become institutionally conferred rights and not natural inherent rights. In our view, it is the moral force of natural rights that is capable to evaluate social practices and confer them as rights or otherwise.

[186] Williams Bruce, *op. cit.* 2009 third edition appendix p. 39.

Creator or nature of human beings, not to the state or society. The state or society must protect and promote these rights for its own smooth governability and in the interests of peace and stability.

The first of the two dimensions of human rights is the subjective, internal or liberal aspect, which regards human being as the subject of rights and confers basic moral judgment to individual human beings. It further claims that each human being is unique, autonomous and dignified. As such, she /he should be free to manifest her or his unique qualities and natural attributes as long as these do not harm others' autonomy, dignity and natural attributes. Also, these rights should be protected by the community and its social and political structures and institutions against any infringements. This concept is promoted in the words of the medieval canonist[187] and in today's Western liberal approach. Moreover, this dimension of human rights is expressed in the three great historic documents of the United Kingdom which regulate the relations between the Monarchy and its people in the Kingdom: the Magna Carta (1297); the Petition of Right (1628); and the English Bill of Rights (1689). The same can be said about the American Declaration of Independence (July 4, 1776) and the French Declaration of Rights of Man (26 August 1789). It is spelt out more distinctly in the United Nations' Universal Declaration of Human Rights (1948).

---

[187] *Ibid.*

The second dimension of human rights is the objective, exterior or communitarian aspect, in contrast to the subjective notion of human rights. It confers the root of moral judgment to the human community or society and places the emphasis on the communal, public and common good. According to this approach, the common good encapsulates and engulfs respect for the individual's rights, dignity and liberties. Hence, if any individual human rights pose a threat to the maintenance of the common good, the restriction or banning of them is justifiable. This restriction is seen as an antidote against the alienation and disintegration of moral and ethical values and social structures and institutions. It is meant to achieve, maintain or restore balance among the elements of the social whole in a bid to secure and protect the common good[188].

This is the approach prevalent in classical and medieval traditions[189]. Some African thinkers, like Leopold Senghor, also believe that this approach was the norm in West Africa: "Negro-African society is collectivist or ... communal, because it is rather a communion of souls than an aggregate of individuals .... Negro-African society puts more stress on the group than on the individual, more on solidarity than on the activity and needs of the individual, more on the communion of persons than on their autonomy. Ours is a community society"[190].

---

[188] *Ibid.*

[189] *Ibid.*

[190] Leopold Senghor (1964) On African Socialism, trans. Mercer Cook New York, Praeger. Pages 93-94. See also Kwame Gyekye "*Person and community: Ghanaian philosophical studies*

For John S. Mbiti, the cardinal point in understanding the African view of the human being is embedded in this statement: "I am, because we are; and since we are, therefore I am"[191].

Human rights can therefore be seen as a 'double edged knife', capable of harming and benefiting both the individual person and the society. On one hand, the subjective approach can protect an individual person against a gross violation of his/her inalienable dignity, rights and honour by the institutional or state powers, but, on the other hand, it can lead to arbitrary individualism with 'rights-talk', which in turn leads to a 'plethora of rights', or 'rights-mania', and can do little to prevent acts such as abortion. It therefore fails to protect the basic human right of the unborn child, that is, its right to life. Over the issue of abortion the subjective approach can only divide people into two camps: pro-life and pro-choice. It can also create a 'disorder in the body politics' and 'standoff of one right against the other'[192].

In the objective approach, however, there is social, institutional and structural stability and enhancement of the common good. Nevertheless, due to its emphasis

---

I", In Cultural Heritage and Contemporary Change Series II Africa Vol.I, published with support of CIPSH/UNESCO the Council for Research and Values and philosophy Washington, 1992, p. 102.

[191] Mbiti S.John, African religions & philosophy, 2nd edition, Heinemann publishers, USA, 1990, P. 106.

[192] Glendon MaryAnn, Rights talk: The impoverishment of political discourse, The Free Press, New York, Macmillan, Inc. 1991 p. x.

on the communitarian nature of justice and social bonds, an objective approach is sometimes likely to be twisted "into rationalization of *de facto* social structures that are oppressive" to political opponents, religious dissidents, ethnic and racial minorities, foreigners, women etc., and can also muzzle social criticism under the cover of institutional and structural stability. To some extent, this approach encouraged slavery and religious persecution in the medieval period[193], and can encourage political oppression and religious persecution today as well.

The two notions of rights mentioned above seem to be divergent and incompatible, and each has its pros and cons. However, the negative, extreme aspect of each can be checked and balanced by the positive, best aspects of the other. These two notions of rights seem to be reconciled in *Pacem in Terris* and are further reconciled in the Catholic concept of common good[194]. In other words, they can be reconciled in: "a firm and persevering determination to commit oneself to the common good. That is to say to the good of all and of each individual, because we are all really responsible for all"[195]. This type of solidarity is the one that "rises to the rank of fundamental social virtue since it places itself in the sphere of justice. It is a virtue directed *par excellence* to the common good, and is found in "a commitment to the good of one's neighbour with the readiness, in the Gospel sense, to 'lose oneself' for the sake of the other instead of exploiting

---

[193] Bruce Williams, *op. cit.*

[194] The Common good is mentioned about 46 times in *Pacem in Terris*.

[195] Compendium of the Social Doctrine of the Church, *op.cit.* 2004, no.193.

him, and to 'serve him' instead of oppressing him for one's own advantage (cf. *Mt* 10:40-42, 20:25; *Mk* 10:42-45; *Lk* 22:25-27)"[196].

The protection of human rights[197] in the view of *Pacem in Terris* is a prerequisite for Peace. This is what we will be analysing in the next segments.

2.3.2 The protection of Human Rights as a pre-requisite for Peace

Some of the rights stipulated in *Pacem in Terris* are, according to Pope John Paul II, similar to the ideological foundation of the Universal Declaration of Human Rights, a document that must have our loyalty, protection and commitment for the establishment of true peace in the world[198]. These rights, as stipulated in *Pacem in Terris*, have their corresponding duties as well. They include: the right to live; the rights pertaining to moral and cultural values; the right to economic rights; the right of meeting and association; the right to emigrate and immigrate; and political rights. These rights are considered to be universal by the United Nations and are stipulated and established by its Universal

---

[196] *Ibid.,* no.193.

[197] The rights portrayed in *Pacem in Terris* are the reflection of those human rights envisaged in 1948 Universal Declaration of Human Rights (UDHR).

[198] Address of His Holiness John Paul II to the 34th General Assembly of the United Nations, New York Tuesday, 2 October 1979 Paragraph 11 accessed at http://www.vatican.va/holy_father/john_paul_ii/, on 1 April 2012 see also AAS 71 (1979), p.1144-1160.

Declaration of Human Rights Charter since 10 December, 1948[199]. According to Pope John Paul II, the UDHR "has struck a real blow against the many deep roots of war, since the spirit of war, in its basic primordial meaning, *springs up and grows to maturity where the inalienable rights of man are violated* [sic]"[200]. The UDHR will no doubt be re-echoed in every genuine document meant for world peace, as it has re-echoed in *Pacem in Terris* fifteen years later. Although duties are not as much expounded in the UDHR as are rights,[201] in *Pacem in Terris* these rights "are inextricably bound up with as many duties, all applying to one and the same person. These rights and duties derive their origin, their sustenance, and their indestructibility from the natural law, which in conferring the one imposes the other"[202]. *Pacem in Terris* calls for reciprocity of rights and duties between persons in a mutually collaborative and responsible manner[203].

These rights, the violation of which allows the spirit of war to appear and grow into maturity, are the most demanding issues of our time. Refusing to acknowledge and guarantee them will make the world ungovernable and the

---

[199] Read articles:3,13,18, 20 and 21 of UDHR.

[200] Address of His Holiness John Paul II to the 34th General Assembly of the United Nations, New York Tuesday, 2 October 1979 Paragraph 11 accessed at http://www.vatican.va/holy_father/john_paul_ii/, on 1 April 2012 see also AAS 71 (1979), p.1144-1160.

[201] Of all the thirty (30) articles of the UDHR the duties are mentioned only in article 29 second but last article.

[202] *Ibid.*, pp. 28.

[203] *Ibid.*, pp. 30-34.

efforts for establishing universal peace an unreachable mirage. Protecting and promoting these rights are pre-requisites for peace. Any efficient, effective, and intelligent strategy to establish world peace cannot ignore human rights issues in this contemporary world. In fact, human rights surfaced internationally as a rationale for averting the replication of the World War II[204] and the atrocities of the Holocaust[205], and to establish world peace in an established public order in a bid to make the world governable, nationally and internationally. This is confirmed in the preamble of the Universal Declaration of Human Rights Charter: "Recognition of the inherent dignity and of the equal and inalienable rights of all members of the human family is the foundation of freedom, justice and peace in the world"[206].

Therefore, virtues, rights and duties are interlocking parts of the overarching principles in maintaining world peace, because "disregard and contempt for human rights have resulted in barbarous acts which have outraged the conscience of mankind"[207] on one hand, while on the other hand, the call for "the advent of a world in which human beings shall enjoy freedom of speech and belief and freedom from fear and want has been proclaimed as the highest aspiration of the

---

[204] Humphery P.John, "*The Magna Carta of Mankind*". In Human Rights, edited by Peter Davies, Routledge London and New York 1988, p. 31.

[205] Weissbrodt David, "*Human Right : An Historical Perspective*" .In Human Rights, edited by Peter Davies, Routledge London and New York 1988, p. 1.

[206] Universal Declaration of Human Rights Charter 10 December, 1948.

[207] *Ibid.*

common people"[208]. The importance of these rights in the realization of world peace must not be minimized, and hence are firmly stated in *Pacem in Terris*.

As mentioned above, the denial of human rights can lead to violence and war and instability among humankind and their society. "The spirit of war, in its basic primordial meaning, *springs up and grows to maturity where the inalienable rights of man are violated* [sic]"[209]. Guarantees of these rights should be established in the order between men and their protection is a pre-requisite for peace. The sections that follow list basic human rights.

2.3.2.1 The Right to Live and Right to Life

The 'right to live and right to life' contain the fundamentals of all human rights. The 'right to live and right to life' are not new-born infants of the 20th century. These are ontological human attributes and are as old as the human being itself. The 20th century did a psychological, political act in recognizing and endorsing them into national and international laws equally applicable to all. The right to live is broader than right to life. The right to life involves protection from the abortion of life, such as abortion of pregnancy, protection from being

---

[208] *Ibid.*

[209] Address of His Holiness John Paul II to the 34th General Assembly of the United Nations, New York Tuesday, 2 October 1979 Paragraph 11 accessed at http://www.vatican.va/holy_father/john_paul_ii/, on 1 April 2012 see also AAS 71 (1979), p.1144-1160.

physically killed and murdered. The right to life presupposes the right to live and presupposes all other rights that can be attributed to a human being. When life is destroyed no other human attribute can sensibly be advocated or protected. Therefore, the deprivation of life can be regarded as the most drastic and total form of violation on human rights.

The right to live entails "the right to bodily integrity and to the means necessary for the proper development of life, particularly food, clothing, shelter, medical care, rest, and, finally, the necessary social services"[210]. The right to live is interpreted in *Pacem in Terris* to cover the right to be looked after in the "event of ill-health; disability stemming from one's work; widowhood; old age; enforced unemployment; or whenever through no fault of one's own one is deprived of the means of livelihood"[211]. This is in line with Article 25 of the 1948 Universal Declaration of Human Rights (UDHR), which stated that: "Everyone has the right to a standard of living adequate for the health and well-being of himself and of his family, including food, clothing, housing and medical care and necessary social services, and the right to security in the event of unemployment, sickness, disability, widowhood, old age or other lack of livelihood in circumstances beyond his control. Motherhood and childhood are entitled to special care and assistance. All children, whether born in or out of wedlock, shall enjoy the same

---

[210] *Pacem in Terris*, pp.11.

[211] *Ibid.* pp.11.

social protection"[212] Pope John XXIII appealed for the protection of these rights by authorities and by all. When the right to life and to live is granted and protected, in order to give it a meaning the rights to moral and cultural values should follow suit.

2.3.2.2 The Rights to Moral and Cultural Values

In the 'order between men', one's aspiration for one's moral and cultural values should not only be respected, but should also be protected. One of the causes of conflict within some countries is the denial of these rights which belong naturally to human beings. The Berbers in the Kabylia region of Algeria and the Southern Sudanese who are struggling against the imposed arabization and islamization policies of their central governments that negate their cultural identity in Algeria and in Sudan, could be some contemporary examples. These policies have resulted in heavy loss of life, material, and even territorial secession in the case of Sudan. But also the conflict of Northern Ireland and people in similar situations in the other parts of the world can be added as many practical examples.

For there to be peace, a human being should be free not only to have access to his or her cultural and moral values, but also to embrace, practise, live and

---

[212] Universal Declaration of Human Rights, (UDHR), 1948.

express them freely without hindrance as long as they do not infringe on those of others. This was made very clear in Pope John XXIII's pedagogy towards the establishment of world peace, hence he would not ignore it[213]. For Pope John XXIII, a human's natural rights that must be respected include his/her right to a good name, freedom of truth investigation, freedom of speech and publication, freedom to pursue whatever profession he/she may choose. In addition, he/she should have accurate information about public events, benefits of culture, and good general education, be it technical or professional training. However, all these have to be "within the limits of the moral order and the common good"[214]. Nonetheless, guaranteeing moral and cultural rights is not enough without guaranteeing religious freedom.

2.3.2.3 Right to Worship God According to one's Conscience

The right to worship God according to one's conscience is one of the most demanding issues of our time. Denials of this right caused many conflicts in history and is still a major issue. Refusal to acknowledge, protect and promote this right will render unrealistic the effort to establish universal peace. For this reason, the 'right to worship God according to one's conscience' should be given a high place in pursuing world peace in our contemporary world. Freedom of

---

[213] *Ibid.,* pp. 12-13.

[214] *Ibid.,* pp. 12-13.

worship in accordance with one's conscience is a prerequisite, not only for realization of inner peace but also external peace. In *Pacem in Terris*, the right to worship according to one's conscience is neither pictured as "erroneous opinion", nor "madness", nor even as "most pestilential error"[215]; neither was it seen as "liberty of perdition," nor "insanity", not even "injurious babbling"[216]. Rather Pope John XXIII affirmed that everyone has the right to encounter God in any religion through the right dictates of conscience and to privately or publicly declare it as one sees it fit and deem[217]. It was on this line of thought that E.E.Y. Hales described Pope John XXIII this manner: "In this remarkable new document [*Pacem in Terris*] ... Roncalli succeeded in lifting himself right out of his political and even out of his clerical environment on to the lofty plane of Father-in-God of all men.... We are allowed, as we read it, to forget, for a time, Pius XII's root assumption that the great apostasy, the withdrawal of so many from allegiance to the Holy See ... has shrouded much of mankind in impenetrable darkness and divided humanity in two. Nor are we any longer in Pius XI's world of sheep within the fold, Communist wolves outside, and the Papacy standing sentinel at the gate. Still less are we in St. Pius X's world of multiplying censorship or Pius IX's *non-possumus* and *non-expedit*. We are looking at the whole world, at Africa, and Asia, and the United Nations, in particular, and we are trying to see

---

[215] *Mirari Vos* on Liberalism and Religious Indifferentism, encyclical of Pope Gregory XVI August 15, 1832, see paragraph 13-15.

[216] Pope Pius IX, *Quanta Cura* Encyclical promulgated on 8 December 1864.

[217] *Pacem in Terris*, pp.14.

what will help to make mankind everywhere have life, in peace, and have it more abundantly"[218].

Right to worship God according to one's conscience is viewed by Pope John XXIII as: "the very condition of our birth that we render to the God who made us that just homage which is His due; that we acknowledge Him alone as God, and follow Him. It is from this ligature of piety, which binds us to God, that religion drives its name"[219]. This is the take of *Pacem in Terris* on worshipping God according to one's conscience.

2.3.2.4 Right to choose freely one's State in Life

Another important right that also has a strong connection to Catholicism is 'the right to choose freely one's state in life'. In Catholicism, it can be part and parcel of religious freedom. Choice is one of the most valuable gifts bestowed on human beings as one of their ontological attributes. In fact it is an essence of humankind. It is free choice that makes us accountable and responsible for our actions. The choice of one's state in life should be left in the hands of the one whose life is to be affected by that choice. Perhaps the Pope has to mention this in solidarity with the persecuted Church and Catholics in some countries whose

---

[218] E.E.Y. Hales Pope John and His Revolution (1965) 63 as cited in http://www.shc.edu/theolibrary/resources/comments_pacem.htm.

[219] Citing the teaching of Lactantius see *Pacem in Terris,* pp.14.

authorities and governments might have banned or made it extremely difficult for a Catholic to choose a consecrated life in Christ. Under this rubric[220], Pope John XXIII mentioned two important areas with regards to Catholic life: priesthood/ordination and founding a family through marriage.

Ordination and marriage are two of the seven sacraments of the Catholic Church. Sacrament, defined conventionally, is "the outward and visible sign of an inward and invisible reality"[221]. From the well of the sacraments spring the mainstream Catholic traditional religious rituals. From the importance and indispensability of ordination and marriage in the Catholic Church, one can infer the importance and indispensability of choice in the authenticity and validity of Catholicism for Catholics[222], but also one can infer the importance and inviolability of choice in maintaining both internal and external peace. 'Right to choose freely one's state in life' should not be limited to ordination and marriage, but should be extended to all spheres of human life. Therefore, in our effort to develop a full universal peace in a fully human being we should create and maintain an atmosphere and an environment in which 'right to choose freely one's state in life' can be fulfilled. No body or authority should deny another of that choice. Moreover, this can be seen as a part of the right to religious freedom with

---

[220] *Pacem in Terris* paragraph 15-17.

[221] Harvey Cox, In *Our religions* edited by Sharma Arvind,etal. Pub. Harper Collins. 1993.

[222] Religion loses its importance, its indispensability, its authenticity and validity in the minds of people if it uses coercion and compulsion to acrue followers. There should be no compulsion in the matters of a genuine faith.

regards to the Catholic Church; denying Catholics a consecrated life in priesthood and sisterhood could not help in promoting world peace. This is an example of how we can link 'the right to choose freely one's state in life' to the establishment of world peace.

2.3.2.5 Economic Rights

Since human beings have both spiritual and material needs, they search for the fulfilment of both to attain a balanced peace. For this reason they must have both spiritual and economic rights; the spiritual rights being religious freedom, the economic rights including the private ownership of property. This signifies the free moral dominion and faculty one has over utility of something. Private ownership has wider freedom than leasing and renting, over which one's freedom of use is limited by certain conditions. Private ownership, with its natural foundation combined with its many advantages, such as guaranteeing personal dignity and freedom over property, incarnation of one's industrious work into tangible assets and the inducement to be industrious, is a contributing factor to social stability, peace and responsibilities. Economic rights do not in any way negate the universal destination of goods in the sense of Catholic social doctrine. For the Catholic Church: "The *right to private property*, acquired or received in a just way, does not do away with the original gift of the earth to the whole of mankind. The *universal destination of goods* remains primordial, even if the promotion of the common good requires respect for the right to private property and its exercise [sic]"[223].

Contrary to communist teaching, Pope John XXIII considered private ownership of property and productive goods as a natural human right and it is a social obligation to recognise it as such[224]. He viewed it as "a right which constitutes effectively and helps one to assert one's personality and responsibility in the field of solidity and security for family life, greater peace and responsibility in the country"[225]. World peace is at stake if the economic security of the people is not ensured. Therefore Pope John XXIII missed no opportunity to assert 'the right to the private ownership of property' and 'productive goods'. He viewed economic rights as a social obligation. Prior to the promulgation of *Pacem in Terris*, the 1948 Universal Declaration of Human Rights acknowledges this fact as it gives everyone the right to own property either individually or as a group, and also recognizes a right to favourable familial remuneration; favourable working condition and economic rights together with social and cultural rights[226], but Pope John XXIII's affirmation of these rights has elevated them to a higher moral ground in Catholicism and Catholic lives.

---

[223] Catechism of the Catholic Church , no. 2403.

[224] *Pacem in Terris*, pp. 22, see also *Mater et Magistra*, pp.19, (1961).

[225] *Ibid.,* pp. 21.

[226] UDHR (1948) article 17, 22 and 23.

By virtue of its importance to the development of world peace, the same rights have been reiterated in the International Covenant on Economic, Social and Cultural Rights (ICESCR) of 1966 that considered and stipulated economic rights together with social and cultural rights. The ICESCR stated that: "All peoples have the right of self-determination. By virtue of that right they freely determine their political status and freely pursue their economic, social and cultural development"[227]. This International Covenant urges state parties to the Covenant to ensure this right by stating that: "The States Parties to the present Covenant undertake to ensure the equal right of men and women to the enjoyment of all economic, social and cultural rights set forth in the present Covenant"[228].

For Pope John XXIII economic rights, which include work opportunity, unearthing one's initiative, and a healthy working environment, are inherent rights of every human being. For him it is also part of the economic right and dignity of everyone to engage in any economic activities that are commensurate to their degree of responsibility. He stated: "The amount a worker receives must be sufficient, in proportion to available funds, to allow him and his family a standard of living consistent with human dignity" [229]. This conviction echoed his predecessor, Pope Pius XII, who stated that it "is the nature itself that imposes

---

[227] International Covenant on Economic, Social and Cultural Rights (ICESCR) of 1966, article 1.

[228] Ibid (ICESCR) article 3.

[229] *Pacem in Terris*, pp. 20, see also Mater et Magistra, 1961, pp.18.

work upon human being as a duty"[230]. Based on this thought, then, each human has the right also to demand that the remuneration of his/her work be commensurate with his/her familial needs. For remuneration of a worker to be commensurate with the worker's familial needs, "is nature's categorical imperative for the preservation of man"[231]. In the encyclical *Pacem in Terris*, Pope John XXIII criticized exploitative and unhealthy working conditions and their systems of remuneration that victimize children, women and low wage earners. Article 22 and 23 of the United Nations' UDHR also appealed for a better system of remuneration.

'Work', as the embodiment of economic security and rights, could mean any kind of input by a human being manually or mentally geared towards unceasingly enhancing the scientific, technological, cultural and moral echelon of the community to sustain living[232]. It could also mean: "activities that harness and shape the material world to build "durable" material objects and products, including constructing and housing a durable space wherein familial action, its practices, traditions and fruits can be nurtured and preserved"[233]. In the interests of peace, economic rights should be extended to all the spheres of *vita activea*:

---

[230] *Ibid.*, pp. 20. Here he quoted Pope Puis XII's broadcast message, Pentecost June 1,1941.

[231] *Ibid.*, pp. 20.

[232] See Pope John II, *Laborem exercens*, 1981, Blessing.

[233] Hinze Firer Christian, "*Women, Families, and the Legacy of Laborem Exercens :An Unfinished Agenda*". In Journal of Catholic Social Thought 6:1, 2009, p. 67.

labor, work and action, the three fundamental human activities intimately connected with existence as advocated by Hannah Arendt[234]. According to Arendt, labor is the biological function which defines life itself, work is the artificial function of human existence and so defined as "worldliness," and action is activity that goes on between man and matter and leads to the permanence of a particular human's existence[235]. In all these spheres of human enterprise just remuneration that is commensurate with dignified human living is required.

Economic rights are sometimes abused and threatened by both political powers and economic institutions such as multinational corporations (MNC), transnational co-operation (TNC) or multinational enterprises (MNE) and others. As a good life is a valuable goal for peace, economic rights too are a valuable agent of peace. Development which has a strong link to economic rights is also another viable element of peace. Against this background, attention should be given to equal access to economic opportunities, equitable distribution of economic resources and social opportunities. Protective security, freedom from arbitrary deprivation of property, conditions of good health, basic education, and cultivation of initiatives should be encouraged, promoted and protected because they are strongly linked to the realization of world peace.

---

[234] Hinze Firer Christian, *op. cit.* P. 67.

[235] *Ibid.* See also Internet Encyclopedia of Philosophy at http://www.iep.utm.edu/arendt/.

Protection of the right of meeting and association is also among the *conditio sine qua non* for peace as will be examined in the segment below.

2.3.2.6 The Right of Meeting and Association

Influenced by their nature and nurture, human beings constitute societies and associations to amend any individual deficiency in obtaining certain necessary aims, services and goods for their own betterment and fulfillment of their needs. These include the formation of multi-political parties, labor unions and other cultural, financial and scientific associations. Associations can be necessary when they are formed by natural necessity or they can be voluntary when they are driven by free choice. They can also be as simple as a family or as complex as a nation. Totalitarian regimes fear freedom of meetings and associations that do not favour them, and in certain situations such associations are heavily repressed and suppressed. Such repression and suppression is a hindrance to both internal and external peace and can be a recipe for instability. It is also in contradiction with the United Nations, whose quest for freedom, justice and peace in the world recognizes the "right to freedom of peaceful assembly and association"[236] as a recipe for world peace. Pope John XXIII considered the right of meeting and association as "absolutely essential for the safeguarding of man's personal

---

[236] UDHR (1948) article 20.

freedom and dignity, while leaving intact a sense of responsibility"[237]. The right

of meeting and association is a recipe for peace and denying it can instigate

conflict and violence.

2.3.2.7 The Right to Emigrate and Immigrate

Again, the right to emigrate and immigrate are seen as recipes of peace in

both UDHR[238] and *Pacem in Terris*[239]. To emigrate is to leave one's own country

in order to live in another country, and to immigrate is to enter into another

country, usually for permanent residence. Regarding peace and the preservation of

life, both rights to emigrate and immigrate are important. In earlier times,

Muslims were able to have peace of mind and preservation of their lives and

religions because of emigration from Mecca and immigration to *Habash*/Ethiopia

and *Yathrib*/Madina respectively. The same could be said about the majority of

the Jews and Christians who had fled nations with harsh and unfavourable

policies against them into more accommodating countries. This applies to many

people today as well; movement could be for political, social or economic

reasons. Many people are living in peace today because of the rights to emigration

and immigration. Pope John XXIII considered the guaranteeing of this right as

---

[237] *Pacem in Terris*, pp. 24 see also *Mater et Magistra* (1961) pp. 22.

[238] UDHR (1948) articles 13 and 14.

[239] *Pacem in Terris*, pp. 25.

another important pre-requisite for peace. For Pope John XXIII, the fact that one is a citizen of a particular State does not deprive one "of membership in the human family, nor of citizenship in that universal society, the common world-wide fellowship of men"[240]. The right to emigrate and immigrate is crucial in saving the lives of many people, especially political dissidents and members of an ethnic minority. Many of these people have been able to live in peace due to international recognition of the right to emigrate and immigrate.

2.3.2.8 Political Rights

Political rights are different from but somehow related to civil rights. Some rights are both political and civil, that is, they are binary or hybrid in nature. For instance, rights such as the right to marry and to institute a family life are binary. That is to say, rights can be simultaneously both political and civil. Rights, economical or political, are part of general human rights. Political rights concern themselves with political measures in the political arena. Such rights include self-determination and self governance. Furthermore, political rights entail a citizen's entitlement to franchise, their participation directly or indirectly in the establishment or administration of government, natural justice, holding public office, petition, freedom of assembly, of thought, of religion and other political

---

[240] *Ibid.*, pp. 25.

activities. Civil rights are meant to protect an individual's mental and physical integrity, protect them from negative discrimination and ensure their entitlement to natural justice[241]. These rights are some of the most demanding rights in the modern world. Therefore, denial of them can be lead to political unrest, civil uprisings and brutal conflict. Since a human being becomes the centre of attraction in the political philosophy of modern political thought, unless a person's political rights are guaranteed, promoted and protected, the state's peace and political stability will be disturbed.

The rights discussed above are summed up in the three instruments of the International Bill of Rights: the Covenant on Civil and Political Rights (CCPR) of 16 December 1966; the International Covenant on Economic Social and Cultural Rights (ICESCR) of 16 December 1966; and the Universal Declaration of Human Rights (UDHR) of 10 December 1948, one of the three instruments and the parent of the other two.

However, these rights are mere lists of entitlements, with no effect unless hinged on or supported by a sense of duty and responsibility. Hence Pope John XXIII regarded rights and duties as "inextricably bound up", and both are pertaining to "one and same person" by way of conferring rights and imposing

---

[241] For more detail reading on political and civil rights see Alex Conte etal. Defining Civil and Political Rights: The Jurisprudence of the United Nations Human Rights Committee, Ashgate Publishing, England, 2004, pages 1-16.

duties. He said: "these rights and duties derive their origin, their sustenance, and their indestructibility from the natural law, which in conferring the one imposes the other"[242]. Thus, for there to be peace on earth, Pope John XXIII opined that rights and duties should be hinged on or supported by reciprocity, mutual collaboration and an attitude of responsibility. And this can be realized by establishing social life in the principles of truth, justice, charity and freedom that are animated by the belief that God is the origin and author of the incorporeal moral order that is supposed to prevail in human society.

In his stress on political rights, Angelo Giuseppe Roncalli, as Pope John XXIII, could not ignore the characteristics of the 1960s, which were humankind's yearning for equal opportunities of sexes and races in political, economic and social arenas. Hence, he had to speak out in favor of 'equality among men' in their political and social aspirations. Therefore every peacemaker should consider the aspirations and circumstances of the era that are prerequisites for realization of peace at a particular time. Pope John XXIII advocated the recognition of the equality of humankind in its natural, inherent and inalienable dignity, and condemned the doctrine, theory and rationale of ethnic, tribal and racial discrimination as intrinsically evil; and that it can in no way be justified at the time[243]. He recognized the equality of humankind as one of the conditions for

---

[242] *Pacem in Terris*, pp. 28.

[243] *Ibid.*, pp. 44.

universal peace. In the 1960s, equality among men in self determination and other issues were the demands of all members of the human family and were seen by Pope John XXIII as the characteristics and signs of the time. The willingness to promote the rights of all people, regardless of color, status, sex and creed, is the supreme test of humanity's commitment to peace, no matter who first said it or initiated it.

2.4 Violence and War among Humankind

Sadly, violence and war are part and parcel of human society, having featured in its history in both ancient and recent times. The first war recorded in the Bible was in the days of Amraphel, king of Shinar; Arioch, king of Ellasar; and Chedorlaomer, king of Elam. Tidal king of nations made war with Bera, king of Sodom; and with Birsha, king of Gomorrah; Shinab, king of Admah; and Shemeber, king of Zeboiim; and the king of Bela, which is Zoar[244].This occurred around 2700 B.C.E. Although, there might have been wars antecedent to 2700 B.C.E., when individuals, families, tribes, cities, and nations had been fighting each other, there are no records of these earlier wars apart from the story of Cain

---

[244] Bible, Genesis 14:1-23.

slaying Abel[245]. War can mean different things to different people and its origin is as controversial as its causes[246].

Wars are always the by-products of violence and conflict. Conflict may happen as a result of incompatibility and discrepancy between the participants over the values and interests in which opponents intend to dominate, harm or eliminate the rivals. Both war and violence occur as a result of conflict. Fink defined conflict as: "situation or process in which two or more social entities are linked by at least one form of antagonistic psychological relation or at least one form of antagonistic interaction"[247]. Violence and antagonism can have destructive consequences, especially when they lead to full-fledged war.

There are many types of wars and violence: international or external war and violence that can occur between two or more sovereign states; intra-national war and violence that occurs within the boundary of a state, especially between ethnic or religious groups; or rebellion within a country. However, one of the concerns of this research is centered on civil violence and wars and the efforts of the world community to avoid war and to preserve peace. To the pacifist, war is immoral

---

[245] Bible, Genesis 4:8.

[246] de Mesquita Bruce Bueno, The war trap, New Haven and London , Yale University Press 1981, pages 1-3). This controversy can be limited depending on our definition of war. Whether it being defined from sociological, legal, technical and psychological perspective (Quincy Wright, *A Study of War,* University of Chicago Press, 1964).

[247] Fink C.F.1968. *"Some Conceptual Difficulties in the Theory of Social Conflict"*. In Journal of Conflict Resolution,Vol.12, p. 456, as cited by M.William Bhaskaran: Role of Academics in Conflict Resolution. http://www.gvpwardha.in/documents/books/conflict/baskaran.html 10/09/10.

and uncalled for, but to many people, war is normal and unavoidable in human society. The question of how and why the war should be conducted led to the formulation of war doctrines, or theories. The theories addressed here are: *Realpolitik*, Pacifism and Just War doctrine.

2.4.1 Realpolitik

Realpolitik takes the view that ethical and moral standards do not apply to the structure of war except for humanitarian needs. *Realpolitik* theory could be in agreement with the statements of Michael Walzer that: "For as long as men and women have talked about war, they have talked about it in terms of right and wrong. And for almost as long, some among them have derided such talk, called it a charade, insisted that war lies beyond (or beneath) moral judgment. War is a world apart, where life itself is at stake, where human nature is reduced to its elemental forms, where self-interest and necessity prevail. Here men and women do what they must to save themselves and their communities, and morality and law have no place. *Inter arma silent leges*: in time of war the law is silent"[248]. However, as mentioned above, this theory of *Realpolitik*, where ethic and moral standards do not apply to warring situations and '*inter arma silent leges*', is not the definition of war in the 21ˢᵗ century. In this century, there are laws of moral

---

[248] Walzer Michael, Just and Unjust Wars: A Moral Argument with Historical Illustrations, Basic Books, USA, 1977, p. 3.

and ethical standards that require that a combatant must not attack Red Cross or Red Crescent in operation, prisoners must not be killed and hospitals must not be bombed, etc..... A just war has rules, based on *ius gentium* morality.

2.4.2 Pacifism

Pacifism can be defined as an "opposition to war or violence as a means of settling disputes; specifically: refusal to bear arms on moral or religious grounds"[249]. Pacifism is a doctrine, "an attitude or a policy of nonresistance" as a method of achieving one's goal without resorting to war or violence and it believes that war and violence as a means of settling disputes is morally wrong. One of the early genuinely pacifist movement was found in Buddhism, whose *ahimsa* principle required its believers to unconditionally refrain "from any act of violence" against creatures. However, "the ancient Greek conception of pacifism applied to individual conduct rather than to the actions of peoples or kingdoms"[250]. It is claim that the word pacifism was invented by Émile Arnaud (1864–1921) the French peace campaigner and widely used after its

---

[249] Merriam Webster Dictionary accessible at http://www.merriam-webster.com/dictionary/pacifism.

[250] *Ibid.*

adoption by some peace activists in 1901at the tenth Universal Peace Congress in Glasgow[251].

Pacifists hold the view that war and violence are 'beyond the pale' under any circumstances, and that all disputes should be settled by peaceful means. The intentional killing of innocent human beings is immoral and uncalled for. War, which by definition involves such killing, must be entirely banned on moral grounds; therefore, for the pacifist, war is immoral and uncalled for. Since both *realpolitik* and pacifism ultimately abandon any ethic of war, they are at two extreme ends of the spectrum, they are both unacceptable, unnecessary and indefensible to many people. Therefore, a third alternative theory, the Just War theory, must be developed. For many people, although war is abnormal, it is also unavoidable in human society. The question now is how and why a war should be conducted; this has led to the postulation of a Just War doctrine which is logical, defendable and necessary.

2.4.3 Just War

The Just War doctrine has basically two main components: *Ius ad bellum*, that entails the justified decision to undertake war; and *Ius in bello*, that implies

---

[251] Keith Robbins, The Abolition of War: the Peace Movement in Britain, 1914-1919, University of Wales Press, 1976, p.10.

right conduct in prosecuting war. Just War doctrine has been developed and theorized by experts from the medieval period through to the contemporary era. One of the most important exponents of Just War theory in the medieval period is Thomas Aquinas, who described both components of Just War doctrine: *Ius ad bellum* and *Ius in bello* [252]. *Ius ad bellum* demands that a war to be waged by a right authority (*auctoritas principis*), for a just cause (*causa iusta*) and for a right intention (*sit intention bellantium recta*). However, in the modern period into mid-20th century, the *Ius ad bellum* principle added three other conditions that must be met before waging a just war: last resort; reasonable prospect of success; and proportionality in the final outcome.

Ius in bello includes the discrimination, that is, the immunity, of the non-combatants and proportionality in collateral damage. Injured soldiers and prisoners of war must be respected and must be treated humanely. Nevertheless, the Just War doctrine in its strictest sense should be seen as merely theoretical and speculative in managing modern warfare. "They were meant,…., to cover warfare of a special kind, that [is] between mercenary armies, and not our mammoth warfare which sometimes entails the total downfall of the nations at grips with each other; the principles, in fact, cannot be applied in the life of modern nations without doing serious damage to the particular peoples

---

[252] Aquinas Thomas, *Summa Theologiae* 2a-2ae. Blackfriars, 1972, Pages 80-83. For more detail reading on Catholic Church's just war theory See also paragraph 2307- 2317 of Catechism of the Catholic Church, http://www.vatican.va.

involved"[253]. In practical terms and with regard to the highly advanced technological warfare of today, Just War theory is also unrealistic and unattainable. Its reality, authenticity and attainability depend on the non-manufacture of those weapons that cannot be used within the context and the legal frame of Just War theory. Modern warfare contravenes some fundamentals of this doctrine, most significantly the principle of discrimination, that is, the immunity, of the non-combatants and proportionality in collateral damage. This was clearly manifested during World War II in the launching of atomic bombs on Hiroshima and Nagasaki in Japan by the United States of America. Moreover, "If one were to chart the percentage of combatants killed as opposed to non-combatants it would be apparent that the trend in warfare was toward the killing of more non-combatants than combatants"[254]. During World War I, for instance, civilian casualties made up fewer than 5% of all casualties. Today, about 75% or more of those killed or wounded in wars are non-combatant civilians[255].

Interstate violence and war are assumed to be unavoidable, and so a large part of the national budget of many states is consumed by defence and the acquisition of weaponry. Since war can be economically lucrative, nations might also set obstacles on the path to peace by continuous development and

---

[253] Ottaviani Alfredo, *"A Classic Text The future of offensive war."* In *Oikonomia, Febbraio,* 2000. Accessible at www.oikonomia.it/pages/febb/classica.htm .

[254] Bemporad Jack, *op., cit.*, 2009, p.1.

[255] Judy A. Benjamin, *op. cit.*

maintenance of high levels of arsenals for economic purposes. The 'military industrial complex' that, according to Pursell C., can be referred to as "an informal and changing coalition of groups with vested psychological, moral, and material interests in the continuous development and maintenance of high levels of weaponry, in preservation of colonial markets and in military-strategic conceptions of internal affairs"[256], certainly does not help in disarmament and arm reductions. Indeed, it can also be an obstacle to peace. Due to the uncertainty of their security, dictators of underdeveloped countries also trade with industrialised nations in a bid to prolong their power by spending large sums of public money building up their arsenals. Dictatorship and long periods in power also generate war and violence in most of the underdeveloped countries.

Violence and war, be it interstate or intrastate, are fuelled also by territorial disputes and ethnic or religious animosities, and have caused unmitigated misery, economic and social destruction in poor nations. Higher scale agricultural productivity, integral human capacity building and development are very low in violent and war-torn countries. Economic growth and progress, and contextual democratization are unattainable in a violent and warring situation. As a result hunger and starvation, and the widespread outbreak of diseases cause much

---

[256] See Muhammad Ahmed Qadri, World Peace Order Towards an International State, Publisher: Islamic Educational & Cultural Research Center, USA, 2008, P. 72.

misery and death around the globe, and in certain cases have threatened the existence of humankind[257], especially in poor nations.

As violence and war are part of human society a solution to minimise them must be developed. There are basically two means: diplomatic negotiation or military force. Cicero, the great Roman orator, offered two means for settling disputes: discussion and force. He said: "Discussion and force are the main ways of settling quarrels, the former of which is peculiar to man, the latter to brute beasts"[258]. Of the two, it is normal to choose the former in a normal circumstance. But at times where diplomacy is exhausted and economic sanctions have failed, military force would be needed as a last resort to bring peace. Violence and wars are undesirable and their consequences are also bitter, but at the same time they are unavoidable between states and between people. Therefore, international systems must find ways and means to solve them when they occur or are about to occur. This is one of the *raisons d'être* of the international systems.

---

[257] The World at War, http://www.globalsecurity.org/military/world/war/index.html (21/11/10.

[258] Ottaviani Alfredo, A Classic Text The future of offensive war. Oikonomia, *Febbraio,* 2000. *op. Cit.*

2.5 Persons, Families, People and States: How to Structure New Relations to Guarantee Peace

The structure of relations between persons, families and state is a vital guarantor for peace and stability within the states. How to construct a structure for new relations in guaranteeing peace and stability nationally and internationally between persons, families and states will be examined below.

2.5.1 Persons, Families, People and States

The relations between persons, families, people and states are important in guaranteeing peace. There are inextricable links and relations between them. It is the coming together of persons that makes up a family, the coming together of families that make up a people, and it is the coming together of a people that forms a state. Peace minded persons can make a peace loving family that can produce a peace loving people to form a peace loving state. A person is the basic unit in guaranteeing peace; hence, its upbringing and formation should be geared toward peace. This logic guides the UNESCO Constitution that stated: "Since wars begin in the minds of men, it is in the minds of men that the defences of peace must be constructed" [259]. Pope John XXIII also stated that: "unless this process of disarmament be thoroughgoing and complete, and reach men's very souls, it is impossible to stop the arms race or to reduce armaments" [260]. When

---

[259] UNESCO Constitution, adopted in London on 16 November, 1945.

[260] *Pacem in Terris,* pp.113.

peace reaches the soul and mind of a person and therein constructs its defences, it can reach the familial, public and state levels. However, in order to ensure wars between the states become obsolete, construction of peace in the minds of the people is not enough. It is in the structures and systems of the states and in the international systems that the defences of peace must be built. At the interstate level these defences can manifest in *pacta sunt servenda*, and in various ways of co-operation and collaboration.

To guarantee the maintenance of peace within and among these four units of persons, families, people and states, new structures and new relations should be formulated. The first step in this structure of relations is the 'authority'. "Every civilized community must have a ruling authority, and this authority, no less than society itself, has its source in nature..."[261]. This authority must be just and truthful. It must not be tyrannical, or dictatorial, and totalitarian in nature. It must derive its binding force from the moral order that is realizable only through appeal to the conscience of the governed. Thus, for Pope John XXIII, any regime that "governs solely or mainly by means of threats and intimidation or promises of reward, provides men with no effective incentive to work for the common good. And even if it did, it would be certainly offensive to the dignity of free rational

---

[261] *Ibid.*, pp.46. See also Immortale Dei, encyclical of Pope Leo XIII on the Christian Constitution of States (1885) , pp.3.

human beings"[262]. On this note, even the electioneering process, which is expected to be a dignified and honorable means to take to the helm of government and is expected to legitimize and authorize one's status in public office, is expected to be free from intimidation, bribery and empty promises or lies.

The goal of public authority is expected to be the attainment of the 'common good', whose essential aim is to facilitate "the *sum total of social conditions which allow people, either as groups or as individuals, to reach their fulfillment more fully and more easily*"[263]. The common good that is mentioned about 46 times in *Pacem in Terris* should be holistic and integral, entailing the spiritual as well as the material prosperity of persons, families and people. The principal responsibility of public authority *inter alia*, is expected to be the recognition, respect, protection and promotion of human rights and the creation of an environment in which performance of civil duties and responsibilities of individuals can be facilitated and coordinated. "To safeguard the inviolable rights of the human person, and to facilitate the performance of his duties, is the principal duty of every public authority"[264]. Social progress, as well as economic progress, is part of the purpose of public authority. For this reason, the public authority must provide essential services such as "road-building, transportation,

---

[262] *Pacem in Terris*,pp.48.

[263] Catechism, *op. cit.* no. 1906.

[264] *Pacem in Terris*, pp. 60.

communications, drinking-water, housing, medical care, ample facilities for the practice of religion, and aids to recreation"[265]. Thus, public authority has failed its moral existence and obligation if it fails to address "those social conditions which favor the full development of human personality"[266]. United Nations Secretary-General Kofi Annan made an insightful statement in this regard by saying that: "State sovereignty, in its most basic sense, is being redefined by the forces of globalization and international cooperation. The State is now widely understood to be the servant of its people, and not vice versa. At the same time, individual sovereignty -- and by this I mean the human rights and fundamental freedoms of each and every individual as enshrined in our Charter - has been enhanced by a renewed consciousness of the right of every individual to control his or her own destiny"[267]. The relations between citizens and public authorities should be deeply rooted in terms of rights and duties[268].

---

[265] *Ibid.,* pp. 64.

[266] *Ibid.*, pp.58 .See also Mater et Magistra, 1961, pp. 65.

[267] Annan A. Kofi, Annual Report to the General Assembly, 20 September 1999 accessed at http://www.un.org/News/ossg/sg/stories/ on 4th May 2012.

[268] *Pacem in Terris*, pp.77.

2.5.2 How to Structure New Relations between Persons, Family, People and States in Order to Guarantee Peace

It is a lesson of history that political, economic and cultural inequities in a society become more obvious when a government fails to take appropriate action in rendering its duties towards the common good. In relation to guaranteeing peace, the structure and operation of the public authority should be based on law and order and conscience. The system, the nature and the principle of government should be left to be determined within the cultural context, the prevailing circumstances and the condition of the people[269]. While the system of government is that which helps the nature and the principle of government to achieve its goals, the nature of government is "that by which it is constituted" or structured; and the principle of government is "that by which it is made to act", or better still, the "human passions which set [the government] in motion"[270].

In the structure and operation of the public authority, the division and separation of powers is important as it can provide checks and balances to protect and safeguard the rights and liberty of the citizenry and fulfillment of their rights in the rule of law. The three basic principles of the rule of law include: the supremacy of law, as opposed to whimsical power; equality of all before the law;

---

[269] *Ibid.*, pp. 68.

[270] Montesquieu, The Spirit of Laws, Book III ,1, p. 37.

and the right of the courts in defining and interpreting what the law is[271]. These basic principles of the rule of law are articulated by Albert Venn Dicey in this manner: "In England no man can be made to suffer punishment or to pay damages for any conduct not definitely forbidden by law; every man's legal rights or liabilities are almost invariably determined by the ordinary courts of the realm, and each man's individual rights are far less the result of our constitution than the basis on which that constitution is founded"[272.]

Power is one of the characteristics of government. However, absolute power can make a good ruler a bad one, as observed by John Emerich Edward Dalberg, Lord Acton: "power tends to corrupt, and absolute power corrupts absolutely. great men are almost always bad men"[273]. Against this background, the principle of separation of powers[274] is then recommended[275]. Separation of powers and functions between the three arms of government (legislative, executive and judicial, which correspond to the three main functions of the public authority) should be instituted.

---

[271] See Albert Venn Dicey, *Introduction to the Study of the Law of the Constitution (LF ed.)* [1915, ed. Roger E. Michener , Indianapolis: Liberty Fund 1982. Accessed at: http://oll.libertyfund.org/simple.php?id=1714, on 9 May 2012.

[272] *Ibid.*

[273] Dalberg Emerich Edward John, 1st Baron Acton (1834–1902), British historian. Letter, April 3, 1887, to Bishop Mandell Creighton. The Life and Letters of Mandell Creighton, vol. 1, ch. 13, ed. Louise Creighton (1904).

[274] See Baron de Montesquieu, *op. cit.*

[275] *Pacem in Terris*, pp.67.

In separation of powers, the function of the executive is the implementation of laws and administration of the country; the legislature's role is to make and amend laws and to scrutinize the policies of the government; the function of the judicial branch is to regulate the application of laws by the executive and declaration of *ultra vires* as unconstitutional[276].

In order to guarantee peace, the laws must safeguard the dignity of its people. The people and 'citizens' of a state should be given the opportunity to participate in public life. When the state is founded and formed by the people, one of the natural consequences of people's dignity is their right to be actively involved in the government of the state[277]. This participation of citizens will open a new and extensive field of opportunity for services towards the common good. It can also help towards a regular succession of public officials and can pump new blood and

---

[276] Separations of powers and checks and balances make it possible for three arms of government to remain in a state of healthy, dynamic and constant display and interaction, with none of the three is supremely advantaged to dominate the others. The judicial is limited by the legislature because it is not empowered to create laws. It is only the legislature that is empowered to create and amend laws. The legislature is also limited since it is empowered to create and amend laws but not directly empowered in application of laws. The executive is also limited as it is not empowered to create or interpret laws. It can only apply them within judiciary interpretation. The scopes, objectives, and procedures of the three arms of governments sometimes can overlap and tense. Hence, separation of powers is necessary for preservation, security, stability and predictability of government which are the supreme goals of every state.

[277] *Pacem in Terris*, pp.73.

new experience in the system for efficiency and effectiveness[278]. It should be a 'pedagogic duty of the state'[279] to encourage the participation of its subjects in public administration by providing capacity-building training. This can increase citizens' confidence in the government and can maintain continuity, security, preservation and stability of the government by taking "on a new vitality in keeping with the progressive development of human society"[280].

However, for this participation to be productive, it should be guided by "a clear and precisely worded charter of fundamental human rights formulated and incorporated into the State's general constitutions"[281]. It "must have a public constitution, couched in juridical terms, laying down clear rules relating to the designation of public officials, their reciprocal relations, spheres of competence and prescribed methods of operation"[282].

When these domestic issues, or internal affairs of the states, are properly taken care of in the interests of peace, the next area to be addressed would be international affairs. This is so because no nation or state is absolutely self-

---

[278] *Ibid.,* pp. 74.

[279] This phrase is taken form Peter Riga's Peace on Earth, A commentary on Pope John's Encyclical. Pub. Herder and Herder N.Y.1964, Page, 103.

[280] *Pacem in Terris*, pp. 74.

[281] *Ibid.*, pp. 75.

[282] *Ibid.,* pp. 76.

sufficient. The states must interact and interrelate to realize both national and international goals. This interaction of the states can only be fruitful in an atmosphere of peace. It is this relation between the states that we will analyze in the segment below.

2.6 Recipes for Peace in International System

Due to our sense of interconnectedness and the interdependency of our nature reflected in our social, political and economic interactions, international relations and an international system has to exist. Relations between the states are the core of international relations[283] and system.

---

[283] "The discipline of International Relations (IR) is the academic study of the origins and consequences (both empirical and normative) of a world divided among states. So defined, IR is a very broad discipline. It includes a variety of sub-fields such as diplomatic statecraft and foreign policy analysis, comparative politics, historical sociology, international political economy, international history, strategic studies and military affairs, ethics, and international political theory. In addition to its wide scope, the study of international relations is shaped by the interplay between continuity and change in its subject-matter". See (Griffiths and Terry O'Callaghan, International Relations: the Key Concepts, First published, Routledge 2002, p. vii). International Relations confirm the existence of sovereign nations in distinct territorial lands outside one's territory, each possessing its own internal laws and exercising authority subject to no restriction except those provided by its constitution, treaty, and pact or by (*ius gentium*) the law of nations. Thomas Jefferson in a nutshell identified three basic sources for the principles of (*ius gentium*) law of nations. The law of nations according to Jefferson is composed of three branches: the moral law of our nature, the usages of nations, and the special conventions. See (Armitage David, The declaration of independence: a global history, Harvard University Press 2007, Page 69). The purpose of international relations for Montesquieu is reciprocity of good in peace times and

A system is an organized, purposeful structure regarded as a 'whole', consisting of interrelated and interdependent components, entities, factors, members, parts etc., which continually influence one another harmoniously, directly or indirectly, to maintain their activities at the existence of the whole, in a bid to achieve the 'common purpose' or the 'goal' of the whole[284]. An international system, therefore, should be complete, coherent and interdependent in its relations among states, organizations, and groups. The role of every nation is a component of the international system, whose aim is to interrelate in order to achieve the international common goal. In the face of the complex relations of the epoch, the international system, without harmfully undermining the rights and self-determination of nations, has to develop a system for the channelling and ordering of any collective efforts to achieve a common objective or to address worldwide problems that go beyond the capacity of individual states to solve.

Due to the importance of peace in international relations, there needs to be an international system in the quest for peace. In this regard, Pope John XXIII stated that relationships between the states "must likewise be harmonized in accordance with the dictates of truth, justice, willing cooperation, and freedom"[285]. However,

---

minimization of damages in times of war: "The law of nations is naturally founded on this principle, that different nations ought in time of peace to do one another all the good they can, and in time of war as little injury as possible, without prejudicing their real interests". Montesquieu, *op.cit.,* p. 22.

[284] Business dictionary, http://www.businessdictionary.com/definition/system.html (01/01/11).

[285] *Pacem in Terris*, pp. 80.

for him "the law of nature that governs the life and conduct of individuals" must be the same laws to "regulate the relations of political communities with one another"[286]. As we will see in this thesis, this is not the predominant concept in international relations at the present time.

A purposeful and successful international system and relations ought to be based on truth. In his era of complex international systems and relations, Pope John XXIII held the view that the states should acknowledge the fact that their relations with one another should emanate from the truth, be based on the truth and end in the truth[287].

2.6.1 Truth

In the quest for justice and peace in international systems, truth, as one of the guarantors of peace, calls for the jettisoning of all kinds of false information, and unjust racial and regional discrimination of the international system and relations, by acknowledging the principle that all nations by nature are equal in dignity. They have the right to existence, development, and possession of the necessary means. They should be primarily responsible for their own development, and are legitimately entitled to their good names[288]. Pope John XXIII compared our

---

[286] *Ibid.*, pp. 80.

[287] *Ibid.*, pp. 86.

[288] *Pacem in Terris*, pp. 86.

individual disparity in the level of knowledge, virtue, intelligence and wealth, to that of nations with a "superior degree of scientific, cultural and economic development". He insisted that this disparity must neither be used in favour of those who hold a superior position in order to "impose their will arbitrarily on others", nor may the scientific, cultural and economic progress of one state be a green light to wield unjust political domination over other states. On the contrary, he urged such men and states to take a lion's share "in the common responsibility" in a form of truth and solidarity to "help others to reach perfection" and to "make a greater contribution to the common cause of social progress"[289].

Since information is very powerful and important in shaping one's relations with the other, objectivity in both national and international media is truly vital. Truth demands "unruffled impartiality" from the media practitioners. Every piece of propaganda that infringes "the principles of truth and justice and injures the reputation of another nation" is utterly rejected by Pope John XXIII[290]. One of the causes of war could be the denial of truth and its replacement with false propaganda. Insisting on truth as one of the guiding principles in quest for justice and peace, the UNESCO Constitution states: "That the great and terrible war which has now ended was a war made possible by the denial of the democratic

---

[289] *Ibid.*, pp. 87-88.

[290] *Ibid.*, pp.90.

principles of the dignity, equality and mutual respect of men, and by the propagation, in their place, through ignorance and prejudice, of the doctrine of the inequality of men and races"[291.]   Equally misleading and dangerous in consequence are the distorted images and reporting practised by both national and international media on a particular entity[292.] The negative consequences of propagating false information are great in the quest for justice and peace[293].

---

[291] Preamble of UNESCO Constitution,1945.

[292] For instance, false propaganda by media in the Rwandan 1994 genocide was a crucial one. According to *Roméo Dallaire* the commander of the United Nations Assistance Mission for Rwanda (UNAMIR) in his article "Media Dichotomy", affirms local media's role in stimulating and aggravating the genocide, while the international media either downplayed or seriously misconstrued the event on the ground. This led to the massacre of thousands of lives. Roméo stated: "The news media – both domestic and international – played a crucial role in the 1994 Rwanda genocide. From my vantage point as commander of the United Nations Assistance Mission for Rwanda (UNAMIR), I was able to watch the strange dichotomy of local media, on one side, fuelling the killing while international media, on the other side, virtually ignored or misunderstood what was happening. The local media, particularly the extremist radio station Radio-Télévision Libre des Milles Collines (RTLM), were literally part of the genocide. The *genocidaires* used the media like a weapon. The haunting image of killers with a machete in one hand and a radio in the other never leaves you. The international media initially affected events by their absence. A tree was falling in the forest and no one was there to hear it. Only those of us in Rwanda, it seemed, could hear the sound, because the international media were not there in any appreciable numbers at the outset". See (Thompson Allan, The Media and the Rwanda Genocide, Pluto Press , London England, Fountain Publishers Kampala, Uganda, 2007, p. 12.ff).

[293] Alison Des Forges confirms this in his article "Hate media in Rwanda: Call to Genocide" in (International Commission 1993: 13–14) by saying: "In March 1992, Radio Rwanda was first used in directly promoting the killing of Tutsi in a place called Bugesera, south of the national capital. On 3 March, the radio repeatedly broadcast a communiqué supposedly sent by a human rights

2.6.2 Dialogue

In a system where actors belong to diverse cultures, customs and orientations, ideological differences over certain values are visible and inevitable. One issue may at the same time be seen or approached from different perspectives. Thus, if cooperation in truth must be the core of an international system in its quest for justice and peace, dialogue and negotiation are important in convincing the other players. This is necessary in promoting the legitimacy and efficacy of an international system as the indispensable factor in the quest for justice, peace, development and the protection of human rights. Dialogue and negotiation can make international system truly international and legitimately lawful. This dialogue can take many forms at many levels: it can be political; religious; social; and cultural. In a nutshell, a dialogue of life for coexistence must be based on the recognition of the standard universal values, such as justice, peace, development, the protection of human rights and the rule of law. A dialogue is required that can open up new opportunities and inject into the system the commitment to protection and promotion of higher human values in support of an international standard and cohesion in the service of the common good.

---

group based in Nairobi warning that Hutu in Bugesera would be attacked by Tutsi. Local officials built on the radio announcement to convince Hutu that they needed to protect themselves by attacking first. Led by soldiers from a nearby military base, Hutu civilians, members of the *Interahamwe*, a militia attached to the MRND party, and local Hutu civilians attacked and killed hundreds of Tutsi". See (Thompson Allan, *op.cit.* p., 41 ff).

In a dialogue of life, people seek to live the life of good neighbourliness in sharing their joys and sorrows, their human problems and preoccupations in all spheres of life. It can enable people, regardless of their religious, political, social and cultural affiliations, to come together in a spirit of solidarity for their integral development and liberation from structural sufferings and injustice. A dialogue can be specific if its issue is specific. For instance, it can be religious if the issue is religious one. In this area interreligious dialogue will be important. The experts and specialists can investigate and deepen their understanding over the issue by sharing from each other's creed, their respective religious heritage and traditions through scriptural reasoning, and harmonize a way forward. It can be a cultural, political or economic dialogue if the issue at hand is cultural, political or economic. Without dialogue and negotiation, other members of the international system may consider those values of the international system as an imposition and hence will not be fully committed to its protection.

At present, the religious sphere of dialogue is desperately needed in the quest for peace and justice in the international system. In principle, all religions are in favour of human coexistence. In practice, however, some religious leaders and, more often, political leaders use religions for the purpose of their selfish political aggrandisement, by igniting common religious sentiments and belief with inflammatory, violent messages, with the promise of the "paradise" every religion promises to the just and faithful. Human history has many episodes where religious militancy and belligerency have been ignited for selfish ends. At the present time in particular, it is some Muslims[294] who are using religion in igniting violence for selfish gain nationally and internationally, in the same way as in the past century it has been the case of some Christians. Violent relations between *Sunni* and *Shi'aite*, and between Christians and Muslims, are extreme in some countries. Elsewhere, excessive threats to religious freedom exist. All these justify the need for intercultural and interreligious dialogue or interreligious diplomacy in international systems. It is expected that a responsive and responsible international system will not ignore these threats, indeed, it is expected to facilitate co-existence between its members. Dialogue in an international system is a *conditio sine qua non* in the pursuit of justice and peace. A contemporary issue would be over the use of nuclear energy, as in the case of Iran and IAEA and in the case of North Korea.

---

[294] In the international system and relations of the day, we are faced with the terror engineered by some Muslims against all nationally and internationally. From 8/7/1998 terror bombing on USA embassies in Nairobi and Daru-salaam in Kenya and Tanzania respectively; 9/11/2001 terrorist attack on USA; 3/11/2004 terrorist attack on Spain; 7/7/2005 terrorist attack on UK; war on Weapons of Mass Destruction (WMD) on Iraq and on terrorism in Afghanistan; to the recent Kenyan intervention in Somalia against *Alshabab* which is alleged to have been kidnapping tourists in Kenyan territory all are religiously connected or inclined. The most recent and most tragic ones are *Boko-Haram* of Nigeria, *Azawad* and *Ansaruddin* of Mali and *Alqaeda Magreb* in North Africa both using kidnapping and killing of international tourists and innocent civilians as their means to justify and achieve their end. All of these are now internationalized. French, ECOWAS and Chadian troops under the mandate of United Nations are in Mali to roll back the insurgency.

Pope Paul VI observed the importance of dialogue in the quest for justice and peace by stating that: "The mere fact that we are embarking upon a disinterested, objective and sincere dialogue is a circumstance in favour of a free and honourable peace. It positively excludes all pretence, rivalry, deceit and betrayal. It brands wars of aggression, imperialism, and domination as criminal and catastrophic. It necessarily brings men together on every level: heads of states, the body of the nation and its foundations, whether social, familial, or individual. It strives to inspire in every institution and in every soul the understanding and love of peace and the duty to preserve it"[295]. This is the type of dialogue that is expectedly necessary in the quest for justice and peace.

2.6.3 Justice

Pacem in Terris "integrates justice as rights and justice as right order[296]". It also considers right order as law. Justice itself is one of the guarantors of peace. "Take away justice, and what are kingdoms but mighty bands of robbers"[297]. According to Edmund Burke, "justice is itself the great standing policy of civil society; and any eminent departure from it, under any circumstances, arouses the suspicion of being no policy at all"[298]. Justice entails recognition, respect and

---

[295] Pope Paul VI, *Ecclesiam Suam*, AAS56 (1964), pp.106.

[296] Hittinger Russell, *op. cit.,* P. 46.

[297] St. Augustine of Hippo, see *Pacem in Terris*, pp. 92.

[298]Burke Edmund (1729-1797) Reflections on the Revolution in France: And on the Proceedings

fulfillment of all human rights, responsibilities and duties. Recognition of rights such as right to existence, to self development, to due honours and dignity, and to the means necessary in fulfilling them are the demands of justice. For this reason, justice become a good guarantor in the quest for peace. It is for justice, if there to be peace, that individual, family and states seek to avoid any action that could violate human rights and state sovereignty. For Pope John XXIII, "just as individual men may not pursue their own private interests in a way that is unfair and detrimental to others, so too it would be criminal in a State to aim at improving itself by the use of methods which involve other nations in injury and unjust oppression"[299].

In the situation of conflict of interests among the states it must be settled neither by military might, nor by 'deceit or trickery', but by justice[300]. Any pollution and global warming that has a negative impact on the ecosystem and the environment, such as rivers, lakes and lands on which others' lives depend, is oppression and suppression that deviate from justice. This is a flagrant violation of justice especially if such attempt is directed at the extinction of a particular community[301].

---

in Certain Societies in London Relative to that Event. Printed for J. Dodsley, in Pall Mall M.Dcc.XC p. 230.

[299] *Pacem in Terris*, pp. 92.

[300] *Ibid.*, pp. 93.

[301] *Ibid.*, pp.95.

The unfolding acrimonious events of the globe committed by human beings against fellow human beings under the auspices of religion, race, ethnicity and politics are caused by lack of justice. Justice is one of the crucial guarantors in the quest for peace. This did not escape the writers of the *Gaudium et Spes*, (the Pastoral Constitution on the Church in the Modern World) as it reads: "Peace is not merely the absence of war; nor can it be reduced solely to the maintenance of a balance of power between enemies; nor is it brought about by dictatorship. Instead, it is rightly and appropriately called an enterprise of justice. Peace results from that order structured into human society by its divine Founder, and actualized by men as they thirst after ever greater justice. The common good of humanity finds its ultimate meaning in the eternal law. But since the concrete demands of this common good are constantly changing as time goes on, peace is never attained once and for all, but must be built up ceaselessly"[302].

2.6.4 Active Solidarity

As mentioned above, from the Catholic social teaching 'active solidarity' can be regarded as "a commitment to the good of one's neighbour with the readiness,

---

[302] *Gaudium et Spes*, op. cit.1965, # 78 accessed at http://www.vatican.va on 18/02/2012

in the Gospel sense, to "lose oneself' for the sake of the other instead of exploiting him, and to 'serve him' instead of oppressing him for one's own advantage"[303]. 'Active solidarity', in other words, is struggling to go beyond one's selfishness to actively participate in liberality, compassion, and reconciliation. This must be achieved by regarding other people and nations as one's neighbours; not to be indifferent to their poverty, sufferings and the deprivation of their basic human rights. The existence of international societies and communities is a manifestation that nation states are moving towards social and communitarian feeling. It is the acknowledgement of their growing interdependence on one another in political, cultural, economic and security spheres. This is a progress and enrichment for humankind in its quest for peace. The partition of the world into territorial states must not stop active solidarity amongst them. The rationality behind the partition was to minimize conflict and generate peace. "Of its very nature, civil authority exists, not to confine men within the frontiers of their own nations, but primarily to protect the common good of the State, which certainly cannot be divorced from the common good of the entire human family"[304].

Active solidarity transcends tribal, ethnic, religious and geographical peripheries. It embraces humanity as a single family and should drive its legitimacy from truth and justice[305]. According to *Pacem in Terris*, aiding and

---

[303] Compendium of the Social Doctrine of the Church, op. cit., 2004, no.193.

[304] *Pacem in Terris*, pp. 98.

[305] Thus, it is indeed contradictory in the light of sincere active solidarity, truth and justice that

assisting the poorer countries by the richer countries should be based on a new world order: "A new order founded on moral principles is the surest bulwark against the violation of the freedom, integrity and security of other nations, no matter what may be their territorial extension or their capacity for defense"[306]. In the view of Pope John Paul II, "It is through culture that man lives a truly human life. Human life is also culture in the sense that it is through culture that man is distinguished and differentiated from everything else that exists in the visible world: man cannot do without culture"[307]. Thinking on this line of thought, 'active solidarity' in everything else, such as collective security, promoting good governance, justice and education is important and should be channeled through the culture of the person in need if we are to quest for peace.

---

only about the richest 25% of the world's population receives 75% of the world's income and the poorest 75% of the population share just 25%. According to Income Inequality, Milanovic research established that: "the richest 25% of the world's population receives 75% of the world's income, even when adjusting for Purchasing Power Parity. The poorest 75% of the population share just 25%. This occurs because a large proportion of the world's population lives in the poorest countries and within the poorest regions of those countries, particularly in the rural areas of China, rural and urban India and Africa". See Income Inequality, accessible at http://ucatlas.ucsc.edu/income.php. Also the insistence on maintaining imbalance world market system and trade policy that spotlight the disparity between the have and have-not countries into a sharper focus have no high moral grounds in active human solidarity.

[306] *Pacem in Terris*, pp.124 see also Pius XII's broadcast message, Christmas 1941, AAS 34 (1942) 16-17.

[307] Pope John Paul II, "*For a World Worthy of Man*", United Nations Educational, Scientific and Cultural Organization, Beugnet S.A. Paris, France, UNESCO,1980, p.38.

2.6.5 Interdependent Cooperation

Willing interdependent cooperation in working towards development and in solving the problems of disease, illiteracy, poverty and security threats is very important in the quest for peace. Interdependent cooperations can be bilateral or multilateral cooperations; they can be regional or interregional, continental or intercontinental, or a universal cooperation. On these forms existed North-South cooperation, South-South cooperation, East-West cooperation - and the biggest of all is the universal cooperation led by United Nations. All of these types of cooperations are contributing factors for realization of political peace between the states. *Pacem in Terris* states: "No State can fittingly pursue its own interests in isolation from the rest, nor, under such circumstances, can it develop itself as it should"[308]. This makes the pursuance of "universal common good", the good of the whole humankind, a necessity, a necessity that cannot be realized by a single nation in its single efforts. As such, the creation of such cooperations at regional, continental and universal levels to pursue 'universal common good' is paramount in the quest for justice and peace- especially during the Cold War period and Turkish-Cuban missile crisis after which *Pacem in Terris* was promulgated.

At the time of the promulgation of *Pacem in Terris*, East-West cooperation was the most needed in the quest for world peace. Historically and at present, there had been and there are still efforts for East-West cooperation. Treaties have

---

[308] *Pacem in Terris*, pp. 130-131.

been signed and diplomats have been reciprocally accredited as the efforts to ameliorate East-West cooperation. Pope John XXIII's appeal in *Pacem in Terris* for cooperation is one of those efforts. However, alongside these treaties and diplomatic relations, there was also a deep political mistrust between USA and USSR, the leaders of the Western and Eastern blocs at the time respectively. For instance, the Soviet's acceptance of an Anglo-American plan for a UN Atomic Energy Agency (that was destined to control the development, proliferation and use of nuclear power), and USSR's concession to make some transformations in the Romanian and Bulgarian parliaments, were regarded by George F. Kennan of the U.S. embassy in Moscow at the time as "fig leaves of democratic procedure to hide the nakedness of Stalinist dictatorship"[309]. On the other hand Andrey Zhdanov, the Communist leader of Leningrad, in 1947 had described the Eastern bloc as "the peace-loving, progressive camp led by the Soviet Union" and the Western bloc as a "militaristic, reactionary camp led by the United States"[310].

Nonetheless, with all such poltical mistrust and conflict of interests in our time, there are still efforts for the East-West cooperation on matters of arms control, nonproliferation, and disarmament. For instance, the Strategic Arms Reduction Treaty (START), which had been signed by George Bush in 1991, is still seen to be on track. Although the USA had decided to withdraw from the Anti-Ballistic

---

[309] Encyclopeadia Britanica http://www.britannica.com/EBchecked/topic/291225/20th-century-international-relations/32928/The-end-of-East-West-cooperation.

[310] *Ibid.*

Missile (ABM) Treaty, it could not prevent the USA from engaging with Russia in a new strategic arms control agreement in the Moscow Treaty, in 2002. This treaty was intended "to address nuclear warheads, setting sharply-reduced ceilings" that both the USA and Russia committed to meeting the treaty's deadline due in, 2012[311]. The United States is also unilaterally reducing and removing some amount of "fissile material from weapons stocks and embarking on warhead dismantlement work, and has also chosen to eliminate delivery systems such as the Advanced Cruise Missile"[312].

Today, cooperation with non-state workers for nuclear security is eminent. Cooperation is expected in trying to prevent nuclear proliferation to non-state participants, such as terrorists, from acquiring nuclear weapons and technology. The East–West economic cooperation through international institutions, cultural exchanges, trade, security and technology can be beneficial to both East and West.

Alongside East-West cooperation in the quest for world peace, regional interdependent cooperations are also important to complement the effort of the East-West cooperation and that of the United Nations. In the quest for

---

[311] See Ford Christopher's presentation at a conference sponsored by the Aspen Institute for Contemporary German Studies, Washington, D.C. (June 10, 2009). Accessible at .//www.newparadigmsforum.com/NPFtestsite/?page_id=1628

[312] *Ibid.*

international peace and security, regional interdependent cooperation such as the Economic Community of West African States (ECOWAS) in a volatile-war continent like Africa is crucial. The aims and objectives of ECOWAS are the: "maintenance of regional peace, stability and security through the promotion and strengthening of good neighbourliness; peaceful settlement of disputes among member States, active co-operation between neighbouring countries and promotion of a peaceful environment as a prerequisite for economic development and the promotion and consolidation of a democratic system of governance in each member State"[313]. Also "to promote co-operation and integration, leading to the establishment of an economic union in West Africa in order to raise the living standards of its peoples, and to maintain and enhance economic stability, foster relations among member States and contribute to the progress and development of the African Continent"[314]. In the 1990s, ECOWAS complemented the efforts of UN in ending the war in both Liberia and Sierra Leone.

Interregional cooperation is also crucial in the quest for political peace and security. This is the type of cooperation that exists between regions of the same continent. Taking the African continent for example, there are many sub-regional organizations in the continent such as the Southern African Development Community (SADC) which was founded in 1980 by nine member States: Angola,

---

[313] ECOWAS Treaty, 1993 Chapter 2, Article 4. Accessible at http://www.comm.ecowas.int

[314] *Ibid.* Chapter 2, article 3:1.

Botswana, Lesotho, Malawi, Mozambique, Swaziland, United Republic of Tanzania, Zambia and Zimbabwe with the aim of promoting deeper economic co-operation and integration inter-alia. There is also the Arab Maghreb Union which was established in 1989 to promote cooperation and integration among the Arab states of North Africa, membering Algeria, Libya, Mauritania, Morocco, and Tunisia. Today, this Magreb Union can be used in the fight against *Alqaeda* Magreb that makes the region its base for its terrorist activities. Moreover, there is also Intergovernmental Authority on Drought and Development (IGADD) that was formed in 1986 and again in the mid-1990s. This transformed itself into a fully-fledged regional, political, economic, development, and trade and security entity. IGADD can also be used to check on the terrorist groups such as Lord Resistance Army (L.R.D) of Uganda and *Alshabab* of Somalia. In doing so, it is complementing the effort of the UN in its quest for international peace.

Cooperation between two or more of these entities could be regarded as interregional cooperation. For instance, cooperation between IGADD and Magreb Union in fights against Alqaeda Magreb (in Northwest Africa) and the Lord's Resistance Army (LRD) of Uganda and *Alshabab* of Somalia (in EastNorth Africa) could be an example of interregional cooperation.

Continental cooperation is a type of cooperation geographically circumscribed to the states on the same continent. The Organisation of African Unity which was consequently established in Addis Ababa, Ethiopia, on May 25, 1963, about 44 days after the promulgation of *Pacem in Terris*, can be seen as one example. The purposes of OAU were to promote the unity and solidarity of the African States, coordinate and intensify their cooperation and efforts to achieve a better life for the peoples of Africa; defend their sovereignty, their territorial integrity and independence, eradicate all forms of colonialism from Africa, and promote international cooperation, having due regard to the Charter of the United Nations and the Universal Declaration of Human Rights[315]. However, the Organization of African Unity (OAU) had to be inherited by the African Union (AU) in 2002 after the adoption of the Consultative Act of the African Union in Lomé, Togo, 2000. The OAU and African Union were also instrumental in ending the war in Liberia and Sierra Leone, between Eritrea and Ethiopia and recently between South Sudan and the Republic of Sudan.

Intercontinental cooperation is the cooperation between the states of two or more continents. This can be seen in the South–South Cooperation which was created by the United Nations in 1978[316]. Its purpose is to promote and encourage exchange of resources, knowledge and technological know-how between developing countries. This is the cooperation between South American countries and African countries. It is also known as 'the countries of the global South. South–South cooperation has been successful in minimising dependency of

---

[315] OAU charter article 2,

http://www.africa-union.org/root/au/Documents/Treaties/text/OAU_Charter_1963.pdf (18/01/11)

[316] See http:www.//ssc.undp.org/

developing countries on the aid programmes from developed countries[317] and can also reduce the international financial burden of the United Nations.

Universal cooperation is the kind of cooperation envisaged in the United Nations where the states of all the continents of the world cooperate in the search for peace, freedom, better living and security for all the states and their people regardless of geography, creed, religion, language, culture and skin pigment. It is the world's largest international cooperation and is instrumental in bringing peace, security, justice, and in providing a level political platform for all the states in world politics.

Therefore, for there to be an interdependent cooperation at regional, interregional, continental, intercontinental and universal levels, striving towards the implementation of international rules and treaties that promote mutual understanding, diversity and pluralism is crucial. This interdependent cooperation has to develop mechanisms for inter-civilizational, inter-cultural, and inter-faith alliances in the quest for interstate peace. This can discourage aggression and injustice between states. Essential in this regard is the cooperation in building a communications and information exchange in international systems that can effectively facilitate defences against terror of any kind and disease that are epidemic and endemic everywhere.

---

[317] http://www.globalenvision.org/library/3/1371.

Through the maintenance of law, order and interdependent cooperation, the European Union is able to make war an obsolete factor in Europe. With reference to the solution to the anarchy within the international system Professor Troiani remarks: "To be successful, we need participation and sharing with hegemony, where the supremacy of the strong operates in the collective interest without the ambition to dominate the others. This can be helped by the further development of cooperative agreements at the regional level: in Europe, the EU [European Union] has rendered war obsolete as an instrument for the solution of controversies"[318].

Fully aware of cooperation as an important factor to a durable world peace, Pope John Paul II remarked: "...there can be no true human progress no durable peace without the courageous, loyal, disinterested search of a growing cooperation and unity among the peoples"[319]. Interdependent cooperation therefore can serve as a guarantor for peace in our quest for justice and peace.

2.6.6 Freedom and Liberty

Freedom and Liberty could be viewed as one of the most fundamental and vital human faculties endowed to humankind. It is to choose and be responsible for the

---

[318]Troiani Luigi, *"La guerra, fattore obsoleto di relazioni internazionali"*. In Oikonomia. Accessible at http://oikonomia.it/pages/2004/2004_giugno/sommari_4.htm

[319] Pope John Paul II's address to various diplomatic missions participating at his installation as Pontiff. See Silvano M. Tomasi, *"Why is the Holy See engaged in International Life"*? In International Catholic Organizations & Catholic Inspired NGOsTheir Contribution to the Building of the International Community, Published, Mathias Nebel, The Caritas in Veritate Foundation, 2012, p. 37.

Chapter 2: The Content of Pacem in Terris

consequences of the choice. According to Thomas Hobbes: "liberty is understood, [to be] the absence of external impediments; which impediments may oft[en] take away part of a man's power to do what he would, but cannot hinder him from using the power left him according as his judgment and reason shall dictate to him"[320]. Hobbean liberty is when "each man hath to use his own power as he will himself for the preservation of his own nature; that is to say, of his own life; and consequently, of doing anything which, in his own judgment and reason, he shall conceive to be the aptest means thereunto"[321]. In the view of John Stuart Mills: "By liberty was meant protection against the tyranny of the political rulers." The aim, of liberty for patriots, Mills stated "was to set limits to the power which the ruler should be suffered to exercise over the community; and this limitation was what they meant by liberty"[322].

Freedom or liberty, which was meant to be one of the guarantors for justice and peace, is the independence of a state from the arbitrary and coercive powers of other states in the international system and relations. *Pacem in Terris* put it in these words: "Relations between States must be regulated by the principle of [liberty] freedom. This means that no country has the right to take any action that

---

[320] Hobbes Thomas, The Leviathans, Chapter XIV. Of the First and Second Natural Laws, and of Contracts, pp. 19. Accessed at http://history.hanover.edu/courses/excerpts/111hob2.html . Also accessible at http://ebooks.adelaide.edu.au/h/hobbes/thomas/h68l/chapter14.html.

[321] *Ibid.*

[322] John Stuart Mill On Liberty, Batoche Books Limited Kitchener, Ontario, Canada, 2001 p. 6.

would constitute an unjust oppression of other countries, or an unwarranted interference in their affairs. On the contrary, all should help to develop in others an increasing awareness of their duties, an adventurous and enterprising spirit, and the resolution to take the initiative for their own advancement in every field of endeavour"[323].

Pope John XXIII's concepts of liberty in interstate relations is based on the teaching of Pope Pius XII that: "A new order founded on moral principles is the surest bulwark against the violation of the freedom, integrity and security of other nations, no matter what may be their territorial extension or their capacity for defence. For although it is almost inevitable that the larger States, in view of their greater power and vaster resources, will themselves decide on the norms governing their economic associations with small States. Nevertheless these smaller States cannot be denied their right, in keeping with the common good, to political freedom, and to the adoption of a position of neutrality in the conflicts between nations. No State can be denied this right, for it is a postulate of the natural law itself, as also of international law. These smaller States have also the right of assuring their own economic development. It is only with the effective guaranteeing of these rights that smaller nations can fittingly promote the

---

[323] *Pacem in Terris*, pp.120.

common good of all mankind, as well as the material welfare and the cultural and spiritual progress of their own people"[324].

However, this liberty and freedom must not be seen as giving a free hand to tyrannical rulers to do whatever they want to do with their people without being checked by other states. The ruthless act of these tyrannical rulers can be checked by other states through 'responsibility to protect'[325]. Under a gross violation of human rights and the common good, the states have the responsibility to intervene in the name of responsibility to protect. Responsibility to protect is usually invoked under the name of 'humanitarian intervention'. Classically, humanitarian intervention is seen as "coercive action by one or more states involving the use of armed force in another state without the consent of its authorities, and with the purpose of preventing widespread suffering or death among the inhabitants"[326].

Freedom and liberty are not just a right; it is an ontological human attribute that justice demands us to recognize, so that it can be transferred to the state as a human institution. The concept of liberty *'liberalitatis'*, a word derived from *'liber'* meaning 'free', implies that an inner attitude of virtue animates one's

---

[324] *Ibid.,* pp.124.

[325] For detail on the history of intervention, see Responsibility to Protect: Research, Bibliography, Background Supplementary Volume to the Report of International Commission on Intervention and State Sovereignty , Volume 2 , International Commission on Intervention and State Sovereignty, International Development Research Center 2001.

[326] *Ibid.,* P. 79.

freedom in giving out one's wealth instead of being stingy on wealth and instead of being avaricious[327]. A liberal person or state in this sense is the one who subdues over-attachment and over aggrandizement by freely sharing and even parting with its possessed wealth to others. That is to say, relations between the states must not be based on the spirit of dominations *animus dominandi*, but on generosity. This caused Pope John XXIII to say: "The wealthier States, therefore, while providing various forms of assistance to the poorer, must have the highest possible respect for the latter's national characteristics and time honoured civil institutions. They must also repudiate any policy of domination"[328].

In both meanings freedom, liberality or liberty is significant in international relations. Because on one hand, it gives a sense of dignity and equality amongst the states and entices them to abide by conventions, treaties and pacts that they signed under freedom and liberty. On the other hand, it can also alleviate the sufferings of the poor nations by the rich ones by sharing their possessions with them in the quest for prosperity and peace. Humankind can only flourish and be dignified in freedom and liberty. However, this liberty must be checked with duties and responsibility. Freedom or liberty without responsibility, without wisdom and virtues, could be a dangerous thing and is described by Edmund Burke as 'an oppressive' and 'degrading servitude'. Burke stated: "The effects of the incapacity shown by the popular leaders in all the great members of the

---

[327] Aquinas Thomas, *Summa Theologica, op. cit.* (118.1,2,3) .

[328] *Pacem in Terris,* pp.125.

commonwealth are to be covered with the 'all-atoning name' of Liberty. In some people I see great liberty, indeed; in many, if not in the most, an oppressive, degrading servitude. But what is liberty without wisdom and without virtue? It is the greatest of all possible evils; for it is folly, vice, and madness, without tuition or restraint. Those who know what virtuous liberty is cannot bear to see it disgraced by incapable heads, on account of their having high-sounding words in their mouths"[329]. This is the logic of *Pacem in Terris* in linking peace to social virtues such as: "truth, justice, charity and freedom." [330]

2.6.7 Development and Democracy as the Guarantors for the International Stability and Peace

2.6.7.1 Defining Development

Development can be defined as: Systematic use of scientific and technical know-how or the use of theoretical or practical aspects of a concept to meet particular goals, standards or requirements of improvement in economic, political and social sectors[331]. Pope John XXIII perceived a link between development and international stability and peace. Therefore, he could not ignore it in *Pacem in*

---

[329] Edmund Burke, " Liberty, Without Wisdom and Virtue, the greatest of Evils". In The beauties of the late Right Hon. Edmund Burke, selected from the writings, Pub. Ann Arbor, Michigan: University of Michigan Library 2011, page 183. Accessed at http://quod.lib.umich.edu/e/ecco/004795912.0001.002/1:12?rgn=div1;view=fulltext

[330] Read *Pacem In Terris*, pp. 35-36.

[331] www.businessdictionary.com/definition/development.html

Terris. Pope John XXIII has reiterated on the assistance for economic development between the states. He remarked: "We appealed to the more wealthy nations to render every kind of assistance to those States which are still in the process of economic development"[332]. Pope John XXIII further stated: "The result We look for is that the poorer States shall in as short a time as possible attain to a degree of economic development that enables their citizens to live in conditions more in keeping with their human dignity. Again and again We must insist on the need for helping these peoples in a way which guarantees to them the preservation of their own freedom. They must be conscious that they are themselves playing the major role in their economic and social development; that they are themselves to shoulder the main burden of it"[333].

There exist many approaches to development. There is a mere economic development that focuses its attention to material gain and infrastructural developments. There is also an integral or holistic development. This does not limit its attention to the material aspect of development. It includes financial aspects as well as health, spiritual, moral, religious, intellectual and cultural well-being of the people.

In some cases, the spiritual, moral, religious and cultural aspects of development are overshadowed by the material, financial and economical aspects.

---

[332] *Pacem in Terris*, pp.121.

[333] *Ibid.*, pp.122-123.

In this case, the full realization of integral or holistic development becomes an illusion. Therefore, development must be a full human development that must entail personal, spiritual, social, economic, financial and political, including that of nations and of peoples. This is the type of development that can serve as a guarantor for international stability and peace. For the Catholic Church, the accumulation of material goods, and technological resources and know-how will be unsatisfactory and debasing if there is no respect for the moral, cultural, and spiritual dimensions of the person[334]. Amartya Sen's "Capability" approach argues that the development of the poor must move beyond narrowly economic analysis of the problem of poverty to tackle "social, cultural, educational and health needs as part of the holistic approach known as social development[335]".

Pope Paul VI also considered development as a guarantor for peace by saying: "Knowing, as we all do, that development means peace these days, what man would not want to work for it with every ounce of his strength"[336]? On integral human development, Pope Benedict XVI is of the view that: "projects for integral human development ... need to be *marked by solidarity and inter-generational justice*, while taking into account a variety of contexts: ecological,

---

[334] *Populorum Progressio, op.cit.*

[335] See Rebecca Todd Peters, In Search of the Good Life: The Ethics of Globalization. Pub. Continuum International Publishing Group, USA, 2004, P.71.

[336] *Populorum Progressio, op.cit.* pp. 87.

juridical, economic, political and cultural"[337]. Development has both moral and economic aspects. Its moral dimension is also emphasised in encyclical *Caritas in Veritate*: "The environment is God's gift to everyone, and in our use of it we have a responsibility towards the poor, towards future generations and towards humanity as a whole"[338]. Integral human development therefore, can be a genuine guarantor for international stability and peace.

2.6.7.2 Defining Democracy

Democracy can be defined as "government of the people, by the people and for the people"[339]. Such a government should be responsive and responsible for the protection of life, liberty, property and progeny of the people. Democracy then is a public authority instituted by popular common consent and not to be imposed by coercion and oppression. Paragaraphs 46 to 79 of *Pacem in Terris* did not mention the word 'democracy' by name, however, it considers therein the democratic values to be the core of relations between people and the public authorities for the purpose of stability and peace. For instance, under the "structure and operation of

---

[337] Pope Benedict XVI, *Caritas in Veritate* AAS 101 (2009), pp. 48.

[338] *Ibid.*, no. 48.

[339] Abraham Lincoln, The Gettysburg Address, Gettysburg, Pennsylvania November 19, 1863. Accessed at http://www.abrahamlincolnonline.org/lincoln/speeches/gettysburg.htm

the public authority" it stated in paragraphs 67 to 68 that: "it is not possible to give a general ruling on the most suitable form of government, or the ways in which civil authorities can most effectively fulfill their legislative, administrative, and judicial functions. In determining what form a particular government shall take, and the way in which it shall function, a major consideration will be the prevailing circumstances and the condition of the people; and these are things which vary in different places and at different times. We think, however, that it is in keeping with human nature for the State to be given a form which embodies a threefold division of public office properly corresponding to the three main functions of public authority"[340]. Furthermore, *Pacem in Terris* calls for the protection of human rights, freedom of conscience and association, justice, constitutional rule which are all features of democracy.

Today tyranny becomes the antonym to democracy in governance. A tyrant (the original Greek τύραννος, *tyrannos*), was used to mean an authoritarian sovereign without reference to character. Its modern English usage designates a ruler of a cruel and oppressive reputation[341], an oppressive, harsh, or unjust ruler [342], an absolute ruler unchecked by law or constitution. It is also used to designate any ruler who usurped legitimate sovereignty. Plato and Aristotle gave a

---

[340] *Pacem in Terris*, pp. 67 to 68.

[341] Encyclopedia Britannica

[342] Merriam-Webster online dictionary. Merriam-Webster.

negative description of a tyrant for them a tyrant is, "one who rules without law, looks to his own advantage rather than that of his subjects, and uses extreme and cruel tactics—against his own people as well as others"[343]. The term tyranny is used to describe such a system of government.

Tyranny in itself is wickedness, worrying and intolerant. It makes a ruler or leader intolerant and wicked towards the ruled/led. It can cause a ruler/leader to break the pens of his/her critics, muzzle their mouths and imprison them by the might of military power. Hence, it is the same military power and might that will ruin a tyrant and bring him/her from the top echelon of the throne to the gutters of political failure. This is historical fact and it is inexpedient to be heedless of the lessons of history. UDHR also confirms this.

Pacem in Terris was not the first document to consider democratic values as one of the guarantors for peace. The United Nations Universal Declaration of Human Rights in 1948 also called for the respect for the rights and freedoms of others; and of meeting the just requirements of morality, public order and the general welfare in a democratic society. Hence, a democratic society is a genuine guarantor for peace. Disregard and contempt of democratic principles and values such as human rights that include freedom of speech and belief and freedom from fear and want, rule of law, justice and separation of powers, resulted in barbarous

---

[343] Glad, B. (2002, March). Why Tyrants Go Too Far: Malignant Narcissism and Absolute Power. Political Psychology, 33. see http://en.wikipedia.org/wiki/Tyrant#cite_note-3

acts which have outraged the conscience of mankind, thus, the cause of wars[344].

For instance, the tragic events of the 1990s in both Liberia and Sierra Leone were due to disregard of democratic values. They were the culmination of a long history of human rights abuses and disrespect for democratic values by the tyranny of Samuel Doe's and Joseph Momoh's governments in Liberia and in Sierra Leone. This fertilized the ground on which the seeds of war have germinated and grown. In Sierra Leone for instance, the years before the outbreak of war witnessed the augmentation of an authoritarian style of regime, "which undermined the authority of many of the nation's institutions and encouraged a system in which irregularities, injustices, and oppression of political opponents were tolerated and even encouraged by the government"[345].

Democracy also entails the peaceful change of government; "those who make peaceful revolution impossible make violent revolution inevitable"[346]. This was the case of Samuel Doe and others on the African continent. As such *Pacem in Terris* calls for a system "which allows for a regular succession of public officials" and that, "the authority of these officials, far from growing old and feeble, takes on a new vitality in keeping with the progressive development of

---

[344] United Nations Universal Declaration of Human Rights, 1948.

[345] S. Rabil & K. Shanahan, "*Sierra Leone a case study in conflict resolution*" accessible at http://64.176.9.117/sl/causes.html (18/11/10)

[346] John F. Kennedy (1917 - 1963) 35th President of US 1961-1963 Address on the First Anniversary of the Alliance for Progress Delivered at The White House, 13 March 1962. Accessible at http://en.wikisource.org/wiki/Address_on_the_First_Anniversary_of_the_Alliance_for_Progress

human society"[347]. At the present, democratic principles and values are said to be the highest aspiration of the common people in the matters of their governments[348]. Moreover, it is on record that one of the causes of World War II was the denial of democratic principles: "The great and terrible war which has now ended was a war made possible by the denial of the democratic principles of the dignity, equality and mutual respect of men, and by the propagation, in their place, through ignorance and prejudice, of the doctrine of the inequality of men and races"[349].

For peace between states to be realized, *Pacem in Terris* is of the view that: "Everyone must sincerely co-operate in the effort to banish fear and the anxious expectation of war from men's minds. But this [according to *Pacem in Terris*] requires that the fundamental principles upon which peace is based in today's world be replaced by an altogether different one, namely, the realization that true and lasting peace among nations cannot consist in the possession of an equal supply of armaments but only in mutual trust"[350]. A similar approach towards realization of inter-state and political peace is echoed in *Gaudium et Spes*: "peace is not merely the absence of war; nor can it be reduced solely to the maintenance of a balance of power between enemies; nor is it brought about by dictatorship.

---

[347] *Pacem in Terris*, pp. 74.

[348] United Nations Universal Declaration of Human Rights, 1948.

[349] Preamble of UNESCO Constitution,1945.

[350] *Pacem in Terris*, pp.113

Instead, it is rightly and appropriately called an enterprise of justice. Peace results from that order structured into human society by its divine Founder, and actualized by men as they thirst after ever-greater justice. The common good of humanity finds its ultimate meaning in the eternal law. But since the concrete demands of this common good are constantly changing as time goes on, peace is never attained once and for all, but must be built up ceaselessly"[351].

Moreover, both development and democracy were considered by David P. Forsythe as guarantors for peace when he said that: "three factors may be reducing the probability of overt international war among the major states: attention to civil and political rights, attention to economic and social rights and modern (post 1945) development"[352]. Countries with democratic administrations are also the envy of many people. USA, Canada, and Netherlands are a few examples. Peace is an enterprise that is strongly connected with development and democratic values as viewed by *Pacem in Terris*. At the time of the promulgation of *Pacem in Terris* there were agitations for decolonization, autonomy and independence all of which are features of democracy[353].

Reading *Pacem in Terris* textually and contextually, one can affirm that its concern was the establishment of the world peace, and the avoidance of war,

---

[351] *Gaudium et Spes, op. cit.*, no.78

[352] Forsythe David, Human Rights and Peace: International and National Dimensions, The University of Nebraska Press, 1993, pages VII- VIII.

[353] *Pacem in Terris*, pp. 39-45.

especially nuclear war, between former USSR and USA in a bid that "Peace on Earth—which man throughout the ages has so longed for and sought after"[354] "may be assured on earth"[355]. This is manifested in the entire encyclical. While the word 'peace' is mentioned about twenty three times[356] in *Pacem in Terris,* the word 'war' is mentioned only about seven times[357] and the consequences of war such as "grip of constant fear" "horrific violence" "the appalling slaughter and destruction" and its means, such as "atomic weapons", "nuclear weapons" and "armaments" are also mentioned therein.

There are both primary and secondary recipes for peace for both micro and macro levels of peace. In the quest for justice and peace on earth, both primary and secondary recipes for peace should be considered. While primary recipes for peace are those basic necessities without which peace and stability are unattainable: such as protection of life, religion, property, intellect, progeny, justice etc.; secondary recipes are those secondary needs, the absence of which do not necessarily and totally obstruct peace and stability: such as a right to ample recreational facilities or equal right in freely accessing a government's confidential information etc. From *fiqhi* terminology we borrow *daruriyyat* to render primary recipes and *hajiyyat* to render secondary recipe for the

---

[354] *Ibid.,* preamble.

[355] *Ibid.,* pp.166.

[356] *Ibid.,* pp.1, 110,113,115,116,117,165, 166,167,169,170, 171, 172,172.

[357] *Ibid.,* pp. 111,112,113,115,116,127.

establishment of peace. Micro level peace is that peace within the limited sphere such as peace within the families, neighbourhoods, institutions; ethnic groups, local communities etc. Macro level of peace refers to that level of peace that begins with the peace within the state as a whole to peace between the states and within the wider international community. The level of implementation of these recipes determines the level of micro and macro peace. These primary recipes of peace are what macro peace and its secondary recipes are expected to be built upon.

Pacem in Terris considered both primary and secondary recipes for peace in the quest for both micro and macro peace. Pope John XXIII in *Pacem in Terris* has called for the establishment of what we call primary and secondary recipes of peace in a bid to achieve what we call micro and macro peace. His pedagogy in the establishment of peace on earth begins, persists and finishes with respect for the dynamics of order in inter-human and inter-states relationships and respect for human dignity and the common good. These dynamics are the primary and secondary recipes for peace, for both micro and macro peace. These recipes for peace include: a well and just order between people, rights and duties, truth and justice, charity and liberty, dialogue, active solidarity and sincere cooperaton and subsidiarity; a well and just ordered relations between individuals and the public authorities, a well ordered and just structure and operation of the public authority; and compatibilty of law and conscience, a well ordered citizens' participation in public life, well ordered relations between the states, and insistence on development and democratic values. Some of these recipes are indispensible in both inter-human and inter-states relationships for establishing durable and genuine world peace.

If the above mentioned recipes for peace (truth, dialogue, justice, active solidarity, interdependent cooperation, freedom and liberty, and development and democracy) are in place in the community of humankind, there will be no need for nuclear proliferation and arms race. This will pave way for the reduction of arsenal. Therefore the reduction of arsenals becomes the first step to political peace and peace between states.

2.7 Reduction of Arsenals as the First Step to Peace

In international or interstate relations and systems, reduction of arsenals is the first step to guarantee peace between the states. This entails either termination of an arms race or simultaneous reduction of the stock-piles of ammunition and nuclear weapons which have been built up. Although advancement in science and technology is doing well in improving human life, it also gives human beings much power to cause more harm on the surface of the earth. Dr. Helen Caldicott, an Australian physician showing her disapproval for the arms race and nuclear weapons, affirmed this when she said: "We hold God's creation in the palm of our hand. This generation will either decide actively to save it, or by passive complicity to destroy it"[358]. Arsenal reduction is necessary not only for preservation of life but also for recognition of human dignity and good living in a good environment. It is unswerving with justice, right reason, and the recognition of human dignity that intelligence, energy, time and the billions of dollars spent on arms can be diverted into more fruitful ventures to ameliorate the worsening conditions of human beings in other parts of the world. From this perspective, Pope John XXIII stated in *Pacem in Terris* that: "justice, right reason, and the recognition of man's dignity cry out insistently for a cessation to the arms race. The stock-piles of armaments which have been built up in various countries must be reduced all round and simultaneously by the parties concerned"[359]. "Nuclear weapons" Pope John XXIII said "must be banned". And that "A general agreement must be reached on a suitable disarmament program, with an effective system of mutual control"[360].

One of the causes of armament and arms race is the concept of Mutual Assured Destruction (MAD), a concept that "peace cannot be assured except on the basis of an equal balance of armaments"[361]. A belief that the states that can equally destroy each other and will hardly attack each other. Political mistrust is

---

[358] Caldicott Helen, *op. cit.*

[359] *Pacem in Terris* pp.112

[360] *Ibid.,* pp.112.

[361] *Ibid.,* pp.110.

another cause of the arms race. This happens when "people are living in the grip of constant fear…that at any moment the impending storm may break upon them with horrific violence"[362]. Pope John XXIII, in calling for disarmament, insisted on the teaching of his predecessor Pope Pius XII that : "The calamity of a world war, with the economic and social ruin and the moral excesses and dissolution that accompany it, must not on any account be permitted to engulf the human race for a third time"[363]. Here he meant that the ruins caused by World War I and World War II must not be permitted to be repeated once again. Two years before the promulgation of *Pacem in Terris*, the former USA president Dwight D. Eisenhower had also appealed for disarmament as he remarked: "Disarmament, with mutual honour and confidence, is a continuing imperative. Together we must learn how to compose differences, not with arms, but with intellect and decent purpose"[364].

Nonetheless, there are two concepts with regards to the reduction of arms and armament: the general acknowledgement that conflict will be resolved by negotiation and agreement and not through physical military might[365] is increasing on one hand, and on the other hand, a concept that a peace can be

---

[362] *Ibid.*, pp.111.

[363] *Ibid.*, pp. 112.

[364] Dwight D. Eisenhower, Military-Industrial Complex Speech, 1961.

[365] *Pacem in Terris*, pp.126.

sustained through a balance of armament[366] is also lingering. Between these two realities, Pope John XXIII recommended the former. He was of the view that: "it no longer makes sense to maintain that war is a fit instrument with which to repair the violation of justice"[367]. Against this background, Pope John XXIII called for the replacement of the arm equilibrium principle with peace by mutual trust: Peace that is fruitful, desirable and dictated by common sense[368].

For Pope John XXIII, disarmament was reasonable, desirable and possible[369]. For him therefore, international relations must not be regulated by armed force, but by "the principles of right reason: the principles, that is, of truth, justice and vigorous and sincere co-operation"[370].

Nevertheless, if the Mutual Assured Destruction theory (MAD) can be accredited it can also be applied to what I call Mutual Assured Co-existence (MAC). That is, a belief that peace can also be realized through mutual assured disarmament emanating from mutual assured coexistence. If, for instance, the USA, UK, France, Russia and China cannot wage war on one another due to the concept of MAD, they cannot as well do so through the concept of MAC. This can be done through cooperation, solidarity, building and sustaining channels that

---

[366] *Ibid.,* pp.128.

[367] *Ibid.,* pp.127.

[368] *Ibid.,* pp. 113.

[369] *Ibid.,* pp. 114-116.

[370] *Ibid.,* pp.114.

can promote political trust and limit political mistrust among them. This is a theory worth following since it is humane, cost effective and can avoid titanic economic and intellectual resources being spent on ammunition, their maintenance and safe keeping. "According to an economic analysis, 196.5 billion dollars were spent in World War I and 2.0913 trillion dollars were spent in World War II"[371]. Diverting this huge amount into capacity building and development projects could break the enemy's resistance. Sun Tzu said: "to fight and conquer in all your battles is not supreme excellence; supreme excellence consists in breaking the enemy's resistance without fighting"[372].

In order to reduce political paranoia and political mistrust, MAC theory is essential in that regard. For the concept of MAC, 'the recent progress in science and technology' that compresses time and space can be used in facilitating the coming together, the movement, the communications and relations between diverse peoples in diverse locations in a form of families, associations, public authorities and states. For MAC, science and technology can also be used in the sphere of growing economic interdependence for progress and prosperity of all and can be best used in international systems and order for collective security and

---

[371] Muhammad Ahmed Qadri, in World Peace Order Towards an International State, Publisher: Islamic Educational & Cultural Research Center, USA,2008, Page 72. Qadri cited Pursell, C. The Military-Industrial Complex. Harper & Row Publishers. New York, New York: 1972,

[372] Sun Tzu, *Art of War*, Trans. From Chinese by Lionel Giles with an Introduction and Critical Notes, Department of Oriental Printed Books and Manuscripts, British Museum, 1910, III:2, p. 46.

peace. This is what the concept of MAC aims at achieving. MAC could serve as an antidote to the causes of the arms race such as paranoia of impending war.

If "the object of war is victory; that of victory is conquest; and that of conquest preservation"[373], then armament in this case has a similar objective to disarmament whose objective is also the preservation of life. If through MAC we can achieve what we can achieve through MAD, then it is logical that we employ MAC as the means rather than MAD. Again to recall Sun Tzu: "To fight and conquer in all your battles is not supreme excellence; supreme excellence consists in breaking the enemy's resistance without fighting"[374].

For this reason, Pope John XXIII in *Pacem in Terris* chooses disarmament in nuclear weapons over war and prefers it to the arms race; and appealed for disarmament in nuclear weapons in international politics especially between the Union of Soviet Socialist Republics at the time and the United States of America. He called for an unsparing effort from "mankind, and above all the rulers of States, to be unsparing of their labour and efforts to ensure that human affairs follow a rational and dignified course"[375]. Again, *Gaudium et Spes* is of the view that peace cannot be brought about by MAD theory. It reads: "Peace is not merely the absence of war; nor can it be reduced solely to the maintenance of a balance of

---

[373] Montesquieu, *op. cit.*, p. 22.

[374] Sun Tzu, *op. cit.* p. 46.

[375] *Pacem in Terris*, pp.117.

power between enemies; nor is it brought about by dictatorship. Instead, it is rightly and appropriately called an enterprise of justice. Peace results from that order structured into human society by its divine Founder, and actualized by men as they thirst after ever-greater justice. The common good of humanity finds its ultimate meaning in the eternal law. But since the concrete demands of this common good are constantly changing as time goes on, peace is never attained once and for all, but must be built up ceaselessly"[376].

---

[376] *Gaudium et Spes, op. cit.*, no. 78.

Chapter III

3.1 Responses and Reactions to *Pacem in Terris*

Pacem in Terris, the second and last encyclical of Pope John XXIII, promulgated in the fifty-third month of his brief[377] pontificate and fifty three days before his demise[378], has attracted many responses and reactions. These responses and reactions are doctrinal and political, national and international, from within and

---

[377] According to J. Grootaers: *"Le pontificat de Jean XXIII à été le plus court du XXe siècle mais probablement un des plus denses. Angelo Roncalli [...] demeure ainsi une des grandes figures de l'Église et du monde du milieu du siècle et l'artisan d'un renouveau de la conception que l'Eglise catholique se forge d'elle-même"*J. Grootaers, voce "Jean XXIII", cit. in, *Dictionnaire d'Histoire et de Géographie ecclésiastiques.* Vol.: 26, a cura di R. Aubert, Paris, Letouzey et Ané, 1997, 1172. See Giulio Cesareo*La riflessione teologico-morale sulla pace a partire da Pacem in Terris e Gaudium et spes,*2008. Footnote 131, p. 39.

[378] Melloni Alberto, *Pacem in Terris Storia dell' ultima enciclical di Papa Giovanni, Editori Laterza*, Italy, 2010, p. v.

outside the Vatican. Responses and reactions can be dichotomized into criticisms of condemnation and eulogies of acclamation. This unprecedented amount of response and reaction was due to the extraordinary nature of *Pacem in Terris*: that is, being unprecedented in the history of papal encyclicals in that it addressed all people of goodwill throughout the world. But also perhaps it was due to its firmness and eloquence in the call for universal peace; its emphasis on the common origin of human kind; its stress on human dignity, and rights, duties and freedoms; its appeal for the establishment of an international political authority for the advancement of common good and human welfare. Moreover, its timing (during the Turkish-Cuban missile crisis) would have contributed to the wider responses and reactions it received.

3.2 Some of the Criticisms against *Pacem in Terris*

Within the religious sphere, the Jesuit Georges Jarlot, a professor at the Gregorian University of Rome, at the time criticized *Pacem in Terris* from the doctrinal perspective. For him, any encyclical must be strictly based on the Catholic doctrine of human rights. For Jarlot, it is a mistake to portray a person as an absolute, because the only absolute is God[379]. The *New York Times* also noted that

---

[379] In the words of Alberto Melloni: *"Jarlot ritiene che l'enciclica dovrebbe "fondare in dottrina" la concezione cattolica dei diritti umana: se cio non accade (ed è cosi: non accade e non*

Pacem in Terris was not strictly following the doctrinal or dogmatic view of its predecessors. It says: "John XXIII's basic doctrine is that the common humanity which binds all men and all nations is more important than the doctrinal or racial differences which divide them. On these premises, he calls for an end to the arms race, for disarmament under effective control, and for voluntary acceptance by all nations of a world law.... It will not be easy to realize this program in a world riddled by suspicions, jealousies and hatreds. But it can be done if the leaders of the world follow the Pope's example and rise above national and doctrinal hatreds that lead only to disaster"[380]. According to Melloni, many readers of *Pacem in Terris* "*condivideranno con Jarlot la sensazione, sottesa a molte delle sue obiezioni, che l'enciclica non abbia sufficiente fondamento dottrinale*"[381]. Loosely translated as: 'many reader of Pacem in Terris, share with Jarlot, many of his objections that the encylical has no sufficient fundamental doctrine'.

Another critic of *Pacem in Terris* was Frank S. Meyer who considered *Pacem in Terris* as an encyclical that "counsels coexistence and collaboration with Communism". He said: "It is one thing to uphold the social primacy of the

---

accadrà nemmeno nel testo finale), egli teme vi si legga una impensabile consacrazione dei principi della dichiarazione dei diritti dell'uomo del 1791. Per Jarlot è sbagliato porre la persona come assoluto, dovendo "l'assoluto essere riservato a Dio". Melloni Alberto, *op.cit*, p. 63. For more on the criticism of Jarlot see Melloni Alberto, *op.cit*. 2010, pages 62-72.

[380] New York Times (14 April 1963) 8E. See
http://www.shc.edu/theolibrary/resources/comments_pacem.htm

[381] Melloni Alberto, *op.cit.*, p. 72.

person. It is another matter altogether, however, when the rights of the person are presented in close symmetry with the egalitarian, anti-capitalist, anti-Western attitudes of Liberalism; when the necessity of order is equated with a moral mandate for 'a world political authority'--an authority which would inevitably, by its very nature, impugn the sovereignties, the freedoms, the diversities, not only of nations but of civilizations, and create the conditions for the most fearsome tyranny in the history of man". And instead of condemning "the greatest danger to freedom, order, justice and peace in our time--the all-encompassing drive of Communism towards world dominion ... the encyclical counsels coexistence and collaboration with Communism" [382]. Rudolf Kraemer-Badoni claimed that Pope John XXIII was abusing his own dignity. He claimed: "I address myself to Pope John, who sits on the venerable throne of St. Peter, with the following warning: You are abusing your dignity politically; you have taken a path leading to the final undermining of our will to ensure liberty, which is already weak; you want to save the Church at the cost of our freedom. You have no authorization from us to conduct such a policy. Give up that approach"[383].

On the diplomatic front, the French were of the view that although the encyclical had been well received broadly in the world, still it was noteworthy

---

[382] Frank S. Meyer. National Review (7 May 1963) 406 see
http://www.shc.edu/theolibrary/resources/comments_pacem.htm.

[383] Rudolf Kraemer-Badoni. *Die Welt*, quoted in *Cross Currents* 14 (Summer 1964) 276 as cited by http://www.shc.edu/theolibrary/resources/comments_pacem.htm.

that none of the college of cardinals praised it or underlined its importance. *Archives du Ministère des Affaires Etrangères* stated: *"on notera également que, si l'Encyclique 'Pacem in Terris' du 11 Avril 1963, a été accueillie, en general, dans le monde entier avec faveur, aucune voix autorisée ne s'est élevée jusqu'à present venant du college des cardinaux, pour en fair l'éloge et en souligner l'importance"*[384]. This can be loosely translated as : 'We will equally point out that the encyclical 'Pacem in Terris' of 11 April 1963, was in general very welcomed in the entire world, but no authorised voice of the college of cardinals have eulogised it or has given any importance to it'. Foy D. Kohler, American ambassador to Russia at the time, remarked: "it is quite possible that the Soviets have in fact opened Pandora's Box in deciding to exploit portions of encyclical rather than simply ignoring it entirely or taking a passive attitude towards it"[385]. Moreover, due to the wider aggressive comments and reaction against *Pacem in Terris*, the then President Kennedy of, USA wrote to Pope John XXIII to disassociate himself from such aggressive comments[386].

---

[384] Archives du Ministere des Affaires Etrangeres-Paris, EU30/19G:n.117, 20/5/1963, La Tournelle, p.21. as cited by Alberto Melloni, *op.cit.* 2010, p. 84, footnote 16.

[385] NARS, Pol 5,Vat, Moscow T.10873, 15/4/1963. As cited by Alberto Melloni, *op.cit.*, p. 85, footnote 23.

[386] Melloni Alberto, *op.cit.*, p.91.

3.3 Some of the Eulogies for *Pacem in Terris*

Alongside the criticism, there was much praise for *Pacem in Terris*. One thing is common and obvious both to its critics and its supporters: the novelty of *Pacem in Terris*. One of the eulogies *Pacem in Terris* received from Peter Riga is as follows:

The novelty of this encyclical is that Pope John presents the church's teaching in a way which is in profound accord with modern aspirations (for international rights, disarmament, independence, the world community, economic and cultural dignity, and so on). It expresses these aspirations in the language of modern man, in his vocabulary. Pius XII had already said many of the things contained here, but for the first time a document from the Holy See uses the modern vocabulary of the rights of man. In fact, it is the first time that a papal document has given so much attention and praise to a secular document such as the Universal Declaration of Man['s rights][387].

The insistence of *Pacem in Terris* on "freedom" and "liberty" is what makes it different from the past papal pronouncements and hence enjoys such a privilege amongst them. This is in line with the view of John Courtney Murray, S.J. when he remarked: "In the past, papal pronouncements on political and social

---

[387] Riga Peter. Continuum (1963) 194. see
http://www.shc.edu/theolibrary/resources/comments_pacem.htm.

order have always been suspended, as it were, from three great words--truth, justice and charity. These three great words are repeated in this encyclical, and the demands of each are carefully particularized. But a fourth word is added, with an insistence that is new at the same time that it is traditional. I mean the word freedom. Freedom is a basic principle of political order; it is also the political method. The whole burden of the encyclical is that the order for which the postmodern world is looking cannot be an order that is imposed by force, or sustained by coercion, or based on fear"[388].

Furthermore, its persistence on human right also made *The Catholic Lawyer* describe *Pacem in Terris* as a solemn declaration of human rights. It stated: "This is the very first time that a document of the Church acclaims a declaration of human rights so solemnly. The main reason would seem to be, from the context, that the Declaration may form the common denominator, the ground for an understanding where men of different ideologies can meet"[389].

"The Nation" (20 April 1963) viewed *Pacem in Terris* as: "the kind of message which befits the most liberal and earnestly religious Pope of this century. It echoes the yearnings of human beings everywhere. Whether the statesmen will dismiss it as the well-meaning declaration of one who has no atomic bombs at his

---

[388] Murray John Courtney, S.J. America (27 April 1963) 613 see
http://www.shc.edu/theolibrary/resources/comments_pacem.htm.

[389] "Catholic Lawyer" (1964) 139 see
http://www.shc.edu/theolibrary/resources/comments_pacem.htm.

command--that remains to be seen. Judging by past reaction, it will not dissuade them from redoubled efforts in the nuclear-arms race"[390].

In the view of Emmet John Hughes, Pope John XXIII in *Pacem in Terris* "assails the shallow moralisms that can denature national policy and world diplomacy.... He insists--finally--upon respect for the rights of all who may be wrong"[391]. Another reacted to *Pacem in Terris* with these words: "Its abiding importance will prove to be something more than specific programs or policies. Ultimately, the encyclical's true greatness may be seen to consist in this, that it gave voice in our day to all mankind's authentic aspirations for lasting peace in a world order based on justice, truth, charity and freedom"[392]. John Cogley saw it as "a soundly realistic document, packed with sound doctrine without being doctrinaire. Its presentation is integral; its directives are put in a context which shows the exquisite conformity between reason and faith. It unmistakably recognizes the need for political action and structural organization if peace is to be served"[393]. A *Washington Post* editorial described *Pacem in Terris* as "not just

---

[390] "The Nation" (20 April 1963) 317 see
http://www.shc.edu/theolibrary/resources/comments_pacem.htm.

[391] Emmet John Hughes. Newsweek (22 April 1963) 19 see
http://www.shc.edu/theolibrary/resources/comments_pacem.htm.

[392] "America" (27 April 1963) 604. see
http://www.shc.edu/theolibrary/resources/comments_pacem.htm.

[393] Cogley John, "Commonweal th"(3 May 1963) 158-59 see
http://www.shc.edu/theolibrary/resources/comments_pacem.htm.

the voice of an old priest, nor just that of an ancient Church; it is the voice of the conscience of the world"[394].

Furthermore, Norman Cousins described *Pacem in Terris* in this way:

In its analysis of the condition of man; in its assertion of freedom of conscience in religious and political matters; in its discussion of the dangers of a runaway nuclear arms race; in its comprehension of the nature of nuclear war; in its call for a strengthened United Nations under law, and responsive to the needs of the world human community--in all these respects, the encyclical letter has historic proportions. It is at once eloquent and practical, diagnostic and therapeutic, historical and contemporary. Most important of all, it sets men's minds in a new direction, enabling them to break loose from notions of inevitability, defeatism, and despair[395].

Although the French and the USA could not praise *Pacem in Terris* at a diplomatic level, it was a different case in Kremlin. There, the text of the encyclical *Pacem in Terris* that was signed by Pope John XXIII and brought to the USSR by Norman Cousins, was published in the Russian language[396]. This

---

[394] See Monsg. Celestino Migliore's intervention as the permanent mission of the Holy See to the United Nations, commemorates the 40th anniversary of the encyclical *"Pacem in Terris"* Tuesday, 7 October 2003.

[395] Cousins Norman, "Continuum" (Summer 1963) 218, see
http://www.shc.edu/theolibrary/resources/comments_pacem.htm.

[396] Melloni Alberto, *op. cit.*, p. 85.

was one of the eulogies *Pacem in Terris* received from Russian authority at the time.

While some see *Pacem in Terris* as a liberal document, slipping away slightly from the traditional doctrine of the Church[397] and its author as 'great liberal Pope', Otto Feinstein reframed the questions and considered him a 'great Christian,' and a 'human pope'. Feinstein remarked:

We live in this world and much of the discussion concerning *Pacem in Terris* and the work of John XXIII reflect these outworn debates. He was a great liberal Pope is the consensus of the mass media and the intellectual commentators. From the holy throne of the church, the liberal forces had received a document to support their side in the debate. But was this really the case? It is my fervent belief that Pope John was not the great liberal pope. He was a great Christian, nay, human pope. He transcended the outworn Liberal-Conservative debate and addressed himself to the issues of the day using the precepts of those human values embodied in Christianity to capture the facts in the form of a problematic, and what is more important, made them real to the individual by pointing out what had to be done[398].

---

[397]Jarlot Georges, see Melloni Alberto,*op.cit.* Pages 62-72.

[398] Otto Feinstein, *Continuum* (Summer 1963) 223 see
http://www.shc.edu/theolibrary/resources/comments_pacem.htm.

Mary McGrory said the following about *Pacem in Terris*: "Pope John's *Pacem in Terris* received instant acclaim here [in Washington, DC], and was the subject of intense discussion and enthusiasm. His magical personality and simply shattering concepts perhaps added to the impact of his most famous message"[399].

From an ideological stance, some see *Pacem in Terris* as a tactic of appeasement with communism[400]. In fact, the French press accused Pope John XXIII's *Pacem in Terris* of having favored the communists[401]. Pope John XXIII has been accused of being a socialist Pope "and his diplomacy has been marked by a series of overtures toward the Communist world.... In line with this diplomatic 'opening to the East,' the new encyclical makes some surprising verbal overtures.... Small wonder that Pope John has been accused of over optimism, even 'softness' toward Communism; and his critics will not be mollified by other 'leftish' pronouncements in the new encyclical, including its favorable references to government welfare services, full employment, complete racial equality, the U.N., disarmament, and even the need for world government"[402].

---

[399] McGrory Mary, " *Pope Paul Speaks for the Have-Nots*". In "America" 116 (15 April 1967) 552. As quoted , see http://www.shc.edu/theolibrary/resources/comments_pacem.htm.

[400] Melloni Alberto, *op. cit.*, pages, 75-78.

[401] *Ibid.*, p. 90.

[402] Life Magazine (26 April 1963) 4. See
http://www.shc.edu/theolibrary/resources/comments_pacem.htm

Pacem in Terris disappointed those who expected a strong condemnation of communism from Pope John XXIII. Against his background *Commonwealth* wrote:

It provides no support for those who would argue that a holy war against Communism is called for; for those who believe that any aid given one nation by another should be determined solely by political and military considerations; for those who believe that a nuclear balance of terror is the best way to preserve peace; for those who would cheerfully resort to nuclear war in the name of 'justice'; for those who would misuse the traditional doctrine of subsidiarity to keep the government out of the areas of social and economic welfare[403].

3.4 The Influence of *Pacem in Terris* in Christianity

The influence of *Pacem in Terris* in Catholicism, and on Christians by extension, is enormous. If *Pacem in Terris* was embraced by both Catholics and non-Catholics, this was largely due to the style, the interest and the timing of the encyclical itself. In style it was addressed to all people of goodwill; in interest it was peace oriented, appealing for disarmament and human rights; and its timing

---

[403] Commonwealth (26 April 1963) 123. See
http://www.shc.edu/theolibrary/resources/comments_pacem.htm

was just after the missile crisis between the two nuclear powers, the USA and USSR.

In Italy, the influence of *Pacem in Terris* was felt in the promotion of the dialogue between Catholics and Communists[404]. Due to the wider influence and effects of *Pacem in Terris*, the French ministry of foreign affairs stated that it would take fifty years to repair the damage that, not only *Pacem in Terris*, but Pope John XXIII's whole pontificate had done: "*Il faudra cinquante ans pour réparer les dommages causés par ce pontificat. Si la forme et le fond de ces propos attestent qu'il est apocryphe, il n'est pas non plus arbitrairement imaginé*"[405]. Loosely trasnlated as : it will take fifty years to repare the damages caused by this pontificate. When the form and the substace of the remarks used attest that it is apocryphal, nevertheless, the thinking was not arbitraly.

Moreover, the influence of *Pacem in Terris* is well felt in the "Declaration on Religious Freedom: *Dignitatis Humanae* on the Right of the Person and of Communities to Social and Civil Freedom in Matters Religious" promulgated by His Holiness Pope Paul VI on December 7, 1965. *Pacem in Terris* is the most cited Papal encyclical in "*Dignitatis Humanae*".

---

[404] Melloni Alberto, *op.cit.* 2010, p. 88.

[405] *Archives du Ministere des Affaires Etrangeres-Paris*, EU30/19G:n.117,20/5/1963, La Tournelle, p.21. as cited by Melloni Alberto, *op.cit.* 2010, p. 91, footnote 49.

Two years after its pronouncement, the Center for the Study of Democratic Institutions in the United States selected *Pacem in Terris* to be the 'centerpiece' of its imposing conference in February 1965. Robert Hutchens, the then head of the Center, regarded it as "one of the most profound and significant documents of our age,… which consigns nuclear arms, nationalism, colonialism, racism, and non-constitutional regimes to the wastebasket of history"[406].

In many parts of the world, Catholics have broken previous doctrinal barriers and are engaging in organizations and structures that facilitate cooperation and dialogue between nations. Catholics, both religious and lay, who are participating in social work and social justice activism through the lens of human rights, in assisting victims whose rights have been violated, are confirmed by the content of the encyclical. It can be said that one of the effects of the text was to increase the Catholic Church's efforts in reducing the widening gap between rich and poor nations. Another effect was the increase in the Church's participation in promoting global interdependence. On April 6, 1964, Holy See became a permanent observer at the United Nations and on July 1, 2004 gained all the rights of full membership, except voting and putting forward candidates[407]. The Church's firm stands on the relationship between justice and peace, and the

---

[406] Steinfels Peter, '*Pacem in Terris* A retrospective'on the 40th anniversary of *Pacem in Terris* at Vincentian convocation on January 30th 2003.

[407] United Nations General Assembly *Resolution* 314 session 58 (retrieved 27 April, 2013).

defence of human rights as the foundational principle of social justice and peace were becoming the core principle of the Church's social teaching.

3.5 The Influence of *Pacem in Terris* in the Muslim World

In *Pacem in Terris,* Pope John XXIII neither mentioned Muslims nor Islam by name. It was addressed to "Venerable Brethren the Patriarchs, Primates, Archbishops, Bishops, and all other Local Ordinaries who are at Peace and in Communion with the Apostolic See, and to the Clergy and Faithful of the entire Catholic World, and to all Men of Good Will"[408].

The influence of the influential on the influenced can only exist when there is a conscious rapport between the influential (in this case *Pacem in Terris*) and the influenced (in this case the Muslim world). The logic here is that Muslims cannot react or respond to *Pacem in Terris* prior to having knowledge about it. It is true that Pope John XXIII in *Pacem in Terris* spoke a universal language which is not exclusively Christian. He had to address and appeal to the heads of states (among whom are some Muslims) because the states are the principal actors in the issue of wars between states and with regards to the their mutual relations. His overall message was to everyone and that is: do not make war, especially not nuclear war. However, the Muslims and Islam are not explicitly mentioned. The only way one

---

[408] See *Pacem in Terries*, preamble .

can implicitly include Muslims is by categorizing them under "all Men of Good Will" and under the heads of states. As the Holy See's Nuncio in Turkey, a Muslim majority nation, the then Angelo Giuseppe Roncalli surely met some Muslims of goodwill in Turkey. However, to exactly state the influence of *Pacem in Terris* in the Muslim world would be a difficult task.

Historically, Christian-Muslim relations existed since the time of Muhammad. However, there were high points and nadirs to these relations. Christian-Muslim relations nationally and internationally have never ceased to exist. There are many Christian influences on Muslims, all of which cannot be displayed here in this thesis. Thomas Aquinas, one of the greatest theologians of Catholicism, also had contact with the works of some Muslim philosophers and *Mutakallimun* such as Ibn Sina [Avicenna] (980–1037) and Ibn Rushd [Averroës] (1126-1198)[409] and this can be used as a point of reference on widening the dialogue between Catholicism and Muslim culture. In this regard, Louis Gardet remarks: "Rather than an encounter between Christian and Islamic worlds, the

---

[409] "Aquinas' own geographic and social origins could well have predisposed him to a closer relationship with thinkers representative of the Islamicate than his contemporaries could be presumed to have had, in Paris at least. For his provenance from Aquino in the region of Naples, itself part of the kingdom of Sicily, reflected a face of Europe turned to the Islamicate, as evidenced in the first translations commissioned from Arabic". (David B. Burrell, C.S.C. Thomas Aquinas and Islam. Modern Theology 20:1 January 2004 ISSN 0266-7177 ,ISSN 1468-0025 Blackwell Publishing Ltd, USA 2004..): "Latin, Muslim, and Jewish culture mingled freely in Sicily in a unique way that was peculiarly Sicilian." (James Weisheipl, O.P., *Friar Thomas D'Aquino: His Life, Thought, and Works* (Washington, DC: Catholic University of America Press, 1983) p. 15, David Burrell, *op.cit.*)

work of Thomas Aquinas bears witness to an encounter between Christian thought and an Islamic philosophy of Hellenistic inspiration, with a few forays into *kalâm*"[410]. Catholic Church official documents and encyclicals that have been addressed to Muslims or mentioned Muslims (rather than Islam) are: Pope Gregory VII's letter XXI to Anzir *(*Nacir*),* King of Mauritania[411], Pope Paul VI's *Ecclesiam Suam*[412], and Vatican II's *Lumen Gentium*[413] and *Nostra Aetate*[414].

---

[410] Louis Gardet, "La connaissance que Thomas d'Aquin put avoir du monde islamique", in G. Verbeke and D. Verhelst, eds., *Aquinas and the Problems of His Time* (Leuven University Press, The Hague: Martinus Nijhoff, 1976), pp. 139–149; citation at p. 149, David Burrell, *op.cit.*

[411] See Pope St. Gregory VII (d. AD 1085), *letter XXI to Anzir (Nacir), King of Mauritania* (Pl. 148, col. 450f).

[412] "Then we have those worshipers who adhere to other monotheistic systems of religion, especially the Moslem religion. We do well to admire these people for all that is good and true in their worship of God". Encyclical of Pope Paul VI *Ecclesiam Suam* (on the church) August 6, 1964 pp.107.

[413] "But the plan of salvation also includes those who acknowledge the Creator. In the first place amongst these there are the Muslims, who, professing to hold the faith of Abraham, along with us adore the one and merciful God, who on the last day will judge mankind" Dogmatic Constitution on the Church *Lumen Gentium* November, 1964, pp.16.

[414] "The Church regards with esteem also the Moslems. They adore the one God, living and subsisting in Himself; merciful and all- powerful, the Creator of heaven and earth, who has spoken to men; they take pains to submit wholeheartedly to even His inscrutable decrees, just as Abraham, with whom the faith of Islam takes pleasure in linking itself, submitted to God. Though they do not acknowledge Jesus as God, they revere Him as a prophet. They also honor Mary, His virgin Mother; at times they even call on her with devotion. In addition, they await the day of judgment when God will render their deserts to all those who have been raised up from the dead. Finally, they value the moral life and worship God especially through prayer, almsgiving and

In the 1960s the level of conscious official interreligious dialogue and rapport between Holy See and Muslim majority states, at an official level, was almost non-existent. Though there were spontaneous dialogues of life between Catholics and Muslims for centuries, these were not considered official. There exists some form of interreligious dialogue between The World Islamic Call Society in Libya and the Vatican since 1976[415] through biannual meetings in Libya and Vatican City. Some dialogue also exists between Holy See's Pontifical Council for Interreligious dialogue and Azhar University of Egypt. There also exist sporadic interreligious dialogues between Christians and Muslims elsewhere. Perhaps one could say that these were the influence of *Pacem in Terris* on Muslim-Christian relations since they came into existence after the promulgation of *Pacem in Terris* in 11 April 1963.

In the 1960s, the remaining Muslim Caliphate (the Ottoman in Turkey) that could have been an official voice for many Muslims had already been dismantled since 1924. Hence, it should not be a surprise that we do not find any official

---

fasting. Since in the course of centuries not a few quarrels and hostilities have arisen between Christians and Moslems, this sacred synod urges all to forget the past and to work sincerely for mutual understanding and to preserve as well as to promote together for the benefit of all mankind social justice and moral welfare, as well as peace and freedom" Pope Paul VI, Declaration on the Relation of the Church to non-Christian Religions *Nostra Aetate* , October 28, 1965, pp.3.

[415] Nayed Ali Aref, Growing Ecologies of Peace, Compassion and Blessing A Muslim Response to 'A Muscat Manifesto', Kalam Research &Media, Dubai, 2010, p. 31.

Muslim response to *Pacem in Terris* or that it is difficult to ascertain the influence of *Pacem in Terris* on the Muslim world.

As we mentioned above, the principal issue that generated the promulgation of *Pacem in Terris* was related to the behaviour of two states with considerable Christian populations. From this perspective, we can say it did not directly affect Muslim majority nations as such. However, for the fact nuclear weapons respect no territorial boundaries or religions, Muslims would be affected by the nuclear war of that magnitude. Moreover, both the USA and USSR had allies among the Muslim majority states, and so their involvement in nuclear war could have affected their allies as well, not forgetting that American missiles were also in Turkey[416], which is a Muslim Majority nation. Nonetheless, Turkey could be affected not only because of its being majority Muslim nation but because of its NATO membership as well.

There are also other issues mentioned in *Pacem in Terris* that were affecting the Muslim-majority nations. These include human rights issues, especially the status and condition of women, and the status of the minorities and *dhimmis*[417] whose conditions were not equal to Muslims'. Moreover, at the time of promulgation of *Pacem in Terris*, many Muslim majority nations were not

---

[416] Hershberg Jim, *op. cit.* see also http://www.crisismagazine.com/2011/preventing-war-pope-john-xxiii-and-the-cuban-missile-crisis.

[417] These are non-Muslims living under Muslim rule and in most cases do not acquire equal political rights compare to their fellow Muslim citizens.

politically settled. They were either searching for a political model for their newly gained independence or were on the path to independence. Muslim majority nations in Subsharan Africa such as the Gambia, Guinea Conakry, Mali, Mauritania, Nigeria and Senegal were yet to achieve their independence from Britain and France.

As far as our finding is concerned, we neither come across any written Muslim response to *Pacem in Terris* at the time nor do we find the certainty of its influence on the Muslim world. Nonetheless, this does not absolutely exclude any Muslim response or reactions around the globe. There could be many reasons for not finding any written Muslim response at the time:

First, Muslims and their religion, Islam, were not mentioned by *Pacem in Terris*. One of the Islamic principles is that: "among the perfection of one's Islam is one's leaving of things that do not concern him/her"[418]. Perhaps this might be the case with regard to Muslim responses and reactions to *Pacem in Terris*. Second, officially, there was a missing link or vacuum in channeling and receiving the information of interreligious concerns between Christians and Muslims in the 1960s.

Third, Islam, unlike Catholicism, has no single spokesperson, no official hierarchy as such. Thus, it would be very difficult to examine Muslims and to gauge their responses at the time.

---

[418] Tirmidhi and others; see 40 hadith of Imam Al-Nawawi.

Fourth, as stated above, one has to know the existence of something or be affected by it prior to responding or reacting to that particular thing, and justice requires that this reaction or response be appropriate and proportionate. Perhaps, Muslims were not appropriately aware of the encyclical *Pacem in Terris* to the extent of responding to it at that level. At this juncture, a good approach could be that of looking at Islamic perspectives[419] that are grounded in the Qur'an[420] and the *Sunnah*[421] and are higly attuned with the teachings of *Pacem in Terris*.

3.6 An Islamic Perspective on the Peace Appeal of *Pacem in Terris*

Islam for Muslims is the system of creed and a code of life revealed by God to humankind as the guidance through Prophet Muhammad. This guidance combines certain principles, rules and regulations either explicitly stated in *Qur'an* and *Sunnah* or implicitly deduce from *Qur'an* and *Sunnah*. Muslim, in a bid to legitimize and authenticate her or his daily life and activities, does struggle to abide by the *Qur'an* and *Sunnah*. Muslim is expected to struggle endlessly to implement Islamic teachings on his/her daily life and activities. He/she could perform below the standard or at the standard. Thus, Islam is the yard stick

---

[419] For definitions of the word 'perspective' see

https://dictionary.cambridge.org/us/dictionary/english/perspective

[420] For more on the Qur'an and its sciences see 'An Approach to the Quranic Sciences',

by Justice Mufti Muhammad Taqi Usmani translated by Dr. Muhammad Swaleh Siddiqui Adam Publishers & Distributors, 2006.

[421] For more on *Sunnah* See 'The Origins of Islamic Law: The Qur'an, the Muwatta' and Madinan Amal' By Yasin Dutton, Curson Press, 1999, pages.161-178. see also 'Is there a difference between the words "hadeeth" and "Sunnah".'? Accessible at https://islamqa.info/en/145520.

against which the action of a Muslim should be measured, not a Muslim to be the yard stick against which the value and authenticity of Islam is to be measured.

By an Islamic perspective, we mean a Muslim's mental vista grounded in *Qur'an* and *Sunn*ah in relation to the understanding and interpretations of the *Qur'an* and *Sunnah* over a certain issue of concern. However, this perspective may not be the Islam in its self-image. If anything, it is none other than human understanding of Islam, and this understanding could be right or err.

Literally Qur'an means 'recitation'. Qur'an is the fundamental Islamic religious text and source of jurisprudence, which Muslims consider to be the verbatim and eternal word of God and final revelation in the matters of religion. For Muslims, the Qur'an is the eternal word of God unbound by time, space, or geography, revealed to the universal humankind through God's universal final prophet Muhammad. However one's understanding and interpretations of this eternal book and one's understanding and interpretations of the *Sunnah* of its universal final prophet are neither eternal nor final nor are they universally articulated in the same way everywhere at every place.   Thus, every understanding, interpretation and perspective on the *Qur'an* and *Sunnah* are largely drawn from orientations, experiences, backgrounds, customs and cultures of the interpreter (I call this the spirit of interpretation). Since the orientation, experience, background, customs and culture of universal humankind are not exactly universally the same, I choose the phrase '*an* Islamic perspective' and not the Islamic perspective..

Sunnah is an Arabic word literally denoting a way or a path. Its derivative is '*Sanan*,' meaning: a road or a path. Sometimes many people confuse between *Sunnah* and *Hadith*. However, *Sunnah* as a religious nomenclature or terminology has many definition depending on the sciences in Islam.   In the language and understanding of the Prophet and his Companions *Sunnah* denotes the whole of licit practices embedded in the Religion (introduced by God or prophets), in humans and in nature:"And you will not find any amendment in Allah's Sunnah. Nor will you find any divergence (and digression) in Allah's Sunnah".(Qur'an/ 35:43). This entails a belief system, religious and social practice, or ethics, morals etc. In its technical usage sunnah has many meanings. For the hadith scholars (*muhaddathin*) Sunnah refers to any saying (*qawl*), action (*fi'l*), approval (*taqrîr*), or attribute (*sifa*), whether physical (*khilqiyya*) or moral (*khuluqiyya*) ascribed to (*udîfa ila*) the Prophet , whether before or after the beginning of his prophet-hood.

In the usage *of Usul al-fiqh* (principles of jurisprudence), sunnah signifies a saying (*qawl*), action (*fi'l*) or approval (*taqrîr*) related from (*nuqila 'an*) the Prophet or emanating (*sadara*) from him other than the Qur'an. In the discipline of fiqh (jurisprudence), sunnah denotes whatever is firmly established (*thabata*) and called for (*matlub*) in the Religion on the basis of a legal proof (*dalîl shar'î*) but without being obligatory, the continued abandonment of which constitutes disregard (*istikhfaf*) of the Religion - also sin (*ithm*) according to some jurists - and incurs blame (*lawm, 'itab, tadlîl*) - also punishment ('*uquba*) according to some jurists. Nevertheless, some jurists made a differentiation within the Sunnah. There is what they called "Emphasized sunnah" (*sunnah mu'akkada*) or 'sunnah of Guidance' (*Sunnah al-huda*), and 'non-Emphasized sunnah' (*Sunnah ghayr mu'akkada*) or 'Sunnah of habit' (*Sunnah al-'ada*). 'Emphasized sunnah' (*Sunnah mu'akkada*) or 'sunnah of Guidance' (*Sunnah al-huda*) (is what has been ordered or emphasized in word or in deed by Prophet, and 'non-emphasized Sunnah' (*sunnah ghayr mu'akkada*) or 'Sunnah of habit' (*sunnah al-'ada*) is the types of sunnah considered less binding in their religious legal status.

These meanings of *Sunnah* are used to make contradistinction to the Qur'an and also to other religious categories for human actions such as :-

177

fard (obligatory),   *mubah* (indifferent), *makruh* (disliked), *haram* (prohibited) - and applies in the usage of jurists from the second Hijri century onwards. However, the jurists have stressed that the basis for all acts of worship categorized as *Sunnah* is 'obligatoriness' not 'permissiveness' *(al-asl fi al-sunnah al-wujub la al-ibaha)*. Sunnah thus, is anything emanated, or ordered, or intended, or accepted by the prophet and promoted by him among all his followers, as a part of God's religion.

Sunnah therefore can bee seen as a categorical issue purely related to the pragmatic aspects of life and is authenticated by the perpetual, universal and consensus devotion of the community to it and has been handed down from generation to generation. Hence its manner in transmission is almost *islamicaly* universal, since universal principles are never devoted or handed- down by one or two individuals. As such *Sunnah* is certainly authentic for Muslims and its authenticity in method is parallel to that of the Qur'an itself. Hence *Sunnah* is regarded as one of the independent sources of Islamic jurisprudence. Antithesis of *Sunnah* is *bid'ah* innovation. *Hadith* can be defined as 'what was transmitted on the authority of the Prophet, his deeds, sayings, tacit approval, or description of his *sifaat* (features) meaning his physical appearance. In other words, whatever was reported from the Prophet Muhammad, be it utterances, acts, or things he permitted to be done or to be uttered by his companions through tacit or explicit approval or criticism either valid or invalid. There are authentic and fabricated ahadith as distinguished by the hadith scholars.

Lexically, *Islam* is derived from the root word *Silm/SLM* or *Salama* which renders surrender, peace, safety and security. In a religious terminology it also means to surrender or submit one's self to the will and plan of God. It is based on the notion that, since God is the omnipotent, the supreme and the creator of the

178

universe, submitting one's self to the will and plan of one's creator will guarantee one peace, safety and security. However, this kind of peace is problematic as far as international peace is concerned: to whose version of God are we to submit internationally in order to have peace? This kind of peace is too personal and is not what the international system requires. The international system seeks peace between states rather than personal or private peace. However, the Muslim has been defined by Prophet Muhammad as: the one who grants safety (SLM) to others, from his tongue and his hand (i.e. who does no harm to others)[422] He summed up the very essence of Islamic faith when he said: "You will not enter paradise unless you believe, and you will not believe unless you love one another. Shall I guide you to what leads to your love of one another? Spread peace between yourselves!"[423]. Therefore, 'spreading of the peace' (*ifsha al-salam*) is absolutely essential to true Islamic faith. "'*Ifsha*' is more than just spreading or dispersing—it is also cultivating and nourishing peace[424]". Therefore, Muslims "are all called upon to spread, cultivate, and nourish peace." Moreover, the culmination of a Muslim's five daily (*salat*) prayers and his or her *tashahhud* (bearing witness to faith in God and the Prophet) entails evoking peace for all servants of God. Furthermore, at the end of every *salat* God's peace, compassion, and blessings are invoked upon everyone on the right and left. The daily greeting

---

[422] Ahmed, no. 7066.

[423] Muslim, no. 157.

[424] Ali Nayed Aref, *op. cit.*

of Muslims is God's peace, compassion, and blessings be upon you. Hence, any attempt against peace and security of the people, irrespective of national or international level, political or social peace is considered to be un-Islamic[425]. This is a brief summary of the etymological and terminological meaning of Islam.

Islam was founded in the 7th century, precisely 610 C.E., in Mecca, Arabia. At the advent of Islam, there had been threats to rights, religious freedom, justice and liberty, and hence a threat to peace. Islam emerged among a people, the majority of whom were hostile to justice, righteousness and freedom of conscience. Oppression, enslavement and exploitation were also rampant in the pre-Islamic society of Mecca[426]. Islam was revealed in one of the darkest periods of human history in Arabia called the period of ignorance—(*Asr ul-jahiliyya*)—a period in which intermittent wars were rampant, women were regarded as objects, burying female babies alive [427] was acceptable, might was right, idolatry was rife

---

[425] By un-Islamic I mean any acts, deeds or behaviour which is in contradiction with the teachings of the Qur'an and the traditions of the Messenger Muhammad.

[426] It is a belief that in history God sent His prophets and messengers to society and nations when a majority departed from the divine order. This was the case in Arabia at the time. See also the speech of Ja`far ibn Abī Tālib in Ethiopia in front of king Negus in Ibn Hisham, *Siratu an-nabawiya*,(the Biography of the Prophet) Darul-Jiel, Lebanon, Beirut ,1975, vol. 2.

[427] "When the female (infant), buried alive, is questioned-For what crime she was killed". Qur'an: At-Takwir/The Overthrowing/ 81:8-9. "When news is brought to one of them, of (the birth of) a female (child), his face darkens, and he is filled with inward grief!-With shame does he hide himself from his people, because of the bad news he has had! Shall he retain it on (sufferance and) contempt, or bury it in the dust? Ah! what an evil (choice) they decide on" Qur'an: Al-Nahal/ The

[428], tribalism, injustice, oppression, immoral business practices, usury, excessive profitmaking, deception and theft, illicit sex, plundering, conceit, unending malice, superstition and credulity, gambling and an unlimited number of wives were the order of the *jahiliyya* period and the society[429].

Prior to the revelation of Islam and the emergence of Muslims as a compelling social and political force, military uncertainty that was accompanied by political instability in both Roman and Sasanian empires was already in existence. Brutal wars were waged between the Roman and Sasanian empires[430]. Although the Byzantine and Sasanian empires had instituted a master-client relationship with some Arab tribes—such as the Ghassanids (with the Romans) and the Lakhmids (with the Persians)—which could serve as a buffer between the imperial provinces and the ungovernable Arab tribes[431], these relations were

---

Bee/16:58-59.

[428] "Have ye seen Lat. and 'Uzza, And another, the third (goddess), Manat? What! for you the male sex, and for Him, the female? Behold, such would be indeed a division most unfair! These are nothing but names which ye have devised,- ye and your fathers,- for which God has sent down no authority (whatever). They follow nothing but conjecture and what their own souls desire!- Even though there has already come to them Guidance from their Lord" Qur'an, An-Najm/ The Star /53:19-23.

[429] Akbar Shah Najeebabadi, *The History of Islam Vl.* 1. Darussalam, Int'l Publishers & Distributors, Riyadh, Houston, New York, Lahore, Dhaka2000, pages 70-77.

[430] Berkey, Jonathan P., *The Formation of Islam: Religion and Society in the Near East, 600-1800* Cambridge University Press, 2003, P. 73.

[431] *Ibid.*, P. 73.

precarious and unstable so they could not guarantee permanent regional peace. For instance: "Khusrau II apparently harbored dreams of restoring the hegemony over the whole of the Near East which Iran had wielded under Cyrus and Xerxes and came close to success: by 620 Sasanian armies, had occupied Syria, Egypt and Asia Minor as far as the Bosphorus"[432].

Moreover, as Jonathan Berkey puts it :"The Roman empire's unsuccessful attempt to force [the Jews] wholesale conversion in 632 is just as telling, if less dramatic, a sign of the culmination of the process of resolving religious identity which had characterized late antiquity as the Arab conquest which followed rapidly upon the death of Muhammad in that same year"[433]. Added to these external wars were the bitter intermittent tribal feuds resulting from weak and fragile intertribal relationships among the pre-Islamic Arabs. The perpetual conflicts of *Aws* and *Khazraj*, *'Abs* and *Dhubyan*, *Bakr* and *Taghlib*, are striking examples.

However, pre-Islamic Arabs instituted four sacred months for secession of hostilities and any breach in this regard was seen as blasphemous. These are: first, seventh, eleventh, and twelfth months of what is now the Islamic lunar

---

[432] *Ibid.,* P. 50.

[433] *Ibid.,*P. 51.

calendar[434]: *Muharram, Rajab, Dhul-Qaʻdah,* and *Dhul-Hijja*[435]. The Qur'an, in

its desire for peace, endorsed these months as being sacred and not appropriate for

hostilities and hence a period of ceasefire[436]. Furthermore, in the interests of peace

and sympathy for his poor and weak followers who had been brutalized and

persecuted by the Meccans, Muhammad, the prophet of Islam, had to choose

migration over war by dispatching some of his followers to Abyssinia

(Ethiopia)[437].

---

[434] Muhamamad Asad, The Message of the Qur'an, commentary on *Al-Baqara*/The Cow /2:194.

[435] "O People! Time has gone back to how it was at the time Allaah created the Heavens and the Earth. A year has twelve months, four of which are sacred, three consecutive, *Thul-Qi'dah, Thul-Hijjah, Muharram*, and *Rajab,* which comes between Jumaadaa and Sha'baan." Al-Bukhaari, Volume 4, Book 54, Number 419.

[436] Qur'an, At-tawbah/ Repentance/9:36 "BEHOLD, the number of months, in the sight of God, is twelve months, [laid down] in God's decree on the day when He created the heavens and the earth; [and] out of these, four are sacred: this is the ever-true law [of God]. Do not, then, sin against yourselves with regard to these [months]".

[437] In a bid to have the fleeing Muslims repatriated to Mecca, the Meccans had sent delegation under the leadership of ʻAmr ibn al-ʻAs and ʻAbdullah ibn Abi Rabia ibn Mughira. However, the repatriation appeal of the Meccans was unsuccessful as the Muslims had already reached the Negus, the Christian ruler of Ethiopia. The following was the speech delivered by Muslims' spokesperson Jaʻfar ibn Abī Tālib in an appeal to King Negus against their repatriation to Mecca: "O king! We were plunged in the depth of ignorance and barbarism; we adored idols; we lived in unchastity; we ate dead bodies; and we spoke abominations; we disregarded every feeling of humanity; and the duties of hospitality and neighbourhood were neglected; we knew no law but that of the strong, when Allah raised among us a man, whose birth, truthfulness, honesty, and purity we were aware of; and he called to the Oneness of Allah and taught us not to associate anything with Him. He forbade us the worship of idols; and he enjoined us to speak the truth; to be

Furthermore, as the Meccan's hostile endeavor to impede Islam and Muslims increased, Muhammad, the prophet himself, for the interest of peace and the safety of his life, had to migrate to Yathrib, a city to be later known as Medina, where he was invited as an arbitrator (*hakam*) over war between certain tribes in Yathrib [438] namely Aws and Khazraj [439]. It was in Medina that Muhammad signed a treaty call *Sahifat ul-Madina*, the Madinan Charter or the Constitution of Madina.

---

faithful to our trusts; to be merciful and to regard the rights of the neighbours and kith and kin; he forbade us to speak evil of women; or to eat the property of orphans; he ordered us to distant from the vices, and to abstain from evil; taught us to offer prayers, to give alms, and to observe fast during Ramadan. We have believed in him, we have accepted his teachings and his injunctions to worship Allah and not to associate anything with Him, and we have allowed what He has allowed, and prohibited what He has prohibited. For this reason, our people have risen against us, have persecuted us in order to make us forsake the worship of Allah and return to the worship of idols and other abominations. They have tortured and injured us, until finding no safety among them; we have come to your country, and hope you will protect us from oppression." See http://www.fountainmagazine.com/Issue/detail/Jafar-Ibn-Abi-Talib. see also Ibn Hisham, *Siratu an-nabawiya* (the Biography of the Prophet, Darul-Jiel, Lebanon, Beirut 1975 vol. 2.) After some queries by King Negus which were answered to his satisfaction he refused to hand over these Muslims to the Meccan delegation. For these queries see Ibn Hisham, *Siratu an-nabawiya* (the Biography of the Prophet Darul-Jiel, Lebanon, Beirut 1975 vol. 2).

[438] His Medinan life commenced with his arrival at Quba' in the oasis of Yathrib around 4 September 622. See W. Montgomery Watt Muhammad at Medina, Oxford University Press, Amen House, London E.G.4 1956, p.1.

[439] Dabashi Hamid Authority in Islam from the Rise of Muhammad to the Establishment of the Umayyad, Transaction Publishers, USA, 1989, p. 65. See also W. Montgomery Watt Muhammad at Medina *op.cit.* page 1 . See also Ibn Hisham, *Siratu an-nabawiya* (The Biography of the Prophet), Darul-Jiel, Lebanon, Beirut 1975 vol. 2.

This was the first supra-tribal and supra-creedal confederal document in Islam, for the establishment of peace and security among the heterogeneous tribes and believers in Yathrib or Madina [440]. In addition, pacts of mutual-non-aggression were made with *Banu Damrah* and *Banu Mudlij* [441]. The treaty with *Banu Ghifar, Juhaynad* and the treaty of *Al-Hudaibiyah* [442] with the Quraish were

---

[440] This document brought to an end the decades-old bitter inter-tribal feud between the two tribes of *Aws* and *Khazraj* in the city of *Yathrib*. This supra-tribal and supra-creedal constitution enshrined the security of the community, religious freedoms, the status of Medina as a sacred city (*haram*) (barring all violence and weapons), tribal coexistence within Medina, parameters for exogenous political alliances, a system for granting protection of individuals, a judicial system for resolving disputes, freeing of war prisoners and also regulated the paying of blood money in lieu of *lex talionis*. The execution and implementation of the constitution shall be in accordance with the recognized principles of law and justice. See Ibn Hisham, *Siratu an-nabawiya* (the Biography of the Prophet), Darul-Jiel, Lebanon, Beirut 1975 vol.2 p. 106. See also http://www.constitutionofmadina.com/blog/2012/02/22/constitution-of-medina-in-63-articles.

[441] W. Montgomery Watt Muhammad at Medina, Oxford University Press, Amen House, London E.G.4 1956, p. 4.

[442] After debating on the text of the treaty, the following content of the treaty were agreed upon by Muhammad, the Muslim representative, and Suhayl bin Amr, the Meccan representative. The following articles were decided upon to be observed: The Muslims shall return to Madina without performing umrah in that particular year. In the following year, they can visit Mecca staying therein for three days bearing no arms except the arms of the traveller with swords remaining in their sheaths. One sided extradition: Muslims of Medina taking refuge in Mecca shall not be extradited; however Muhammad must extradite every Meccan arriving in Medina if the master of such Meccan wishes so. (For instance during the negotiation of the treaty, Abu Jandal, son of the Quraish delegate Suhayl bin Amr wished to take refuge as a Muslim under the Muhammad's protection and asked Muhammad to save him from extraditing him to Meccans. The Prophet could not accept Abu Jandal's appeal emphasizing that *pacta sunt servanda* must be observed. Abu Basir, who fled from Meccans to Muhammad in Medina, had to be handed over by Muhammad to the two agents of Meccans who pursued him to Medina). Muhammad will not

some of the peace treaties Prophet Muhammad concluded. It is important to note that one of the most important peace treaties in Islamic history is the *Al-Hudaibiyah* Treaty [443] signed in the 6th year after *Hijra* and Muhammad gave his highest *pacta sunt servanda*[444] to this treaty.

---

repatriate anyone from the Meccan society along with himself and will not prevent the believers [in Islam] who wish to remain in Mecca. People who wish to join Muhammad's alliance are free to do so and those who wish for the solidarity and the alliance with the Quraish are free to do so. Ten years of truce have been signed between the Meccans and Muslims. The allies of the treaty signing parties are included within this treaty. The treaty offered that each of the parties be provided safe passage through their lands for the people of the other party, and if one of the parties is at war with a third party, the other party is obliged to remain neutral. (See Ibn–Hisham, op., cit.1975 vol.2 page 106.) See also http://www.constitutionofmadina.com/blog/2012/02/22/constitution-of-medina-in-63-articles.

[443] This treaty came into being as a result of barring Muhammad and his followers from entering into Mecca for the lesser pilgrimage (*Umrah*). *Hudaibiyah* Treaty with all its seemingly unfavorable conditions and terms for Muslims was accepted by Muhammad despite the initial disapproval of his followers. However, *Hudaibiyah* Treaty was later turned out to be a victory for Islam because by 628 it led to the continual opening of Mecca for Muslims and their continual residence therein up to this time. It was the harshest treaty for Muslims and the greatest of results unprecedented. It was the Banu Bakr tribe, the ally of the Quraish tribe that breached the pact by attacking the Huzaa tribe, the ally of the Muhammad. This breach eventually led to the conquest of Mecca.

[444] It is a principle that expresses one of the fundamental principles of international laws, treaties and agreements. It refers to the duty of every state, person and organization, to conscientiously and completely fulfill its international obligation. Failure to observe the principle of *pacta sunt servanda* is considered a sin in Islam that could attract Divine punishment.

Furthermore, shortly after the *Al-Hudaybiyah* Treaty, it is on record that Muhammad had sent out six messengers with epistles to rulers in the region[445]. Muhammad also signed a treaty with the Christians of Najran. In his prophethood, Muhammad signed many treaties and sent many letters inviting people to Islam, the ultimate aim in this was peace, safety, security and preservation of himself, his people and his new religion. It is a general practice that peace pacts maintained peace, and that, in theory at least, war is less likely to happen among the co-religionists, hence, he either signed pacts or invited other peoples to be his own co-religionists.

Nonetheless, despite all these treaties signed and epistles sent, wars and expeditions were inevitable. The circumstances, the milieu, the socio-political context of the era as mentioned above, made it logical for Prophet Muhammad to engage in war for self-preservation. As such he probably carried out seventy-four expeditions, seven of which were undertaken during the first eighteen months of the *Hijrah*[446]. However, Muhammad is recorded to have participated in at least

---

[445] Such as the Najashi or Negus of Abyssinia, to the governor of Bostr'a (*Busra*) to hand on to the Byzantine emperor, to the Persian emperor (perhaps sent by way of the Yemen), to the *Muqawqis* or ruler of Egypt, to *Al-Harith b. Abi Shamir,* prince of Ghassan, and to *Hawdhah b. 'Ali,* chief of *Hamfah.* According to Montgomery "the critical discussions of European scholars have shown that, while the story cannot be taken as it stands, there is a kernel of truth in it." see W. Montgomery Watt Muhammad at Medina, Oxford University Press, Amen House, London E.G.4 1956, P. 4.

[446] W. Montgomery Watt, *Muhammad at Medina,* Oxford University Press, Amen House, London E.G.4 1956, p. 2.

twenty seven expeditions and to have been represented in some fifty nine others[447].

The abovementioned etymological and terminological definition of Islam and historical events, together with interpretation of the Qur'an and *Sunnah*, provide the foundation for contemporary Islamic and Muslim perspectives on war and peace as with regards to its perspective to *Pacem in Terris*. With regards to war and peace, there are many perspectives from Islam. "Islamic approaches to peace [and war] are based on the Quranic verses, the Hadith (sayings of Prophet Mohammed), and Sunna (deeds and examples of Prophet Mohammed). Since Quranic verses, Hadith, and Sunna refer to particular historical events, at times, they seem to contradict one another. Therefore it has not been possible to develop a single Islamic tradition of peace, and war"[448] "Instead, there are a number of

---

[447] David Cook *Understanding Jihad*, University of California Press 2005 –see acknowledgment. Among the most decisive battles were the battle of *Badr* which occurred around 17th, 19th, or 21st of Ramadan in the 2nd year of *Hijra* 13, 15, or 17 March 624. (see W. Montgomery Watt, *op. cit.* P.12), the battle of *Uhud* occurred in 3rd year of *Hijra* Saturday, 23 March, 625 (W. Montgomery Watt, *op. cit.*.p. 22), the fortnight siege of Medina known to Muslims as the expedition of the *Khandaq* or Trench, began on 5th year of *Hijra* (31 March 627), (*ibid.* P. 35) and the battle of *Hunayn* at the south-east of Makkah occured in February 1st 630 (Sir William Muir, Thomas Hunter Weir, The Life of Moḥammad from Original Sources, Princeton University Elizabeth Foundation, P.430.)

[448] Kadayifçi-Orellana, "Religion, violence and the Islamic Tradition of Nonviolence". In *The Turkish YearBook* [VOL. XXXIV, 2003] p. 40.

different traditions, each of which draws selectively on the Quran to establish legitimacy for its view of war and peace"[449].

Among these perspectives, there can be found the militant/militaristic perspective, the non-violent perspective, and the defensive perspective.

3.6.1 Militarist-Militant Perspective

This perspective theorizes '*jihād*' as 'armed struggle' to extend Muslim political domain *dar-al-islam* (abode of peace) against the political domain of the enemies *dar-al-harb* (abode of war). This theorization existed already in the works of Shafi'i and Sarakhsi, the jurists of the 9th and 10th centuries C.E. respectively. Their interpretation of *jihād* justifies fighting on the part of *dar-al-islam* against the *dar-alharb* territories[450]. Sarakhsi stated: "to sum up, the command of *jihad* and fighting (for Muslims) had been revealed in stages... (the final stage) the absolute order to fight (non-believers).... this means an obligation but this obligation is meant to exalt religion (of Islam) and to subdue the associators"[451]. For Shafi'i "Allah made *jihād* an obligation after it had been a

---

[449] Tibi, Basam, "*War and Peace in islam*" in The Ethics of War and Peace: Religious and Secular Perspectives Terry Nardin, eds. (New Jersey: Princeton University Press, Princeton, 1996), 129. As cited by Kadayifçi-Orellana, *op.cit.* 2003] p. 40.

[450] Ibrahim Kalin, *Islam and Peace* The Royal Aal Al-Bayt Institute for Islamic Thought, Amman 11195, Jordan, 2012, pages 37-39.

[451] Ayse S. Kadayifci Orellana, *Standing on an Isthmus: Islamic Narratives on Peace and War And Peace In Palestine Territories*, Lexington Books, UK, 2007, p. 92.

matter of choice"[452]. The view of these jurists could also serve as a classical juridical source for this Militarist-Militant perspective.

This perspective is rooted in the ideology of Islamic universalism. This ideology holds that Islam is the best solution to the world's problems of injustice, oppression and war. Hence, Islam must be the only religion to which the world systems must succumb. For the protagonist of this perspective, the *raison d'être* of Islam is to dominate not to be dominated, to rule not to be ruled. In order to achieve this, offensive wars are permitted from their perspective. For them: "Islam spread by means of proof and evidence to those who listened to the message and responded to it, and it spread by means of force and the sword to those who were stubborn and arrogant, until they were overwhelmed and became no longer stubborn, and submitted to that reality"[453].

This perspective could also be backed up by certain verses in the Qur'an that explicitly command Muslims to murder the idolaters[454]. The critics of Islam [455]

---

[452] *Ibid.*, P. 92.

[453] Fataawa al-Lajnah al-Daa'imah (12/14) as cited in http://islamqa.info/en/ref/43087/

[454] "Then kill the polytheists wherever you find them and capture them and besiege them and sit in wait for them at every place of ambush. But if they should repent, establish prayer, and give *zakah*, let them [go] on their way. Indeed, Allah is Forgiving and Merciful" (Qur'an, Atawba/ Repentance/ 9:5). "Fight those who believe not in Allah and the Day of Judgment" (Qur'an, Atawba/ Repentance/ 9:29). "and fight in God's cause against those who wage war against you, but do not commit aggression – for, verily, God does not love aggressors. And slay them wherever you may come upon them, and drive them away from wherever they drove you away – for oppression is even worse than killing. And fight not against them near the Inviolable House of

and some Muslim extremists[456] hold that these verses everlastingly and indiscriminately enjoin Muslims to wage war on non-Muslims whoever they may be and where ever they may be. In a bid to find an islamic justification for their actions, they use the 'verses of sword' to chronologically abrogate all the previous verses praising tolerance, forgiveness, justice, reconciliation, patience, inclusiveness, compassion, co-existence and peace. However, extremists are not alone in this view. David Bukay claims so by stating: "Coming at or near the very end of Muhammad's life,… this verse [Surah Al-Tawbah, 9] trumps earlier revelations. Because this chapter contains violent passages, it abrogates previous peaceful content"[457]. However, contrary to the view of Bukay, British scholar Dr. Zakaria Bashier asserted that all the Qur'anic verses which enjoin Muslims to be

---

Worship unless they fight against you there first; but if they fight against you, slay them: such shall be the recompense of those who deny the truth. But if they desist – behold, God is much-forgiving, a dispenser of grace. Hence, fight against them until there is no more oppression and all worship is devoted to God alone; but if they desist, then all hostility shall cease, save against those who [willfully] do wrong" (Qur'an, Baqara/The Cow/ 2:190-193)

[455] David Bukay, "Peace or Jihad: Abrogation in Islam," in *Middle East Quarterly*, Fall 2007, pp. 3-11, Robert Spencer, The Truth About Muhammad, Founder of the World's Most Intolerant Religion (Washington, DC: Regnery Press, 2006). Religion of Peace? Why Christianity Is and Islam Isn't (Regnery, 2007). The Myth of Islamic Tolerance, pp. 43-44. Majid Khadduri, The Islamic Conception of Justice (Baltimore: Johns Hopkins University Press, 1984), p. 165.

[456] Osama Bin Laden and Ayman al- Zawahiri and their associates come to mind.

[457] David Bukay, "Peace or Jihad: Abrogation in Islam," in *Middle East Quarterly*, Fall 2007, pp. 3-11, accessible at: http://www.meforum.org/1754/peace-or-jihad-abrogation-in-islam. Access date: 1 April 2011.

peaceful, tolerant and non-aggressive are: *Muhkam* [unambiguous and unequivocal] and are not known to have been abrogated, so they are naturally still in force up to the present. He sees no reason to think that these verses have been overridden[458]. He further stresses that their contextual information leads to the inescapable conclusion that the verses commanding fighting are time-bound and circumstantial, and so any claim that they abrogate the established policy of tolerance is historically incorrect[459].

The militarist-militant perspective attributes poverty, economic exploitation, oppression, injustice and political instability in the world in general, and in Muslim-majority states in particular, to the international system that dominates the world. Since *la hukma illa li-llah* or the theory of *Hakimyyah* (all ruling and governance belong to Allah), the uprooting of this international system and the substitution of it by God's governance becomes necessary by any means. The end justifies the means. According to this perspective, "offensive wars and even attacks on civilian targets are necessary evils to bring God's rule to earth"[460]. Muslim movements such as *al-Qaeda* and their supporters uphold this

---

[458] Bashier Zakaria, War and Peace in the Life of Muhammad Islamic Foundation , UK, 2006,, page 284. Sohaib Nazeer Sultan, *The Koran for Dummies* (Hoboken: Wiley, 2004) (pp. 278, 281). Both are in agreement that the martial verse and the sword and those like it do not abrogate the numerous peaceful, tolerant and peace inclusive verses.

[459] Bashier Zakaria, *op.cit.* 2006, p. 288.

[460] Kadayifçi-Orellana, *op. cit.* 2003, p. 40.

perspective. The protagonists of this perspective as mentioned above could have legitimized their perspective from the interpretation of certain Quranic verses[461], *ahadith*[462] and historical events[463]. Also early Muslims' involvement in territorial

---

[461] "Then kill the polytheists wherever you find them and capture them and besiege them and sit in wait for them at every place of ambush. But if they should repent, establish prayer, and give *zakah*, let them [go] on their way. Indeed, Allah is Forgiving and Merciful" (Qur'an, Atawba/ Repentance/ 9:5). "Fight those who believe not in Allah and the Day of Judgment" (Qur'an, Atawba/ Repentance/ 9:29). "And fight in God's cause against those who wage war against you, but do not commit aggression – for, verily, God does not love aggressors. And slay them wherever you may come upon them, and drive them away from wherever they drove you away – for oppression is even worse than killing. And fight not against them near the Inviolable House of Worship unless they fight against you there first; but if they fight against you, slay them: such shall be the recompense of those who deny the truth. But if they desist – behold, God is much-forgiving, a dispenser of grace. Hence, fight against them until there is no more oppression and all worship is devoted to God alone; but if they desist, then all hostility shall cease, save against those who [willfully] do wrong" (Qur'an, Baqara/The Cow/ 2:190-193).

[462] Muhammad is on record to have said: "I have been sent ahead of the Hour with the sword so that Allah will be worshipped alone, and my provision has been placed in the shade of my spear, and humiliation has been decreed for those who go against my command, and whoever imitates a people is one of them"(See Ahmad, 4869; Saheeh al-Jaami', 2831. See also http://islamqa.info/en/ref/43087. Ibn Umar also narrated that: Allah's Apostle said: "I have been ordered (by Allah) to fight against the people until they testify that none has the right to be worshipped but Allah and that Muhammad is Allah's Apostle, and offer the prayers perfectly and give the obligatory charity, so if they perform that, then they save their lives an property from me except for Islamic laws and then their reckoning (accounts) will be done by Allah"(*Sahih al-Bukhari*, Volume 1, Book 2, Number 24).

[463] Muhammad is also on record to have charged Qurayza a Jews tribe with treason and ordered the killing of most of them (with exception of those surrendered and converted to Islam) at the Battle of the Trench in 627 and accordingly all the women and children were taken captive and enslaved. (See Ibn Hisham, *op. cit*. See also Peterson, *Muhammad: the prophet of God*, p. 125-127. See also Hodgson, *The Venture of Islam*, vol. 1, p. 191. (as cited in

expansion[464] through war give the impression that "the only reason Islam is a world religion is because it spread by the sword"; and that it was also Muhammad's choice to preach his message through sword. Perhaps these sources made people like Watt and Williams believe that Muhammad's expeditions were offensive. Watt remarks: "The chief point to notice is that the Muslims took the offensive. With one exception these seven expeditions were directed against Meccan caravans.... Although there was no fighting on any of these seven expeditions, they were not without positive result for the Muslims"[465]. These are

---

http://en.wikipedia.org/wiki/Banu_Qurayza) accessed on 13-05-13) Several authors have challenged the veracity of this incident, arguing that it was exaggerated or invented [perhaps to intensify anti-Semitism among Muslims]. (Arafat, "New Light on the Story of Banu Qurayza and the Jews of Medina", p. 100-107. Arafat relates the testimony of Ibn Hajar, who denounced this and other accounts as "odd tales" and quoted Malik ibn Anas, a contemporary of Ibn Ishaq [the original source for the story], whom he rejected as a "liar", an "impostor" and for seeking out the Jewish descendants for gathering information about Muhammad's campaign with their forefathers. Meri, *Medieval Islamic Civilization: An Encyclopedia*, p.754.) as cited in http://en.wikipedia.org/wiki/Banu_Qurayza accessed on 13-05-13).

[464] After the death of Muhammad, "Islamic expansion truly began in the early 630s, [C.E] Campaigns against the Byzantine and Sassanid (Persian) Empires were initiated which pitted this new religion of Islam, with its desert Arabian warriors against the established and ancient empires centered in Constantinople and Ctesiphon. ....Syria was under Muslim control by 638, Egypt by 642, and Iraq/Persia by 644. The Byzantine Empire, having lost its religious base in Syria, as well as its commercial base in Egypt was greatly weakened. The Sassanid Empire, on the other hand, completely ceased to exist after the Muslim conquest. Politically, it was a disaster for these two giant empires". See Firas Alkhateeb in " Did Islam Spread by the Sword"

At http://lostislamichistory.com/did-islam-spread-by-the-sword/ accessed on 10-05-2013.

[465] W. Montgomery Watt, 1956 ,*op. cit.*, p. 2-3. See also Sir William Muir, Thomas Hunter Weir, The Life of Moḥammad from Original Sources, Princeton University Elizabeth Foundation,

some of the scriptural sources for Muslims' conventional *Shariah* and jurisprudence that has to be struggled with in the face of religious freedom, human rights and international relations. This perspective creates obstacles to international security and peace and also threatens both national and international systems of the world and their stability.

3.6.2 Nonviolence Perspective

Another perspective on war and peace is the non-violent perspective. Etymologically, 'non-violence' refers to the negation of use of violence to accomplish one's objective. Developing the *Satyagraha* and *Ahimsa* paradigm of Ghandi's nonviolence, Martin Luther King Jr. described the qualities of nonviolence as follows: nonviolence negates physical aggression, but is spiritually dynamic and aggressive; it negates the humiliation of the opponent, and upholds creating change in the opponent by persuading the opponent to accept the moral shame of his/her action in a bid to build beloved communities, by attacking the evil forces but not the persons overwhelmed by the evil forces; avoidance of "both external physical and internal spiritual violence" and "the conviction that the universe is on the side of justice"[466]. However, when nonviolence is

---

p. 211.

[466] See Kadayıfçı-Orellana, *op. cit.* 2003, p. 37. See also http://satyagrahaandahimsa.blogspot.it/2007/05/six-principles-and-six-steps-of.html.

understood as passivity, inaction or indifference to the structures of injustice, sufferings and oppression, then it becomes a misunderstood concept. On the contrary, nonviolence is a proactive strategic process of resisting injustice and oppression without resorting to physical, verbal or even spiritual violence[467]. Daniel L. Smith-Christopher defined nonviolence in these words: "nonviolence implies an active commitment to social change that would ultimately result in a fair distribution of world resources, a more creative and democratic cooperation between peoples, and a common pursuit of those social, scientific, medical, and political achievements that serve to enhance the human enterprise and prevent warfare"[468]. Simith added: "nonviolence includes not only the refusal to engage in lethal activities, but it also presumes a commitment to strive for conditions of fairness, justice, and respect in human relations"[469]. Mohammed Abu Nimer, a Muslim protagonist for nonviolence, defines nonviolence as "a set of attitudes, actions, or behaviors intended to persuade the other side to change its opinions, perceptions and actions" and he views pacifism as "the overall principle that guides the application of nonviolent strategies"[470]. The nonviolence paradigm in

---

[467] *Ibid.* p. 36.

[468] Smith-Christopher, Daniel L., *Subverting Hatred: The Challenge of Nonviolence in Religious Tradition* (Cambridge MA, The Boston Research Center for the 21st Century, 1998) p. 10 as cited by Kadayıfçı-Orellana, *op. cit.* 2003, p. 38.

[469] Smith-Christophe, 1998, *op.cit.* page 10, as cited by Kadayıfçı-Orellana, *op. cit* 2003, p. 36.

[470] Abu-Nimer Mohammed, Nonviolence and Peacebuilding in Islam University Press of Florida, USA, 2003, p. 14. See also Kadayıfçı-Orellana, *op. cit* 2003, p. 37.

Islam is not different from that of the non-Muslims' such as Ghandi, Martin Luther King Jr., Smith-Christopher and others.

The proponents of the nonviolence perspective of Islam see the above mentioned qualities of nonviolence as Islamic; and not in any way contrary to Islam; and hence consider the incorporation of nonviolence traditions into Islam as Islamic. They claim that there is no scriptural or textual reason for Muslims not to prefer and adopt nonviolence over violence. For them "in fact, not to adopt nonviolence is antithetical to Islam"[471]. For Wahiduddin Khan the only three real battles in which Muslims and their prophet participated when it became absolutely inevitable were the Battles of *Badr, Uhud,* and *Hunayn.* These battles, according to him, lasted only for half a day, each beginning from noon and ending with the setting of the sun. Against this background, Wahiduddun Khan deduced that the Prophet of Islam had actively engaged in war for a total of a day and half, and it was the principle of nonviolence that was practiced throughout his 23 year prophethood[472]. The proponents of nonviolence among Muslim scholars includes Wahiduddin Khan, Mohammed Abu-Nimer, Jawdat Sa'id and others.

This Islamic perspective sees the attainment of durable and substantive peace as being embedded in truth and justice. According to this perspective, this is why

---

[471] Khan, Maulana Wahiduddin "Non-Violence and İslam", paper prepared for the symposium: *Islam and Peace in the 21 Century*". D.C. February 6-7, 1998. As cited In Religion, Violence and the Islamic Tradition of Nonviolence Kadayıfçı-Orellana, *op. cit.,* 2003, p. 42.

[472] Kadayıfçı-Orellana, *op. cit.,* 2003, p. 49.

the establishment of truth and justice is a central message of Islam and the Qur'an as well. From this perspective, peace is central in Islam and nonviolent means are preferable to violent means in addressing social injustice. This perspective could be grounded on the observation that Islam flourished more in a state of peace than in a state of war. It is obvious that Islam has achieved within the seventeen months of *Hudaybiyyah* Peace Treaty what it had not achieved in the seventeen years preceding that treaty. The Qur'an enjoins Muslims to enter into peace completely[473]. The Qur'an commands Muslims to incline to peace even during the war[474]. The prophet of Islam, prior to his engagement in any military encounter with his enemies, had chosen peace treaties over peace wars[475].

In addition, the Qur'an urges Muslims always to accept peace if peace is offered by the enemy, even if the enemy is assumed to be inwardly deceitful in that offer of peace. Inferring from this Qur'anic injunction (8:61), a mere mistrust about the enemy's sincerity for peace cannot be a plausible excuse for Muslims to reject an enemy's offer of peace[476]. This is so because in Islam, all judgment must be based on outward evidence alone; internal evidence is known only to God. If

---

[473] "Oh you who believe enter into peace, all of you, (completely) and do not follow the footsteps of the Satan"Qur'an, Al-Baqara/ The Cow/2:208.

[474] "But if the enemies incline towards peace, you too should incline towards peace, and trust in God: Surely, He is the All-Hearing, the All-Knowing." Qur'an, al-Anfaal/Booty/ 8:61.

[475] By peace wars, I mean those wars that are waged only to attain peace and security for the people. In Islam, war is seen as a last resort to attain peace.

[476] See Muhamamad Asad, *op. cit.*, commentary on Qur'an, Spoils of War/8:61-63.

there is any risk in accepting an enemy's offer for peace, it can be inferred that

that risk must be taken by the Muslims: because Muslims are expected to rely on

Allah's help and the strength of righteousness. For this reason the Qur'an says:

"And should they [enemies] seek but to deceive you [by their show of peace] –

behold, God is enough for you! He it is who has strengthened you with His

support and by giving you believing followers"[477.]

Furthermore, the Prophet of Islam is on record as having urged Muslims to

spread peace: "O (my) people, spread greetings of peace, feed people (in need),

and keep ties of kinship and pray during the night while the others sleep, and you

will enter paradise in peace"[478.] Peace of mind can hardly be achieved under

suffering and injustice. One of the greatest sufferings and injustice is to suppress

people's freedom of conscience, a conscience that is connected to peace of mind.

As such Qur'an protected this conscience by saying "Let there be no compulsion

in religion"[479]. In *Pacem in Terris*, freedom of worship is considered among the

recipes for peace.

The Qur'an also requests Muslims to compete in doing good: "Then strive

together (as in a race) towards all that is good"[480]. The good here includes peace

---

[477] Qur'an, Anfaal/Booty/ 8:62.

[478] *Fiqh-us-Sunnah*, Volume 2, Number 21.

[479] Quran, Al-Baqara/The Cow/ 2: 256 .

[480] Qur'an, Al-Baqara/The Cow 2:148 and 5:48.

and nonviolence. In addition, the prophet of Islam signed and respected twenty three peace and nonviolence treaties and agreements, and exhorted his followers to observe them diligently[481]. All of these treaties were reached through negotiation, one of the principles to which *Pacem in Terris* appealed in the settling of disputes.

Moreover, according to the Qur'an, God does not only describe Himself as peace or prince of peace, but also the source of peace[482]. In addition, since peace and mercy are inextricably linked, God in Islam has prescribed mercy as an obligation for Himself[483]. Furthermore, the overall mission of the prophet of Islam is to be peace and a mercy for the whole creation[484]. It is part of Muslim belief that the mercy and grace of God overspreads everything[485]. Hence manifestation of peace and mercy must be among the Muslim's attributes, and these attributes are incompatible with violence and war.

---

[481] Karl-Wolfgang Troger, Islam and Christian Muslim Relations: Peace and Islam in theory and Practice, 1990-91 Vol. I-II.

[482] "The Source of Peace (and Perfection) Qur'an, Al-Hashr/The Exile/ 59:23.

[483] "Who has willed upon Himself the law of grace and mercy" Qur'an, Al-An'am/Cattle/6:12.

[484] "We sent thee not, but as a Mercy for all creatures" (Qur'an, Al-Anbiya'a/The Prophets/21:107).

[485] This echoed in the authentic Tradition in which, according to the Prophet, God says of Himself, "Verily, My grace and mercy outstrips my wrath" Bukhārī and Muslim. See Muhamamad Asad, *op. Cit.* commentary on verse 6:12.

From an Islamic point of view, the condition of our 'being on earth' is to make peace on earth[486]. This includes the protection of life and order. This implies that mischief, disorder and corruption should not be done on earth. Worship, which is also the *raison d'être* of the whole creation[487], cannot be fully realized in warring and violent situations. Since war produces mischief, disorder and corruption, it is a threat to worshiping God, which is Muslims' *raison d'être* on earth. Islam, understandably, sees war as a threat to its own propagation, and Muslim empires have generally pursued peace through peaceful means. Although Islam is a religion of peace, it is not a pacifist religion[488]. However, if the enemies

---

[486] Qur'an stated: "Do not cause disorder and mischief on earth after it has been made good". Qur'an, Al-A-araf/The Heights/7:56. See also Qur'an, Al/Baqara/The Cow /2:11.

[487] The Qur'an reported the God of Islam to have said: "I have not created the jinn and humankind but to worship me" Qur'an, At-tur/ The Mount/52:56.

[488] Hence: "permission [to fight] is given to those against whom fighting is being wrongfully waged…" (Qur'an, Al-Hajj/The Pilgrimage/ 22:39). According to this verse fighting can only be waged for self-defence – and only in self-defence. The statement as in the passive voice, "against whom fighting is wrongly wage" and not for those who take arms against the other because the other is different in religion, race and nation. In the same way Qur'an advise Muslims to prepare against their enemies: "Prepare against them [their enemies] whatever force you [Muslims] can, and the trained horses whereby you frighten Allah's enemy and your own enemy and others besides them whom you do not know. Allah knows them…." (Qur'an, Anfaal/Booty 8:60) . Here again Islam asks its adherents to prepare for any unavoidable war that is forced upon them. These verses also discredited the claim that Islam is a pacifist religion. Nonetheless, Islam prefers peaceful settlements, peaceful relations and co-existence rather than to fight, war and violent conflict.

incline towards peace, the Qur'an commands Muslims to incline towards peace[489]. Islam sees no good point in war and violence, not even in hardheartedness, because this would separate people from Muhammad in particular and from Islam in general [490]. Islam's aim in war is sincerely to establish the reign of justice, peace and righteousness on earth. For this reason, the prophet of Islam preferred peace through treaties to peace through wars; hence, he entered into numerous peace treaties with his opponents at tribal, national and international levels as mentioned above.

This analysis is derived from Muslim and Islamic sources on one hand. On the other hand, there are also some non-Muslim scholars who seem to acknowledge the non-violent paradigm in Islam and who have refuted the claim that Islam was spread by the sword. Among these scholars are Mahatma Gandhi who remarked: "I became more than ever convinced that it was not the sword that won a place for Islam in those days in the scheme of life. It was the rigid simplicity, the utter self-effacement of the prophet, the scrupulous regard for his pledges, his intense devotion to his friends and followers, his intrepidity, his

---

[489] "But if the enemies incline towards peace, you too should incline towards peace, and trust in God: Surely, He is the All-Hearing, the All-Knowing". Qur'an, Anfaal/Booty 8:61.

[490] "It was by the mercy of God that you were lenient with them; had you been harsh and fierce of heart, they would have dispersed from about you. So pardon them, and ask forgiveness for them, and consult them in the matter. And when you are resolved, rely on God; for God loves those who rely [upon Him]"Qur'an, Al Imran/Family of Imaran/3:159.

fearlessness, his absolute trust in God and in his own mission. These and not the sword carried everything before them and surmounted every trouble"[491]. Edward Gibbon stated: "The greatest success of Mohammad's life was effected by sheer moral force without the stroke of a sword"[492]. A.S. Tritton claimed that: "The picture of the Muslim soldier advancing with a sword in one hand and the Qur'an in the other is quite false"[493]. On a similar view, De Lacy O'Leary remarked: "History makes it clear, however, that the legend of fanatical Muslims, sweeping through the world and forcing Islam at the point of sword upon conquered races is one of the most fantastically absurd myths that historians have ever repeated"[494]. These are the perspectives of some of the non-Muslim scholars on the spread of Islam.

3.6.3 Defensive Perspective

The third perspective on war and peace in Islam is the 'defensive perspective'. Some Muslim scholars are of the view that all the battles fought by

---

[491] Young India, 1924. (10)

[492] Edward Gibbon, History of the Saracen Empire, London, 1870. As cited in (http://www.islam101.com/dawah/sword_islam.html) accessed on 10-05-2013.

[493] A.S. Tritton, *Islam*, london, 1951, p. 21. As cited in (http://www.islam101.com/dawah/sword_islam.html) accessed on 10-05-2013.

[494] De Lacy O'Leary *Islam at Crossroads*, London, 1923, p. 8. As cited in (http://www.islam101.com/dawah/sword_islam.html) accessed on 10-05-2013

Prophet Muhammad were defensive or at least preemptive raids on an impending palpable threat from the enemies whose plans were to eliminate Islam and Muslims. Muhammad Abu Zahra is of the view that: "Prophet Muhammad fought only to repulse aggression"[495]. Eminent and erudite Muslim jurists such as Al-Thawri and Abu Hanifa argued in favour of *jihad* as self-defence. Al-Thawri stated that "Fighting against the associators [polytheists] is not an obligation unless they [polytheists] start the fight, then it is an obligation to fight back against them"[496]. For Abu Hanifa "*jihad* is duty on Muslims but they are not required to fight unless they are needed"[497]. For instance, Muslims are also urged in the Qur'an to bring peace to the door steps of the weak and oppressed[498]. Muslims on the basis of this verse (4:75) are divinely enjoined to carry out what is now known in international relations as the responsibility to protect helpless men,

---

[495] Muhammad Abu Zahra, Concept of War in Islam (Cairo: Ministry of Waqf, 1961), p. 18, quoted in Hashmi, ed., Islamic Political Ethics, p. 208. Also quoted in"*Qur'anic Concepts of the Ethics of War: Challenging the Claims of Islamic Aggressiveness*" in The Journal of Faith and War, page 2. Accessible at http://faithandwar.org/index.php?option=com_content&view=article&id=125%3Aquranic-concepts-of-the-ethics-of-war-challenging-the-claims-of-islamic-aggressiveness-&catid=42%3Agod-and-human-nature&Itemid=58&limitstart=1.

[496] Ayse S. Kadayifci, Standing on an Isthmus: Islamic Narratives on Peace and War And Peace In Palestine Territories, Lexinton Books, UK, 2007, p. 92.

[497] *Ibid.*, p. 92.

[498] "And how could you refuse to fight in the cause of God and of the utterly helpless men and women and children who are crying, "O our Sustainer! Lead us forth [to freedom] out of this land whose people are oppressors, and raise for us, out of your grace, a protector, and raise for us, out of your grace, one who will bring us relief!" Qur'an, Al-Nisa'/The Women/4:75.

women and children, and in the terminology of *Pacem in Terris* "active solidarity". If there is any authentic reason for war in Islam, is to avert tumult or oppression[499]. Religious freedom according to Qur'an is also grounds for a defensive war[500].

---

[499] Qur'an, Al-Baqra/The Cow 2:193. "And fight them on until there is no more tumult or oppression, and until there prevail *Din* for God [justice and faith for God] but if they cease [oppression], Let there be no hostility except to those who practice oppression" The Arabic word *Din* in this verse which is simply rendered by some as the religion includes Justice and faith. "It implies the ideas of indebtedness, duty, obedience, judgment, justice, faith, religion, customary rites, etc." (Yusuf Ali, Glorious Qur'an). The clause: "until there is Din for God, means "until God can be worshipped without fear of persecution and none is compelled to bow down in awe before another human being". (Muhammad Asad, The Message of the Qur'an).

[500] "The ones who were expelled from their homes without any just reason, except that they say 'Our Lord is Allah.' Had Allah not been repelling some people by means of some others, the monasteries, the churches, the synagogues and the mosques where Allah's name is abundantly recited would have been demolished. Allah will definitely help those who help Him (by defending the religion prescribed by Him.) Surely Allah is Powerful, Mighty" Qur'an, Al-Hajj/The Pilgrimage/ 22:40). This could imply the defence of all pious institutions of worship, for Jews, Christians and Muslims. From this verse one can deduce the view that instead of burning monasteries, synagogues, churches and mosques Muslim should protect them. And hence the protection of unused monasteries, synagogues, churches and mosques is useless without mentioning and reciting God's names and His moral laws, the protection of the lives of the followers of these religions to enable them to recite God's names and His moral laws becomes a Muslim religious duty that should be taken seriously by all Muslims. Furthermore, Prophet Muhammad in 628 C.E. has signed a charter guaranteeing religious freedom to Christian monks of St. Catherine's Monastery at Mt. Sinai, giving them all aspects of religious freedom inalienable from human dignity and human rights. The charter reads: "This is a message from Muhammad Ibn Abdullah, as a covenant to those who adopt Christianity, near and far, we are with them. Verily I, the servants, the helpers, and my followers defend them, because Christians are my citizens; and by Allah! I hold out against anything that displeases them. No compulsion is to be on them.

Moreover, there is wider agreement amongst Muslim researchers that the essence of *jihad* is for defence and self-preservation, and that proper *jihad* must not be motivated by aggression or self-aggrandisement to the detriment of the opponent, lest it be regarded as tyranny and oppression[501].

Therefore, the Qur'anic notion of *jihād* and Islamic universalism, unless hijacked, can neither be an obstacle to the values in *Pacem in Terris* nor to the establishment of world peace. Islamic universalism means here that there should be no obstacle to the message and practice of Islam anywhere. It does not, however, mean the universal conversion of the whole world to Islam[502]. The

---

Neither are their judges to be removed from their jobs nor their monks from their monasteries. No one is to destroy a house of their religion, to damage it, or to carry anything from it to the Muslims' houses. Should anyone take any of these, he would spoil God's covenant and disobey His Prophet. Verily, they are my allies and have my secure charter against all that they hate. No one is to force them to travel or to oblige them to fight. The Muslims are to fight for them. If a female Christian is married to a Muslim, it is not to take place without her approval. She is not to be prevented from visiting her church to pray. Their churches are to be respected. They are neither to be prevented from repairing them nor the sacredness of their covenants. No one of the nation (Muslims) is to disobey the covenant till the Last Day (end of the world)" Accessed at http://www.antiochgate.com/about_charters.htm, on 4th October, 2012. See also http://muslim-canada.org/chater1.hml1

[501] Ayatullah Morteza Mutahhari, Jihad The Holy War of Islam and Its Legitimacy in the Quran Translated by: Mohammad Salman Tawhidi Published by The Islamic Propagation Organization, P.O. Box No. 11365/7318, Islamic Republic of Iran Printed by Sepehr, Tehran, Iran1405-1985, Third Lecture: Defense - the Quiddity of Jihad. See also Sayyid Muhammad Rizvi How did Islam Spread? By Sword or By Conversion Publ. North American Shia Ithna-Asheri Muslim Communities (NASIMCO) 2006 / 1427.

[502] This is historical fact; Muslims in their history have lived and are still living in a world full of

Shafi'i-Sarakhsi expansionist theory in the 9th and 10th century C.E. was not

without political stimulus. It was formulated in an era of protracted wars between

Muslims and non-Muslims[503]. Perhaps it was the political and sociological

---

non-Muslims. Both *Qur'an* and *Sunnah* confirm the continual existence of non-Muslims in Muslim lands in particular and in the world in general. This is also the logic behind the Islamic articles of faith such as accountability in the hereafter and existence of paradise and hell. If *jihād* and Islamic Universalism were to mean fighting for the conversion of the whole world, then Islam as a religion would be obsolete and the whole Muslim *ummah* and its history would be a failure, because the whole world has never been converted to Islam by Muslims. What Islam aims at is a substantive and positive peace that is dynamic, vibrant, enduring and living to allow one to freely of worship and express one's faith. As such Islam favours certain recipes for peace and enjoins its followers to constantly pursue them individually or collectively, nationally or internationally. Islamic pedagogy towards peace targets human being as an individual first and then the community as a whole. It does this by defeating harmful propensities within the individual and then within the society. Because if peace can be built in the hearts of an individual people, it will be reflected at the communal level and international level; this is sure because policies at the international level are formulated by people.

[503] Although, despite the justification and legitimization of their expansionist policy in the lands of non-Muslims "they were also adamant about the observation of *jus in bello* norms, i.e., avoiding excessiveness, accepting truce, sparing the lives of noncombatants, women, children, etc." (Ibrahim Kalin, Islam and Peace, The Royal *Aal Al-Bayt* Institute for Islamic Thought, Amman 11195, Jordan, 2012, p.38.) Their observation of *jus in bello* and the political condition of their era does not mean that their views were anchored in or derived from the Qur'anic notion of *jihād*. David cook, is of the view that: "The prophet Muhammad never formally declared a jihad – not, at least, using that term; yet the many campaigns that he undertook on behalf of his faith are the prototypical jihad wars. In the same way the label of jihad has been attached to the great Islamic conquests of the seventh and eight centuries, but long after the fact. We do not know what the Muslim participants called these wars. For centuries Muslims have fought each other, sometimes describing these conflicts as jihad, sometimes not. On some occasion the use of the term to describe warfare against other Muslims was rejected by the community as a whole, or by part of the community, or by historians recording these conflicts. In other instances, such as Ottoman

environment of the Muslim world at the time that made some Muslims interpret the Qur'anic jihād in the light of the expansionist milieu which existed at the time in the order of the international affairs, and which had existed already in the region before the rise of Islam. However, this theory of Shafi'i and Sarakhsi is neither a mainstream stance nor an 'orthodox' stance of the jurists and hence lacks both orthodoxy and orthopraxy. As such it is not in line with the views of Abu Hanifah, Malik Ibn Anas, Abu Yusuf, Shaybani, Awzai, Ibn Rushd, Ibn Taymiyyah, Ibn Qayyim al-Jawziyyah and is also incongruent with historical facts and experience of Muslims[504]. Jihad has many meanings, but the concept of Jihad that refers to "the unilateral use of force by Muslims in pursuit of political objectives and outside the institutional framework of international legality and the rule of law in general since the framework of legality and the rule of law is lacking in 'the real world', there would be no basis for expecting Muslims to

---

conquest of southeastern Europe from the fourteen to the sixteenth century, there is no secure evidence that the dynasty called for a jihad, and yet from outsider's point of view the conquests were unambiguously grounded in religion." (See David Cook, Understanding Jihad, University of California Press, 2005, p. 2). Furthermore, Pickthall after quoting the Qur'an: 2:190, said: "There are many texts that I could quote to prove that Muslims are forbidden to use violence towards anyone on account of his opinion, and I can find not a single text to prove the contrary...the wars of Islam in the Holy Prophet's life and in the life time of his immediate successors were all begun in self-defence". See Muhammad Marmaduke Pickthall, The Cultural Side of Islam, pub. The Committee of Madras Lectures on Islam, 1937, p. 24.

[504] Ibrahim Kalin, *Islam and Peace*, The Royal Aal Al-Bayt Institute for Islamic Thought, Amman 11195, Jordan, 2012, pages 37-39.

abandon jihad, as defined here"[505]. However, now that there is an "institutional framework of legality of the rule of law in international relations" Muslims are expected to abandon such concept of Jihad[506], and they should help and use such international frameworks in resolving disputes, and in the protection of human rights as well. The absence of such willingness and cooperation undermines the credibility and viability of quests for international peace and the things that contribute to it, such as the protection of 'human rights norms'.

Pacem in Terris calls for peace, religious freedom, prevention of war, cooperation and active solidarity regardless of one's faith or religious affiliation. On this ground *Pacem in Terris* can be a facilitating factor for universal international relations. If *Jihad* means to fight the non-Muslims in order to make them Muslims by force, and if Islam calls only for the cooperation and solidarity based on faith, then Islam cannot be a facilitating factor for universal international relations, and it would be an obstacle to international peace as envisaged in *Pacem in Terris*.

While in the 21st century, the *Shafi'i-Sharaksi* expansionist theory and by extension the militarist-militant approach is an obstacle to international peace, the nonviolent and defensive perspectives may not be seen to be so, because "International norms, institutional and discursive continuities (such as the United

---

[505] Abdullahi Ahmed An-Na'im, "Why should Muslims abandon Jihad ? Human rights and the future of international law." In *Third World Quarterly*, Vol. 27, No. 5, pages 785 – 797, 2006"

[506] *Ibid.*

Nations Charter, the Geneva Convention, ete.) enable the persistence of war and violence as a legitimate form of action under certain circumstances. However, 'self-defense' is a loosely defined concept that is subject to manipulation in conflict situations. At times of war, quite often, parties attempt to justify terrorist attacks, collateral damage, preemptive strikes, and acts of revenge with the concept of self-defense"[507].

Faced with the missile crisis and nuclear threats, Islam would not encourage nuclear war but would discourage it as does *Pacem in Terris*. This statement is sustainable by looking at the spirit and objective of Islam. On one hand Prophet Muhammad's choice of migration over war by sending his followers to Abyssinia (today's Ethiopia), his migration to Yathrib (today's Medina), his peace treaties with tribes and regional powers all show Muhammad's peace doctrine; on the other hand, his engagement in wars for self-preservation with strict moral rectitude (just war) discredits the claim that Islam is a pacifist religion. Even so, admiration for pacifism and non-violence is expressed in many Qur'anic verses and in many of Muhammmad's utterances and deeds. This wisdom provides Muslims with the opportunity of picking either pacifism or just war depending on what is necessitated by the circumstances.

In a similar manner, the encyclical *Pacem in Terris* avoided mentioning pacifism or non-violence as the only suitable Christian positions. However,

---

[507] Kadayifçi-Orellana, *op. cit.* 2003,

Gaudium et Spes expresses admiration for those who adopted non-violence as their way of life. It remarks: "We cannot fail to praise those who renounce the use of violence in the vindication of their rights and who resort to methods of defence which are otherwise available to weaker parties too, provided this can be done without injury to the rights and duties of others or of the community itself"[508]. This prudent statement provides Catholics with the opportunity of choosing either pacifism or just war doctrine depending on what is necessitated by the circumstances.

3.7 An Islamic Perspective on Some of the Specific Principles of *Pacem in Terris* with Regard to the Establishment of World Peace

3.7.1 Human Rights

With regard to the protection of human rights as a way of "order" among humankind, Islam's recognition of such "order" with regard to social stability and peace is not against the teaching of *Pacem in Terris* (pp. 8-45). With respect to the protection of human rights, Islam makes its primary objective the protection of one's right to faith, to life, to intellect, to property and to progeny. Islam makes it obligatory for every authority and power to protect the interests of the people and to relieve them of hardship. Muslim jurists agree on this. Abu Hamid Al-Ghazali (450-505 AH/1058-1111C.E), a great Islamic thinker, stated that

---

[508] *Gaudium et Spes, op. cit.*, pp. 78.

promoting the welfare of the people by safeguarding their right to faith, to life, to intellect, to progeny, and to property is a basic objective of Islam and that guaranteeing these five objectives is the responsibility of every Muslim and, of course, of the state[509]. These five universal categories (*al-kuliyyatu al-khamsa*) embrace all other needed rights humankind can claim. Thus, these rights are part of the basic objectives of Islam.

It is true that in certain Muslim majority states, such as Saudi Arabia, perhaps due to their political, cultural, social, traditional and educational background, certain articles of UDHR (e.g. article 16) were not acceptable. However, this should not mean that the content of UDHR is not acceptable to Islam. Abdul Rahman Kayala, a Syrian delegate to UDHR, accepted UDHR in his claim that: "Civilizations had progressed slowly through centuries of persecution and tyranny until finally the present declaration had been drawn up" and that the Declaration was not "the work of a few representatives in the Assembly or in the Economic and Social Council; it was the achievement of generations of human beings who had worked towards that end. Now at last the peoples of the world would hear it proclaimed that their aim had been reached by the United Nations"[510].

---

[509] Al-Ghazali, *Al-Iqtisad fi-l-I'tiqad* (Beirut, Darul-Amanah 1969) taken from Islam and its Quest for Peace: Jihad, Justice and Education, by Mustafa koylu, by The Council for Research in Values and philosophy, 2003,p. 75.

[510] Morsink Johannes, *The Universal Declaration of Human Rights: Origins, Drafting, and Intent,* University of Pennsylvania Press, 1990, p. 12.

This shows that it is important to make a distinction between Islam and Muslims. In a nutshel, Islam is the religious belief and code of life as God's commands sent down by God through His messenger Muhammad to humans and jins. A Muslim struggle to impliment such commands on his/her self in a bid to make him/herself a better person spiritually and socially.

Therefore some Muslims' rejection of the UDHR is due to their political, cultural, social, traditional and educational background or their understanding of Islam, and not because Islam in itself finds the content of UDHR unacceptable. Riffat Hassan, a Muslim, argues on the basis of her research and reflection as well as her deepest faith, "that the Qur'an is the Magna Carta of human rights and that a large part of its concern is to free human beings from the bondage of traditionalism, authoritarianism (religious, political, economic or any other), tribalism, racism, sexism, slavery or anything else that prohibits or inhibits human beings from actualizing the Qur'anic vision of human destiny embodied in the classical proclamation: towards Allah is thy limit"[511]. Among those Muslim jurists who claim the compatibility of Islam with UDHR is Khaled Abou El Fadl. He states: "the commitment to human rights does not signify a lack of commitment to God but is instead a necessary part of celebrating human diversity,

---

[511] Riffat Hassan, "Rights of Women Within Islamic Community," in *Religious Human Rights in Global Perspectives: Religious Perspectives*. Ed. John Witte Jr. and John D. Vander, pub. Kluwer Law International, Hague, Netherlands, 1996. Volume 1, pages 370-71.

honoring God's vice-regents, achieving mercy, and pursuing the ultimate goal of justice"[512].

Furthermore, the understanding and interpretation of Islam in some Muslim majority countries, such as some of those in Sub-Saharan Africa, allows them to accept the UDHR and recognize it for themselves and for others. Moreover, Muslims[513] of different countries and nations gathered in Paris, France to declare a 'Universal Islamic Declaration of Human Rights' thirty-six years after the declaration of the UDHR. This shows that Islam is not against the UDHR in principle. This Universal Islamic Declaration of Human Rights asserts that: "Islam gave to mankind an ideal code of human rights fourteen centuries ago. These rights aim at conferring honour and dignity on mankind and eliminating exploitation, oppression and injustice. Human rights in Islam are firmly rooted in the belief that God, and God alone, is the Law Giver and the Source of all human rights. Due to their divine origin, no ruler, government, assembly or authority can curtail or violate in any way the human rights conferred by God, nor can they be surrendered. Human rights in Islam are an integral part of the overall Islamic order and it is obligatory on all Muslim governments and

---

[512] Khaled Abou El Fadl, 'Islam and the Challenge of Democratic Commitment' in *Does Human Rights Need God*. Ed. Elizabeth M. Bucar and Barbra Barnett , William B. Eerdmans Publishing company, Grand Rapids, Michigan, 2005 p. 91.

[513] These Muslims may not necessarily be heads of state. They are Muslim intellectuals, scholars and spiritual leaders. See "Universal Islamic Declaration of Human Rights" 21 Dhul Qaidah 1401/ 19 September 1981

organs of society to implement them in letter and in spirit within the framework of that order"[514] .

Nine years after this declaration, the "Cairo Declaration on Human Rights in Islam" followed a similar pattern by stating that: "Believing that fundamental rights and freedoms according to Islam are an integral part of the Islamic religion and that no one shall have the right as a matter of principle to abolish them either in whole or in part or to violate or ignore them in as much as they are binding divine commands, which are contained in the Revealed Books of Allah and which were sent through the last of His Prophets to complete the preceding divine messages and that safeguarding those fundamental rights and freedoms is an act of worship whereas the neglect or violation thereof is an abominable sin, and that the safeguarding of those fundamental rights and freedom is an individual responsibility of every person and a collective responsibility of the entire *Ummah*. . . ."[515]

However, Abdullahi Ahmed An'Naim (one of the great sons of the African continent and one of the the foremost academic thinkers about human rights in Islam) believes that: "The claim that *Shari'a* is fully consistent with and has always protected human rights is problematic both as a theoretical and practical matter. As a theoretical matter, the concept of human rights as rights to

---

[514] Universal Islamic Declaration of Human Rights 21 Dhul Qaidah 1401/ 19 September 1981

[515] See preamble of the Cairo Declaration on Human Rights in Islam, Aug. 5, 1990.

which every human being is entitled by virtue of being was unknown to Islamic jurisprudence or social philosophy until the last few decades and does not exist within *Shari'a*"[516]. The difference between Abdullahi Ahmed An'Naim and the signatories of the "Universal Islamic Declaration of Human Rights" and of the "Cairo Declaration on Human Rights in Islam" is due their understandings of Islam, *Shari'*a in general, and human rights in particular. One of the most disturbing issues of rights in some Muslim majority countries, especially in the Arab countries then and now, is the condition of women.

The World Bank publication, "Gender and Development in the Middle East and North Africa: Women in the Public Sphere," (2004), affirms that: "Decades of investment and improved policies have greatly increased women's education and health and have reduced their fertility rate. However, the expected payoffs in higher employment and economic growth have not materialized. Because of cultural and political barriers, only a third of women are in the labor force - the lowest rate in the world. Future economic growth must rely on human resources rather than on the natural resources relied on in the past. Women remain a huge, untapped reservoir of human potential. Gender issues have been seen as a peripheral concern that resided mainly within the realm of the social sectors"[517.] It also "recognizes the complexity of gender issues, explores the causes of gender

---

[516] Abdullahi Ahmed An-Na'im, *"Human Rights in the Muslim World: Socio-Political Conditions and Scriptural Imperatives A Preliminary Inquiry"*. In *Harvard Human Rights Journal*, Vol. 3, (1990), p. 22.

[517] See https://publications.worldbank.org/index.php, accessed on 13-05.-13.

inequality, and proposes an agenda for change" [518] affirming that Arab countries have to overcome the problem of the condition of women in order to solve the problem of their intrinsic underdevelopment. Rania Al-Abdullah of Jordan, President of the Arab Women's Summit, affirmed that: "Gender inequality has a negative impact not only on women but also on society as a whole. It restricts the ability of a country to efficiently allocate and use its most valuable resource, its human capital. Restricting the participation of women in public and economic life limits economic development and national potential. Empowering women and providing opportunities for their full integration into all aspects of society is not just an issue of justice for women. It is a vital factor in creating a climate favorable to achieving sustainable progress and development.... Empowerment of women ... means stronger families and a richer sense of national community and pride....Encouraging and empowering women to take their place as an integral part of regional growth and progress is the wisest and most effective means of closing the development gap" [519].

In the debate at the UN on the human rights declaration, some states with Arab leaders opposed article 16 because they did not want to consider women's concerns as a matter of human rights. However, it is important to point out here

---

[518] *Ibid.*, accessed on 13-05.-13.

[519] Rania Al-Abdullah of Jordan, President of the Arab Women's Summit, as quoted in https://publications.worldbank.org/index.php?main_page=product_info&cPath=0&products_id=23366, accessed on 13-05-2013.

that Arab culture or Arabism is not necessarily Islamic culture or Islam. In some non-Arab Muslim countries, there have been women prime ministers. Both Pakistan and Bangladesh are examples. In the Gambia at present there is a woman vice president and many female ministers. Senegal, too, has many female ministers. Each of these are Muslim majority countries and they are no less Muslim than the Arab countries. Islam is not limited to the Arab region or ethnicity. In fact there are more non-Arab Muslims than Arab Muslims. Arabs form only about 18 to 20 percent of the world's Muslim population. The biggest Muslim country in the world is Indonesia, a non-Arab country. The remaining 80 percent of Muslims[520] are not part of the Arab Region and Arab league. Muslim populations, cultures, and customs are not monolithic; they are complex and diverse, going beyond any single ethnicity.

In Islam, both the right to life and the right to live are seen as natural attributes of a human being. As such, Islamic *Shari'a* makes the protection of life and living one of its fundamental tenets. The Qur'an states that the destruction of a single life is tantamount to the destruction of the life of the whole people[521]. In

---

[520] The Pew Forum on Religious and Public Life, *The Future of the Global Muslim Population Projections for 2010 2030*, accessed at http://www.pewforum.org/future-of-the-global-muslim-population-regional-middle-east.aspx, on 13-05-13.

[521] "If anyone slew a person- unless it be for murder or for spreading mischief in the land- it would be as if he slew the whole people: and if anyone saved a life, it would be as if he saved the life of the whole people" (Qur'an, Isra'e/ The Night Journey/ 17:33.) Qur'an even forbids suicide: "And kill not your selves. Truly, God has been compassionate to you". (Qur'an, Al-Nisa'e/Women 4:29).

Islam, the giving and taking of a soul is incontestably reserved for God. Killing violates this reservation; hence it is considered to be the second greatest sin, just after idolatry. For peace to prevail in any society, the protection of faith, life, intellect, progeny and property, all of which are inextricably linked to the right to live, must be guaranteed. Islam encourages its followers to give *zakat* [522]and *sadaqa* or *eleemosyna* to those without wherewithal in order to secure their right to life and live. The right to live is a prerequisite for peace. Ali Ibn Abi Talib, the fourth Muslim caliph, once said: "No one has rights towards others unless they have rights towards them"[523]. This means that rights and duties are inextricably linked.

3.7.2 Right to Emigrate and Immigrate

"Hijrah" is the Arabic word for emigration. It means to abandon. *Hijrah* and its derivatives are mentioned about 27 times in the Qur'an. To give it an Islamic nomenclature, it means to flee from religious persecution and oppression to a place of religious freedom and protection or fleeing from insecurity and violence to security and non-violence. In this sense, the basis of *Hijrah* is

---

[522] *Zakat* which is sometimes referred to as *sadaqa* or alms is designed for eight categories: " the poor and the needy, and those employed to administer the (funds); for those whose hearts have been (recently) reconciled (to Truth); for those in bondage and in debt; in the cause of God; and for the wayfarer: (thus is it) ordained by God, and God is full of knowledge and wisdom" Qur'an, Repentance/At-tawbah/9:60.

[523] Nahj al-Balaghah, Sermon 34, pages. 332 - 333.

monotheism and monotheism is inextricably linked with peace. It is to leave for a place where peace and justice prevail, where one is able to exercise his/her monotheistic duties and aspirations[524]. Emigration and immigration have been fundamental for Islam and are expected to remain so at least doctrinally until the end of time[525].

From an Islamic perspective, the right to emigration and immigration contributes to the pacification and humanization of internal and international relations in times of war and peace. For instance, during war the Qur'an gives rights to emigrate and immigrate to fugitives and urges Muslims to respect and protect the fugitive even if he/she happens to be an enemy[526].

---

[524] This is the reason behind the emigration and immigration of the early Muslims. The prophet of Islam asked his persecuted followers to emigrate to Abysinia, present Ethiopia, that had a Christian leader at the time and the majority of its inhabitants were assumed to be Christian. Earlier, Muslims had been able to have peace of mind and to preserve their lives and religion by emigrating from Mecca to *Habash*/ Ethiopia and *Yathrib*/ Madina respectively.

[525] According to the reported statement of the prophet of Islam: "Migration will not end until repentance ends, and repentance will not end until the sun rises in the west". The rising of the sun in the west in Islamic eschatology designates the end of human life in this world. For this *hadith* see Al-Musnad , Vol.4/99, Abu Dawud, Kitab al-Jihad, Vol.3/7, *Hadith* 2479, and ad-Darami, Kitab as-Siyyar, Vol.2/239. Albani classifies it as *Sahih*. See: "Sahih al-Ja'mi' as-Sagheer", Vol.6/186, *Hadith* 7346

[526] "If one amongst the Pagans ask you for asylum, grant it to him, so that he may hear the word of God; and then escort him to where he can be secure. That is because they are men without knowledge". (Qur'an, Al-Tawba/ The Repentance/9:6). According to Yusuf Ali "Even among the enemies of Islam actively fighting against Islam, there may be individuals who may be in a position to require protection. Full asylum is to be given to them, and opportunities provided for hearing the Word of Allah. If they accept the Word, they become Muslims and brethren, and no

In Islam it is both an individual and a collective duty to protect and assist asylum seekers and immigrants. In other words, both the political institutions of Islamic communities and individual persons living in Muslim lands are obliged to grant asylum to asylum seekers regardless of religion, race, ethnicity, sex, social, economic or political status as long as they are not criminals[527]. In comparison, the protection guaranteed to refugees and forced migrants under modern law is more limited and restrictive than what is offered by the ideal of Islam.

---

further question arises. If they do not see their way to accept Islam, they will require double protection: (1) from the Islamic forces openly fighting against their people, and (2) from their own people, as they detached themselves from them. Both kinds of protection should be ensured for them, and they should be safely escorted to a place where they can be safe. Such persons only err through ignorance, and there may be much good in them". See his commentary on Qur'an 9:6. Abu Hurairah relates that the holy Prophet said: "One who believes in Allah and the Day of Judgement must not cause hardship and inconvenience to his neighbour; and he who believes in Allah and the last Day must respect his guest; and he who believes in Allah and the Day of Judgement must speak well or keep quiet!". (This *hadith* is reported in both Bukhari and Muslim.) The Prophet Muhammad (peace be upon him) once told his wife: "Do not turn away a poor man...even if all you can give is half a date. If you love the poor and bring them near you" the *hadith* continued "...God will bring you near Him on the Day of Resurrection" (Al-Tirmidhi, Hadith, no.1376) A fugitive or immigrant is no less than a guest, and is no less than a poor person. Hence, fugitive, immigrants and asylum seekers need Muslim solidarity.

[527] The Prophet is reported to have said, "*Aman* [protection] given by Muslims is allowed. So, if anyone violated the protection granted by a Muslim, he [the violator] is cursed by God, angels and all the people" (*Sahih Bukhari*, ed., Muhammad Daib, (Beirut: Dar ibn Kathir, 1987), 3rd edn., 3:1160, *hadith* no. 3008. See also Ahmad ibn Ali ibn Hajr, *Fath al-Bari Sharh Sahih al-Bukhari*, ed., Ahmad ibn Hajr al-Asqalani, (Beirut: Dar Ma,,rifah, 1379), 4: 81, see also *Sahih Muslim*, ed., M. Fu"ad Abdul Baqi, (Beirut: Dar Ehya al-Torath al-Arabi, n. d.), 2: 999, *hadith* no. 1371.

The Islamic concept of emigration is much more comprehensive than the definition of refugees given in the 28 July 1951 'Geneva Convention Relating to the Status of Refugees'[528]. Islam on one hand, considers emigration and asylum as a God given right since it is God who created the earth and who asks humans to emigrate through it. Many Qur'anic verses attest to this [529]. On the other hand, it makes it a responsibility and duty for those from whom asylum is requested to grant it within their capacity. Modern national and international laws regarding emigration and immigration do not give individuals the right to offer and grant asylum.

---

[528] This document defines refugees: "As a result of events occurring before 1 January 1951 and owing to well-founded fear of persecution for reasons of race, religion, nationality, membership of a particular social group or political opinion, is outside the country of his nationality and is unable or, owing to such fear, is unwilling to avail himself of the protection of that country; or who, not having a nationality and being outside the country of his former habitual residence as a result of such events, is unable or, owing to such fear, is unwilling to return to it. In the case of a person who has more than one nationality, the term 'the country of his nationality' shall mean each of the countries of which he is a national, and a person shall not be deemed to be lacking the protection of the country of his nationality if, without any valid reason based on well-founded fear, he has not availed himself of the protection of one of the countries of which he is a national." <http://www.unhcr.org/3b66c2aa10.html>.

[529] "He it is who has made the earth easy to live upon: go about, then, in all its regions, and partake of the sustenance which He provides: but [always bear in mind that] unto Him you shall be resurrected." (Qur'an, Al-Mulk/The Sovereignty/67:15). "When angels take the souls of those who die in sin against their souls, they say: 'In what (plight) Were ye?' They reply: 'Weak and oppressed Were we in the earth.' They say: 'Was not the earth of God spacious enough for you to emigrate therein?' Such men will find their abode in Hell,- What an evil refuge!" Qur'an, Al-Nisa'e/Women/ 4:97.

Modern refugee laws reserve the right to offer and grant asylum to the State and they make the state sovereign in granting or refusing asylum to those who seek it. In our secular laws, only the State has the right to choose to whom refugee status can be granted. In Islamic law and tradition, any person fleeing and seeking protection has the right to enter an Islamic community and ask for protection (*aman*) from State leaders or from common individuals, men or women, Muslims or non-Muslims, residing in Muslim lands. In Islam, both individuals and the state are equally obliged to grant asylum and to protect asylum-seekers[530] and emigrants. Seeking asylum in Islam can be a duty and likewise to grant it is an obligation[531].

However, it is important to note that this Islamic legacy in the field of migration and refugee protection is honoured more in theory than in practice. It has been abandoned by the Muslim majority states and their politicians today. Nonetheless, we can say that an Islamic perspective gives no less concern to the

---

[530] Munir Muhammad, *Refugee Law in Islam* available at http://works.bepress.com/cgi/viewcontent.cgi?article=1017&context=muhammad_munir, accessed on 1st November 2012.

[531] It can be said that the above mentioned verse (4:97) urges Muslims to forsake places of injustice, insecurity, and oppression for places of justice and security. The below mentioned verse also urges Muslims to deliver the oppressed from the oppression: "And what is [the matter] with you that you fight not in the cause of Allah and [for] the oppressed among men, women, and children who say, 'Our Lord, take us out of this city of oppressive people and appoint for us from Yourself a protector and appoint for us from Yourself a helper?'." Qur'an, Al-Nisa'e/Women/ 4:75.

plight and rights of emigrant and immigrants than that which is stated in *Pacem in Terris*. As such, Christians and Muslims can work hand in hand to ameliorate the condition of emigrants and refugees nationally and internationally.

3.7.3 An Islamic Perspective on Political Rights with Regard to World peace

The principle of political rights (see *Pacem in Terris* pp. 26) from an Islamic perspective can be deduced from *(haqq al-hurriyah)*, the right to freedom, a term used in Islamic jurisprudence. *Haqq-al-hurriyah* can entail the right to self-determination for both individual persons and communities. In Islam, these rights are offered by God and their protection becomes a duty and an obligation, a unilateral divine duty for human beings. Just as Islam stipulates the relationship between God and humans, so does it stipulate the relationship between humans, and between humans and nature. These relationships between human beings with regard to the governance of their society is what is called politics and to be able to participate in this governance is a right, hence political rights in non-religious terminology.

Safeguarding the political rights of people in Islam is a double command, from human beings and from the Divine, and its violation also attracts both human and Divine condemnation. Hence it becomes a duty and an obligation. If the political rights of the people are seen as religious, their protection becomes a sacred obligation for the faithful. As such, a religious society is expected to observe the rights of people more than other societies. In a similar vein, if it is seen as secular, its protection is expected to prevail in secular society more than in other societies. In Islam, denying the legitimate rights of people, whether they be political, social, economic, religious or cultural, is in itself tantamount to encroachment upon Islam and its tenets. In an Islamic perspective, political rights are public rights and there should be no interference in the public sphere except by consent of the public. God is sovereign in the public sphere and next to God's sovereignty is that of the public itself.

In Islam, *Shura* (consultation), *ijma`a* (*consensus*) and *ijtihad* (independent thinking) ensure the highest level of human sovereignty in politics, subject only to God's sovereignty. However, Islam does not impose or attempt to shape a certain unchangeable system of political government. Rather, it sets up basic principles, such as justice, equality, the common good, and freedom, that should guide a government's general character. Beyond that, people have the right to choose the system and form of government that suits their time and circumstances[532]. However, when we look at political rights in Muslim majority countries today, we cannot help but remember the words of Ali ibn Abi Talib, the fourth Muslim Caliph, who said: "Right is the easiest thing to describe and the hardest to find at the moment of action and the search for justice"[533]. Indeed, in theory, the Qur'an, *Sunnah,* and Islamic tradition assert people's political rights;

---

[532] Gülen, M. Fethullah, Essays, Perspectives, Opinions, The Light, Inc. 2000, pages 14-17.

[533] *Nahj al-Balaghah*, Sermon 34, pages 332 - 333.

alas, in majority Muslim countries, rights are in fact the rarest thing. This shows us that what Muslims should do is different from what Muslims actually do.

Again, when we distinguish Islam from the culture of many Muslim majority nations, we conclude that political rights as described by Pope John XXIII in *Pacem in Terris* are not incompatible with Islamic teaching even though this ideal is rarely seen in Muslim politics of the day. Political rights are part of human rights and many times they are encroached upon in many cultures. Many cultures also aspire to safeguard them, although with different methods. In this regard, we cannot help agreeing with Robert Dickson Crane that: "What we today call human rights were always conceived of as the result of virtues. The goal was not to pursue freedom from moral values, but to practice the values that produce freedom. Within this context, which is universal in history, human rights have always been explored and developed as part of the higher concept of justice, perhaps the most universal value in all civilizations"[534].

3.7.4 An Islamic Perspective on Relations Between Individuals and Public Authorities with Regard to World Peace

In an Islamic perspective, Pope John XXIII's concept of 'relations between individuals and the public authorities'[535] should be based on *Bai'ah*[536]

---

[534] Crane, Robert Dickson, "*Human Rights in Traditionalist Islam: Legal, Political, Economic, and Spiritual Perspectives*". In The American Journal of Islamic Social Sciences 25:1 p. 86. Accessible at http://i-epistemology.net/attachments/925_ajiss-25-1-stripped%20-%20Crane%20 %20Human%20Rights%20in%20Traditionalist%20Islam.pdf.

[535] *Pacem in Terris*, pp.47.

and *Shura*[537]. *Bai'ah* and *Shura* are permitted, authorized and islamized[538] by the Qur'an[539]. The only legitimate public authority from an Islamic perspective is the authority consented to by *Shura*. Muhammad Asad argues that *Shura* must be considered "as fundamental, operative clause of all Islamic thought relating to statecraft" and it encompasses all aspects of political life[540]. He further argues

---

[536] *Bai'ah* is a free-will transaction between two or more individuals where each becomes reciprocally obligated to the other. If an agreement is met, it can define and limit the rights and duties of the would-be ruler and the would-be ruled. In other words it is freely and willingly pledging a firm allegiance to a person or persons in which both are mutually bound to observe the conditions of such pledge of allegiance. It is a mutually obligating agreement or allegiance which implies that if one party does not fulfill its obligation, the whole transaction is then rendered null and void and unbinding to the other party or parties. This is the process of choosing a would-be leader in an Islamic public authority.

[537] *Shura* is an open inclusive mutual consultation in conducting all the affairs of life. This could be private consultation (as in private domestic family affairs between spouses or other responsible members of the household) or public consultation between the enfranchised or between rulers and ruled, and also within and between different ministries of administration, to preserve checks and balances and the smoothness of administration.

[538] The pledging of faith and allegiance was by placing hand on hand in the Arab custom even before the advent of Islam and it was later islamized when the Qur'an accepted its islamicity or legitimacy. This implies that non-Arab cultures that are not against the spirit of Islam can be islamized as well.

[539] Qur'an, Al-Fath//48:10 : "Verily those who pledge their allegiance to you do pledge their allegiance to God: the hand of God is over their hands: then any one who violates his oath, does so to the harm of his own soul, and anyone who fulfils what he has covenanted with God, God will soon grant him a great Reward". Qur'an, Al-Shura/ The Consultation/42:38 : "and whose rule in all matters of common concern is consultation among themselves".

[540] Muhammad Asad, *The Principles of State and Government in Islam*, Dar Al-Andalus, 1980, pages. 44-45.

that the *shura* verse "is so self-expressive and unequivocal that no attempt at abitrary interpretation can change its purport" [541]. "This principle [of *shura*] was applied to its fullest extent by the holy Prophet in his private and public life, and was fully acted upon by the early rulers of Islam. Modem representative government is an attempt-by no means perfect-to apply this principle in State affairs"[542]. Mawdudi deduced four things from the *shura* verse: "The executive head of the government and the members of the assembly should be elected by free and independent choice of the people. The people and their representatives should have the right to criticize and freely express their opinions. The real conditions of the country should be brought before the people without suppressing any fact so that they may be able to form their opinion about whether the government is working properly or not. There should be adequate guarantee that only those people who have the support of the masses should rule over the country and those who fail to win this support should be removed from their position of authority"[543]. Ali Ibn Abi Talib's dictum that: "I have no authority without your support,"[544] indicates the respect of the political rights and the participation of citizens in public life.

---

[541] *Ibid.* pages. 44-45.

[542] Abdullahi Yusuf Ali's, *op.cit.*, commentary on Qur'an 42:38.

[543] Mawdud Abu al-'A'la, Human Rights in Islamal Tawhid Journal, vol. IV No. 3 Rajab-Ramadhan 1407.

[544] Ibrahim bin Ali Alwazir *"The Relationship between the Ruler and the Ruled: A Mutually Obligating Agreement"* accessible at www.alhewar.com. Mr. Alwazir is the President of the Union

Another well-known incident in Islamic history is when Omar Ibn Al-Khattab, the second Caliph, proposed that a limit be set regarding dowries. A woman brought to his attention that his proposal goes against the Quranic text. Omar then admitted his mistake and succumbed to the position of the lady[545].

It is unanimous among Muslim jurists that the purpose of public authority in Islam is to protect the interests of the people as manifested in the protection of their life, faith, intellect, property, progeny and dignity. One can also see a *de facto* separation of powers between the scholars and kings in the *Umayyad* kingdom thirty years after the prophet's death and also in the kingdoms that followed. This might be called an initial separation of powers between mosque and court and between secretaries and scholars[546]. With this background, Mallat Chibli writes: "The lessons of the classical age, [of Islam] to sum up, are: the rule of law is established as a principle, so is the concept of the right of man.... At the same time, there is a dimension of civil society with its own autonomous regulation which can be found, in first approximation, in the importance of custom [*uruf*] and its legal recognition, and in an identifiable sphere of separation of powers with the ruler on the one hand and ulama, muftis and qādīs, on the

---

of Supportive Shurists. This article is part of his publication "Two Testimonies: A Charter for the Good Life".

[545] *Ibid.*

[546] The Royal *Aal Al-Bayt* Institute for Islamic Thought Jihad and the Islamic Law of War, 2007, Jordan. P. 51.

other" [547]. Although the word 'democracy', and the terms 'separation of powers' and 'rule of law' might not be seen in the Qur'an and *Sunnah,* their spirit is always present therein.

They also provide the moral and ethical bases for the interactions between communities and their socioeconomic life and their political enterprises nationally and internationally. Schact describes the purpose of sharia as: "In the field of penal law, it is easy to understand that the Qur'ān laid down sanctions for transgressions, but again they are essentially moral and only incidentally penal, so much so that the Qur'ān prohibited wine-drinking but did not enact any penalty, and the penalty was determined only at a later stage of Islamic law[548]. The reasons for Qur'ānic legislation on all these matters were, in the first place, the desire to improve the position of women, of orphans and of the weak in general, to restrict the laxity of sexual mores, to strengthen the marriage tie, to restrict private vengeance and retaliation, and to eliminate blood feuds altogether; the prohibition

---

[547] Mallat, Chibli, "Islam and Public Law, Introduction: On Islam and Democracy", In Centre of Islamic and Middle Eastern Law. Accessible at http://www.soas.ac.uk/cimel/materials/public.html. see also SOAS/Institut du Monde Arabe, June 1990.

[548] The punishment for drinking is said to have established by *hadith* as forty lashes. Under the Caliphate of Abubakar, the first Caliph, the punishment remained forty lashes but under Omar, the second Caliph, the punishment was eighty lashes and Ali, the fourth Muslim Caliph, enacted both forty and eighty. See Ahmad ibn Abdul Halim ibn Taymiyyah, *Assiasatu Ashari'ah* fil islahi raie wal- ra'iah (the politics of Shariah for the betterment of the leader and the led) also accessible at www. Al-mostafa.com, p. 56.

of gambling, of drinking wine and of taking interest are directly aimed at ancient Arabian standards of behaviour"[549].

3.7.5 An Islamic Perspective on Relations Between States with Regard to World Peace

Muhammad b. Ahmad b. Abi Sahl Abu Bakr al-Sarakhsi, an outstanding hanafi jurist who died around 490AH/1096 C.E, describes *siyar,* Islamic International law governing Islamic international relations, to mean "the attitude adopted by the ruler towards aliens in the state of war and peace"[550]. We can say that the conduct, pronouncements, practices and endorsement of the prophet Muhammad in his relations with other nations in times of war and peace provide the basis for *Siyar,* Islamic international law. To put it succinctly, *Siyar* is the totality of the principles, set of laws, and practices that govern a Muslim nation's (*Ummah's)* relationships with other nations[551.] *Siyar* acquired a distinct character and became an analytical tool in the study and application of *shariah*[552]. The

---

[549] Schact, J., Cambridge Encyclopedia of Islam, vol. II, pt. VIII/chpt. 4, p. 539.

[550] Muhammad Hamidullah, The Emergence of Islam: Lectures on the Development of Islamic World-View, Intellectual Tradition and Policy. Translated and edited by Afzal Iqbal, Adam Publishers & Distributors, Delhi India, 1995, p. 110.

[551] Khadduri Majid, The Islamic Law of Nations: Shaybàni's Siyar, John Hopkins Press Baltimore, 1966, p. 8.

[552] "*Shari'a,*" literally "The path", or guidance for appropriate Muslim conduct or a Muslim's code of life, and *fiqh* (its method of understanding) concern themselves with the common good of

Qur'an, the *Sunnah* and the *hadith*, practices of the four rightly guided caliphs, practices of the later caliphs, opinions of the learned, treaties and agreements, official instructions to the military, ambassadors, to other state officials and customs are the sources of *siyar*.

Law and order is the basic characteristic of every human society nationally and internationally, between people and between states. Islam derives its laws primarily from the Qur'an and *Sunnah* beside them, *ijtihad* (deducing of an appropriate rule through the exercise of reason and conscience)[553], *Uruf* (custom), *qias* (analogy) and *ijma'* (consensus) are also methods of making Laws in Islam. Even though laws existed before the advent of Muslim, their religion and their society were firmly founded on the concept of *shari'ah* or 'rule of law'. Hence Muslim jurists contributed greatly to the principle of jurisprudence[554].

---

humanity socially, economically, physically, intellectually, and spiritually in: Islam - (Divine commandment) Imān - (Belief) and Iħsān - (ethics and moral excellence).

[553] *Ijtihad* is confirmed by the prophet in a *hadith* related by Muadh ibn Jabal: "Muadh ibn Jabal relates that when the Prophet sent him to Yemen, prophet asked, 'What will you do if a matter is referred to you for judgment?' Muadh said, 'I will judge according to the God's Book.' The Prophet asked, 'What if you find no solution in God's Book?' Muadh said, 'Then I will judge by the *Sunnah* of the Prophet.' The Prophet asked, 'And what of if you do not find it in the *Sunnah* of the Prophet?' Muadh said, 'Then I will make *Ijtihad* to formulate my own judgment.' The Prophet patted Muadh's chest and said, 'Praise be to Allah who has guided the messenger of His Messenger to that which pleases Him and His Prophet'". See *Sunan* Abū Dāwūd.

[554] Makdisi, John A. "The Islamic Origins of the Common Law", *North Carolina Law Review* 77 (5): 1635–1739 (June 1999). See also Manlio Lima "English Common Law and Islam: A Sicilian Connection" at www.bestofsicily.com/mag/art283.htm. accessed on 6 November 2012.

The primary objective of this Islamic *shariah* (*Maqasid al-Shari'ah*) is Mercy to all creatures: "We sent you [Prophet Muhammad] not, except as a Mercy for all creatures" [555] and also to bring benefit to them (*maslaħ*) and to protect them from harm. This objective is summarized under the following universal categories: protection of religious freedom, protection of life/soul, protection of the intellect, protection of reproduction and protection of property[556]. Providing conditions within which these categories can be fulfilled is no less a common good. As such, the domain of Islamic jurisprudence is geared towards bettering the behaviour of Muslim private and public, national and international relations.

Classical Muslim jurists in their efforts to shape the nature of relations between their nations and other non-Muslim nations had basically divided the world into the following camps: *dar al Islam*-the abode of peace, (the Muslim territories) and *dar al harb*-the abode of war (territory not in treaty with the Muslims and with whom war can break out at any time*), dar al-Sulh*-the abode of reconciliation and *dar al-ahd*-the abode of treaty, (designating those territories not ruled by Muslims but with whom a Muslim nation has some sort of peace agreement)[557]. However, this classical division in the law of nations by the

---

[555] Qur'an, Al-Anbiya'a/the prophets/ 21:107.

[556] See Shatibi's *Maqasid Al-shari'a* (the objectives of shari'a).

[557] The Royal Aal Al-Bayt Institute for Islamic Thought, Jihad and the Islamic Law of War, 2007 Jordan, Pages 26-29. Majid Khadduri, 1966, and Muhammad Abu Zahara, (Imam) *Al-a'laqatu al-*

Muslim jurists is neither grounded on nor found in the Qur'an nor in the *Ahadith*. It was a Muslim juridical speculation with assumptions influenced by the political circumstances of their times[558]. "Although its basic assumptions were derived from these authoritative sources, it was rather the product of Islamic juridical speculation at the height of Islamic power"[559]. From an Islamic perspective the application of justice is indiscriminate regardless of *dar al Islam*-the abode of peace, dar *al harb* -the abode of war, *dar al-Sulh*-the abode of reconciliation and *dar al-ahd* -the abode of treaty[560]. The same rules that govern the relations between individuals should govern the relations between states since the states start with people. Against this background, Islam exhorts that the relations between human beings, including all levels of relationship between individuals,

---

dualliah fil-Islam pub, publ. Dar al fikra al-Araby1995, are recommended for further reading on the relations between Muslim states and non-Muslim states.

[558] The Royal *Aal Al-Bayt op.cit.* 2007 Jordan. Pages 26-29. See also Khadduri Majid, *The Islamic Law of Nations Shaybàni's Siyar. Op.Cit.*

[559] Khadduri Majid ibid, *Op. Cit.* 1966 , P. 19.

[560] This is deduced from the Qur'anic verse: "O ye who believe! stand out firmly for Allah, as witnesses to fair dealing, and let not the hatred of others to you make you swerve to wrong and depart from justice. Be just: that is next to piety: and fear Allah. For Allah is well-acquainted with all that ye do". Qur'an, Al-Maida/The Table Spread/5:8. This verse is fundamental and pivotal in Muslim relations with others be it private or public, national or international. Reflecting on this verse Yusuf Ali stated: "To do justice and act righteously in a favourable or neutral atmosphere is meritorious enough, but the real test comes when you have to do justice to people who hate you or to whom you have an aversion. But no less is required of you by the higher moral law" . See Abdullahi Yusuf Ali's commentary on Qur'an, Alma-eda/The Table Spread/5:8.

groups and states, should be deep rooted and anchored in truth, justice and solidarity.

3.7.6 An Islamic Perspective on Truth as A Principle of International Relations

"The first point to be settled is that mutual ties between States must be governed by truth. Truth calls for the elimination of every trace of racial discrimination, and the consequent recognition of the inviolable principle that all States are by nature equal in dignity"[561] Pope John XXIII asserted.

According to Qur'an, people are lost and in a state of destruction unless they practice and speak the truth in their relations nationally and internationally. The Qur'an says: "[I swear] by Time! Verily man is in [a state of] loss, except those who believe, and perform righteous deeds, and enjoin one another to [follow] the truth, and enjoin one another to patience" [562]. "A most excellent *Jihad*" the prophet Muhammad said: "is when one speaks a word of truth in the presence of a tyrannical ruler"[563]. Furthermore, the Qur'an urges Muslims to establish the truth from the information we receive and give: "Oh you who

---

[561] *Pacem in Terris*, pp. 86.

[562] Qur'an, Al-Asr/The Declining Day/103:1-3.

[563] This *hadith* is narrated by Abu Sa'id al-Khudri and collected by Abu Dawood and Trimithi. See also Muhammad Sa'id R. Al-Buti, *Jihad in Islam, How to Understand and Practise It.* Translated and abridged by Munzer Adel Absi, pub. Dar Al-Fikr Publishing House, Damascus Syria, 1995, p. 17. .

believe if *fasiq* [a liar, evil person] comes to you with any news, verify it, lest you should harm people in ignorance and afterwards you become regretful for what you have done"[564]. In the 21st century the role of information in international relations is pivotal. For this reason, news or reports on national and international media should be based on truth that must be ascertained before despatching them for public consumption. Otherwise much harm may be done to the reputation and dignity of peoples and nations out of ignorance. This verse signifies the moral imperative of safeguarding the honour, dignity and reputation which is the human right of every member of the community, nationally and internationally. From an Islamic perspective, truth should be the basis for international relations and agreements. There are many instances in the Qur'an that urge Muslims to be truthful in their dealings with people. Therefore, for truth to be the principle of international relations is not only compatible with Islam but it is an Islamic injunction.

3.7.7An Islamic Perspective on Justice as a Principle of International Relations

In Islam, Justice is another core principle in international relations. Justice, which could mean placing things in their rightful place or giving everyone his/her/its due, is one of the foundations upon which the Islamic code of belief is

---

[564] Qur'an, Al-Hujurat/The Private Apartments/49:6.

built. This is the fundamental nature of (*tawheed*) monotheism. Injustice is to put

a thing in an inappropriate place. *Shirik* (Polytheism) is seen by Islam as the grave

injustice, because it is giving to creatures that which absolutely and exclusively

belong to the Creator. Islam sees Polytheism as an injustice against the Creator. In

Islam "Idolatry is indeed a great injustice"[565]. The Qur'an enjoins Muslims to be

just at all costs[566]. To stand for God in Islam is to stand for justice[567]. The verses

mentioned in the footnote with regard to justice include all sorts of relationships

from interstate relations to relations of individuals and families.

Islam urges that both national and international judiciary systems be

centered on justice.[568]. Second only to the principle of monotheism, justice is the

most emphasized principle in the Qur'àn and the traditions[569]. Words derived

---

[565] Qur'an, Luqmân /31:13.

[566] "O ye who believe! Stand out firmly for justice, as witnesses to God, even as against
yourselves, or your parents, or your kin, and whether it be (against) rich or poor: for God can best
protect both. Follow not the lusts (of your hearts), lest ye swerve, and if ye distort (justice) or
decline to do justice, verily God is well- acquainted with all that ye do" Qur'an, Al-Nisa/Women/
4:135.

[567] "O believers, stand out firmly for Allah, as securers of justice, and let not the hatred of others
to you make you swerve to wrong and depart from justice. Be just: that is next to piety: and fear
Allah. Allah is well-acquainted with all that ye do" Qur'an, Al-Maeda /The Table Spread/5:8.

[568] "But if you judge, judge between them with justice. Surely, Allah loves those who do justice"
Qur'an, Al-Maeda / The Table Spread/ 5:42.

[569] Koylu Mustafa, *Islam and its Quest for Peace: Jihad, Justice and Education*. The Council for
Research in Values and philosophy, 2003 P.72. See also M.K.N. Belkacem's "The Concept of
Social Justice in Islam" in "The Challenge of Islam," (Islamic Council of Europe 1978) P.72.

from the root *àdl* (justice) occur about 46 times in the Qur'an, and from *alqist* (dispenser of justice) occur 20 times. One of the many names and attributes of God in Islam is (*Adl*) just and (*almuqist*) dispenser of justice. Therefore, justice captures the essence of all Islamic laws, all Islamic teachings, and must permeate Muslim international relations. Justice is the overarching value that prevents international relations from falling into disorder. The Qur'an says: "Indeed, we sent our messengers with the clear signs, and we sent down with them the book and the balance so that men might uphold justice"[570]. Thus, from this verse one can deduce that the sole purpose of sending the prophets, the clear signs, the book and balance is to establish justice in the world and to make an end to injustice. Justice and peace are interconnected; calling for justice is calling for peace. From this perspective we can say that the whole Islamic edifice and that of international relations rests on peace. This peace cannot be realized without justice. Justice then, for Islam, is the secret of the existence and the progress of nations and the symbol of virtues.

Because of the loss of justice, great powers can collapse and glorious civilizations can be reduced to rubble. To avoid this scenario, Islam aims at creating a society where rich and poor, friend and foe, Muslim and non-Muslim, the ruler and the ruled, will all be treated equally and all of them can count on receiving justice whenever their due is taken away from them. Again, we

---

[570] Qur'an, Al-Hadeed,/The Iron /57:25.

conclude this segment by saying that justice as one of the principles of international relations is not only in harmony with Islam; it is an Islamic injunction as well.

3.7.8 An Islamic Perspective on Active Solidarity as a Principle of International Relations

Active solidarity in truth and justice, where States pool their material and spiritual resources in mutual collaboration "primarily to protect the common good of the State, which certainly cannot be divorced from the common good of the entire human family"[571] is suggested by Pope John XXIII as one of the principles of international relations.

In Islamic international relations 'active solidarity' in truth and justice is highly recommended. This drives from the belief that God created human beings from a single soul[572] and as such, human beings should live in active solidarity with one another. From an Islamic perspective, the Qur'an conferred upon all human beings equal dignity and honour. As such, they are morally bound to relate to each other with dignity and honor, be it between the individuals, tribes,

---

[571] *Pacem in Terris*, pp. 98.

[572] "O mankind! Be conscious of your Sustainer, who has created you out of one living entity, and out of it created its mate, and out of the two spread abroad a multitude of men and women. And remain conscious of God, in whose name you demand [your rights] from one another, and of these ties of kinship. Verily, God is ever watchful over you! " (Qur'an, Al-Nisae/The Women/4:1).

ethnicities, communities or states. Since people equally share that inviolable honour and dignity and together they are all created from a single soul of the same origin, the Qur'an commands Muslims to help in the 'common good' by saying: "And never let your hatred of some people that shut you out of the Sacred Mosque lead you to transgression (and hostility on your part). Help ye one another in righteousness and piety, but help ye not one another in sin and rancour: fear Allah for Allah is strict in punishment"[573].

The above injunction should not be limited exclusively to *dar al Islam* or to any historical event; it is inclusive, timeless and general[574]. It urges Muslims to cooperate with every nation in solidarity for common good; it urges cooperation and solidarity with anyone who endeavours to establish world peace. Muslims' disapproval of others' systems and ways of life must not deter them from working

---

[573] Qur'an, Al-Maida/ The Table Spread/5:2.

[574] "Inasmuch as this *sūrah* was undoubtedly revealed in the year 10 H. (Tabarī, Ibn Kathīr), it is difficult to accept the view of some of the commentators that the above verse alludes to the events culminating in the truce of Hudaybiyyah, in 6 H., when the pagan Quraysh succeeded in preventing the Prophet and his followers from entering Mecca on pilgrimage. At the time of the revelation of this *sūrah* Mecca was already in the possession of the Muslims, and there was no longer any question of their being barred from it by the Quraysh, almost all of whom had by then embraced Islam. We must, therefore, conclude that the above injunction cannot be circumscribed by a historical reference but has a timeless, general import: in other words, that it refers to anybody who might endeavour to bar the believers – physically or metaphorically – from the exercise of their religious duties (symbolized by the "Inviolable House of Worship") and thus to lead them away from their faith. In view of the next sentence, moreover, this interpretation would seem to be the only plausible one. 3- See 2:173". See Muhammad Asad's commentary the Qur'an, Al-Maida/The Table Spread 5:2.

in solidarity with them for the common good. This is the kind of solidarity Muslims are expected to do: helping others because one is to fulfill a divine duty. This help is extended to political and economic refugees, to widows, the poor, and orphans as well as the sick and the weak. "If one amongst the pagans asks thee for asylum, grant it to him, so that he may hear the word of Allah; and then escort him to where he can be secure that is because they are men without knowledge"[575].

Muslims are expected to be in solidarity with others in righteousness and piety, not in perpetuating feuds of hatred and enmity. They are expected to cooperate with the coalition of the willing to establish justice, peace and stability and are expected to cooperate in the sharing of intelligence in the interest of international security[576].

---

[575] Qur'an, Al-Tawbah/The Repentance/9: 6 .

[576] "And how could you refuse to fight in the cause of God and of the utterly helpless men and women and children who are crying, "O our Sustainer! Lead us forth [to freedom] out of this land whose people are oppressors, and raise for us, out of Thy grace, a protector, and raise for us, out of Thy grace, one who will bring us *succour!"Qur'an (add space)*, Al-Nisa'e/ The Women/4:75. From an Islamic point of view, the cause of Allah is the cause of justice, hence, Muslims have no moral ground in refusing to rescue the oppressed who is denied justice. Therefore Muslims are divinely enjoined by this verse to carry out what is now known in international relations as the responsibility to protect utterly helpless men, women and children in solidarity with any people of goodwill. Furthermore, the Qur'an urges Muslims to "Serve God alone and do good- to parents, kinsfolk, orphans, those in need, neighbors who are near, neighbors who are strangers, the companion by your side, the wayfarer (you meet), and what your right hands possess. For God loves not the arrogant, the vainglorious" Qur'an Al.Nisaa'e/Women/4:36

Moreover, there are many a*hadith* that can be interpreted in the sense of active solidarity in interstate relations.[577.] The Prophet of Islam always stressed a Muslim moral obligation towards neighbours, regardless of the faith of the neighbours by saying: "Whoever believes in God and the Last Day let him do good unto his neighbour"[578]. There is also neighbourliness in statehood. The Qur'an exhorts Muslims to be in active solidarity with all people of goodwill in promoting peace in the world.

3.7.9 An Islamic Perspective on Reduction of Arsenals in International Relations

From an Islamic perspective, reliance on Mutual Assured Destruction (MAD) for peace is "religiously unacceptable, morally untenable and militarily unjustifiable". However, there is a verse in the Qur'an that can be interpreted in favour of arms race[579].

---

[577] For instance: "None of you has faith until you love for your brother what you love for yourself" (Sahih Al-Bukhari,Kitabal-Iman, Hadith no.13). And "None of you has faith until you love for your neighbor what you love for yourself"(Sahih Muslim, Kitabal-Iman 67-1, *Hadith* no.45). Prophet of Islam Muhammad is also on record to have said: "Ibn Abbas reported: The Prophet, peace and blessings be upon him, said, "He is not a believer whose stomach is filled while the neighbor to his side goes hungry." (Al-baihaqy Sunan al-Kubrā, 19049).

[578] Agreed Upon.

[579] "Against them make ready your strength to the utmost of your power, including steeds of war, to strike terror into (the hearts of) the enemies, of God and your enemies, and others besides, whom ye may not know, but whom God knows. Whatever you shall spend in the cause of God,

For Abdullahi Yusuf Ali, the immediate occasion of that verse "was the weakness of cavalry and appointments of war in the early fights of Islam. But the general meaning follows. In every fight, physical, moral, or spiritual, arm yourself with the best weapons and the best arms against your enemy, so as to instil wholesome respect into him for you and the cause you stand for"[580]. Furthermore, looking at the verse that follows one can deduce that the verse calls for armament only in times of self defense and not a perpetual arms race. The Qur'an continues: "But if the enemy incline towards peace, incline you [also] towards peace, and trust in God: for He is One that hears and knows (all things)"[581].

Hermeneutically speaking there are many *ahadith* that can be used in support of disarmament[582]. These *ahadith,* coupled with the hermeneutic

---

shall be repaid to you, and you shall not be treated unjustly. But if the enemy incline towards peace, incline you [also] towards peace, and trust in God: for He is One that hears and knows all things" Qur'an/Al-Anfaal/ The Spoils of War/ 8:60-61. Muhammad Asad interpreted this by saying: "tethering of horses" in Arabic rendered as (*ribāt al-khayl*) as it appears in this verse signifies "holding in readiness mounted troops at all points open to enemy invasion (*thughūr*)"; hence, tropically, the over-all maintenance of military preparedness" See Muhammad Asad's commentary on Qur'an/Al-Anfaal/ The Spoils of War/ 8:60-61.

[580] Abdullahi Yusuf Ali, *op. cit.*, Commentary on 8:60.

[581] Qur'an/Al-Anfaal/ Spoils of War/ 8:61.

[582] Among them are: Sa'd Ibn Abu Waqqas' statement upon the ordeal of Uthman Ibn Affan that reads: "I testify that Allah's Messenger (Peace be upon him) said: 'There will be soon a period of turmoil in which the one who sits will be better than one who stands and the one who stands will be better than one who walks and the one who walks will be better than one who runs.' Someone

243

interpretation of the verse: "If you stretch your hand towards me to kill me, I am not going to stretch my hand towards you to kill you. Indeed, I fear Allah, the Lord of the worlds"[583] and many other verses, would favour arms reduction if not disarmament. The arms race is built on a philosophy contrary to that of Abel whom the Prophet of Islam asks his followers to imitate. Advising Muslims to be like Abel and not Cain is to advise them not to be aggressive, wicked, violent and murderers. As such this can be interpreted to encourage a reduction of the arms

---

said: 'Allah's Messenger! What is your opinion if someone entered my home and stretched his hand to kill me?' Allah's Messenger (Peace be upon him) said: 'Be just like the son of Adam (Abel)'" Ibn Mardwiyah who took the *hadith* from Hudhaifah Ibn Al- Yaman narrated it in another wording: "Be just like the best of Adam's two sons". Narrated by Imam Ahmed, Abu Dawud and At-Tirmidhi on the authority of Sa'd Ibn Abu Waqqas see ibn kathir *The Story of Habil and Qabil* (Able and Cain). Accessible at www.islambasics.com. In another *hadith* reported by Abu Bakr, in a time of tumult and affliction, the prophet of Islam urges Muslim that: "He should take hold of his sword and beat its edge with the help of stone, and then try to find a way of escape". (Jawdat Sa'id, *Non-Violence The Basis of Setting Disputes in Islam*. Translated by Munzer A.Absi H.Hilwàni. Revised by Anas an-Rifa'i .Dar al Fikr in Damascus Syria. First Edition January 2002. P.28.) He quoted the *hadith* from Sahih al-Bukhari and Sahih al-Muslim). In a similar circumstance when the prophet Muhammad was asked by Abu Dhar al-Ghifari :"But what if someone entered my home (to kill) me?" the prophet replied: "If you fear to look upon the gleam of the sword raised to strike you, then cover your face with your robe. Thus will he bear the sin of killing you as well as his own sin". (Abu Dawud Sulayman ibn Ash'ath, *Sunan Abu-Dawud*, bk. 35, no. 4246, reviewed and verified by Muhammad 'Awwamah, *Kitab al-Sunan: Sunan Abu Dawud* (reprint, Jiddah: Dar al- Qiblah lil-Thaqafah al-Islamiyah 1998). Furthermore, Prophet Muhammad also told Abu Musa al-Ash'ari: "Break your bows, sever your strings, [and] beat stone on your swords (to break the blades); and when infringed upon by the one of the perpetrators, be as the best of the Adam's two sons". (Mohammed Abu-Nimer, *Nonviolence and Peace Building in Islam Theory and Practice*. University Press Florida 2003, p.44.)

[583] Al Ma'eda/ The Table Spread/5:28.

race. This Qur'anic verse is no less important in legitimizing disarmament from an Islamic perspective: "Because of this did We ordain unto the children of Israel that if anyone slays a human being – unless it be [in punishment] for murder or for spreading corruption on earth – it shall be as though he had slain all mankind; whereas, if anyone saves a life, it shall be as though he had saved the lives of all mankind. And, indeed, there came unto them Our apostles with all evidence of the truth: yet, behold, notwithstanding all this, many of them go on committing all manner of excesses on earth"[584].

In this verse, a particular reference is made to the children of Israel, but it is not exclusive to them; it includes every human being. Israelites being a particular reference does not exempt a Muslim from obeying this instruction and it does not change its "universal validity" and continuity[585]. For Yusuf Ali there is no "stronger condemnation of murder and revenge" than this verse. In their Disarmament Statement, the Military Professionals and Religious Leaders stated that "A peace based on terror, a peace based upon threats of inflicting annihilation and genocide upon whole populations, is a peace that is corrupting, a peace that is unworthy of civilization... [and] it defies all logic to believe that nuclear weapons can exist forever and never be used"[586]. Muslims were among the

---

[584] Al Ma'eda/ The Table Spread/5:32.

[585] See also Muhammad Asad, op., cit. comments on Al-Maida/ The Table Spread /5:32.

[586] Joint Nuclear Reduction/Disarmament Statement Military Professionals and Religious Leaders www.nrdi.org/nuclear/Nuclear02.html . Accessed on 18 -02 -2008.

religious leaders who drew this decision from their religious scriptures and traditions. However, as mentioned earlier, this does not make Islam a pacifist religion.

3.7.10 An Islamic Perspective on Freedom as a Principle of International Relations

Pacem in Terris states that "relations between States must be regulated by the principle of freedom" [587]. From an Islamic perspective, freedom can be seen as the unrestricted will that can make actors and stakeholders responsible for their actions and utterances and attaches liability for valid contracts in any relations. For Islam, freedom is important in personal and international relations and the validity of any transaction, convention, treaty and agreement is derived from freedom. The validity of international agreements also hinges on freedom. International principles that aim at establishing peace on strong and righteous foundations must be based on freedom of the States who are to observe such principles. However, from an Islamic perspective, the word Justice overshadows the word freedom. Freedom is hardly mentioned in the Qur'an and *Hadith*. According to Mohamed Shahrour,[588] "Throughout various historical eras to the present day, there seems to have been little trace of freedom in the Arab Muslim collective consciousness. There are two reasons – epistemological and political –

---

[587] *Pacem in Terris*, pp.120.

[588] Mohamed Shahrour, (PhD) is an engineer and Islamic thinker resident in Damascus, Syria.

for the lack of this value in Arab Muslim culture. The epistemological reason is that the term "freedom" is not mentioned in its literal sense in the Qur'an, the only reference being to the abomination of slavery. The phrase 'freeing a slave' appears five times in Surahs 4, 5 and 58. It also appears once in the following verse: O you who believe! The law of equality is prescribed to you in cases of murder: the free for the free, the slave for the slave. (2:178) Other than these indirect references to freedom, we can find no mention of the term in the revealed Book of God the Omniscient"[589]. Sharour went further to say that: "Freedom in Islamic historical literature is mentioned only in the sense of detesting the servitude of a slave. There is clearly no reference to its social, political and other dimensions. The only institution that has survived unharmed to the present day is that of tyranny and repression, especially the Pharaonic type (political) and, in second place, the Hamanic type (religious)"[590].

Nonetheless, 'Umar ibn al-Khattab said "Since when did you enslave people, whose mothers had given birth to them as free beings"[591]. According to Shahrour "free being" in this statement means justice and equity. Nevertheless, the Qur'anic emphasis on the concept of (*Adl* and *qist*) 'justice' and, (*iradah* and

---

[589] Shahrour Mohamed, "The Concept of Freedom in Islam". accessed at www.globalwebpost.com/farooqm/.../islam/freedom/shahrour_freedom.doc on 22-05-13. This article is said to have been based "on a paper presented to the Institution of Ibn Khaldun for Developmental Studies at the conference on "Islam and Reform: Workshop", Cairo, 5–6 October 2004 .

[590] *Ibid.*

[591] *Ibid.*

mashi'ah), 'human will'[592], are meant, for the realisation of Freedom. In the Qur'an, "oppression" is condemned no less than three hundred times[593]. In all of these condemnations, it is enjoined that justice be practiced and hence freedom realised. Negating freedom of choice is tantamount to ridiculing the Day of Judgment (accountability, reward and punishment), one of the articles of Islamic faith. Against this background, one can claim that the "concept of freedom is the main objective of creation, as described in God's Holy Book"[594].

Justice and Freedom are inspirational and motivating factors in the contemporary Arab uprising. This shows the lack of justice and freedom in the political institutions of these countries. With the magnitude of its importance, Islam will surely accommodate freedom in international relations instead of negating it.

In his book (*Al-alaqatu al-duwaliyyah fil-Islaam*) "International Relations in Islam," Muhammad Abu Zaharah identifies (*al-huriyyah*) freedom, (*karamatul-insaniyyah*) the dignity of humankind, (*al-naas jami' ummah wahidah*) the oneness of humankind, (*al-ta'awun al-insaniy*) humanitarian assistance, (*tasamah*) tolerance, (*al-fadilah*) honour, (*al-adalah*) Justice, (*Aalmu'a'maltu bil mithil*) reciprocal transactions, (*al-wafa'a bil-ahad*) fulfillment of promises, (*al-mawadah wa-man'u al-fasad*) and amicability and prevention of mischief, as the

---

[592] "Let him who will, believe, and let him who will, reject [it]". Qur'an 18:29.

[593] Shahrour Mohamed, *op.cit.*

[594] *Ibid.*

principles of international relations. Some of these principles are also mentioned in *Pacem in Terris*. For Zaharah, "the real and true (*huriyyah*) begins from the emancipation of soul from the dominium of vanity and sensual pleasure to subdue only to the dominium of the intellect and faith"[595]. Zahara is of the view that Islam also guarantees freedom to people to decide their way of life; it also gives them freedom of thought and creed[596]. For him, the basis of all relations is peace. He maintained the juridical distinction of world politics into *dar-ul-harb*, (abode of war), *dar-ul-salaam* (abode of peace), *dar-ul-ahad*, (abode of treaty), and (*al-siyadah*) Sovereignty, (*al-mu'ahadat-wa-sulhu*) treaties and reconciliation in international relations[597].

3.7.11 An Islamic Perspective on the Relationship of Men and of Political Communities with the World Community

In Islam, the relationship of men and of political communities with the world community should be based on the "common good". The Madinian Charter (*Sahifatul Madina*), a treaty between the prophet of Islam and the different tribes of Medina including Jewish and Arab tribes, approves Muslims' involvement in any kind of community, movement or organisation working on the model

---

[595] Zaharah Abu Muhammad, *Al-alaqatu al-duwaliyyah fil-Islaam* "International Relations in Islam" Dar-ul-fikru-al-Arabi, Egypt 1995, p. 29.

[596] *Ibid.*, p. 32

[597] *Ibid.*

portrayed in *Pacem In Terris.* (see *Pacem in Terris* pp. 103-145). The Qur'anic injunction: "Help one another in righteousness and piety, and do not help one another in furthering evil and enmity"[598] is another justification in that regard. Helping one another in justice and eschewing injustice remains the bedrock of all Muslim relationships and membership in any organization.

It is against this background that Marmaduke Pickthall claimed: "A League of Nations has been started to try to do a part of the work Islam has done, to bring the varying nations into unison and frame a code of international law conducive to peace and progress. But it is starting at a disadvantage for it admits the principle of aggressive nationalism and imperialism"[599]. By analogy we could arguably say that United Nations is pursuing the standard set by Islam for equity, justice, solidarity, and human rights for the interest of world peace but has yet to achieve it. Moreover, every Muslim signatory to any agreement, such as the Charter of the United Nations, Geneva Conventions or to any other national and international treaty or agreement, is obliged to abide by it as Prophet Muhammad abided by the treaties with pagan Quraish, with other inhabitants of Arabia and beyond[600].

---

[598] Qur'an, Al-Maida/The Table Spread / 5:2.

[599] Muhammad Marmaduke Pickthall ,*The Cultural Side Of Islam,* Publishers, The Commitee of Madras Lecture in Islam, Lahore in 1937, p. 58.

[600] See Qur'an, Saff/ The Ranks /61:2-3. See also Qur'an, Al-Mā'idah /The Table Spread/5:1

Thus, there is an Islamic perspective that does not contradict *Pacem in Terris* "towards the establishment of a juridical and political ordering of the world community"[601] in the United Nations whose objective is to "maintain international peace and security for the interest of universal peace"[602]. Such an Islamic perspective aims to establish peaceful community in the world, and it expects Muslim majority states to cooperate in the realization of international peace. This Islamic perspective will embrace participation in organized national and international action for justice, liberty, charity, love, disarmament, collective security, human solidarity and collaboration in establishing world peace as envisaged in *Pacem in Terris*.

Muslims and their states are expected not to cooperate with or join in any organisation promoting injustice, exploitation and or terrorism on earth. This is what the Islamic notion of *al-wala'a- wa- al-bara'a* (obedience and disobedience/loyalty and disloyalty) stands for[603]. In his search for a

---

[601] *Pacem in Terris* pp.144.

[602] See the aims of the UN in UN Charter .

[603] Nonetheless, some Muslim extremists corrupted this notion and took up arms against their countries for having cooperated with non-Muslim authorities. Allama Sheikh Abdullah bin Bayyah, one of Islam's foremost living Sunni scholars, criticized Somali extremists in Somalia, on the notion of "loyalty and disloyalty". The extremists are disloyal and disobedient to the Somali's internationally legitimate "government on the pretext that it has relations with non-Muslim powers or with the Pan-African peace-keeping force that is stationed in the country", he said. Bayyah rejected the extremists' claim by emphasizing that "loyalty to the faith of Islam is at the level of creedal belief and is not to be broadened to all human dealings". He cited corruption in fundamental notions such as *Jiha*d (striving), *al-wala wa- al-bara* (loyalty and enmity), *al-hukum*

"comprehensive strategy for overcoming extremism and for safeguarding the original teachings of Islam: peace, compassion, and blessings", 'Allama Sheikh Abdullah bin Bayyah, one of Islam's foremost living Sunni scholars, urges Muslims to work towards international conventions, covenants, and agreements that encourage mutual understanding, and prevent aggression and unfair dealings; and asks Muslims to encourage respect for diversity and pluralism, and to develop inter-civilizational, inter-cultural, and inter-faith dialogues; and together to address problems of disease, illiteracy, and poverty. In protecting and defending nations against terrorism, he calls for building communications and information-exchange, and international infrastructures to that effect[604].

Against this background, Pope John XXIII's appeal for the establishment of universal peace in truth, justice, charity and liberty can be expected to be a Muslim duty. However, nations that aim to establish universal peace should do so through diplomatic means. No nation can exclusively claim to uphold the establishment of this universal peace through a monolithic approach to peace. Some nations seem to take it for granted that it is only through their own monolithic political vision that all human beings must be governed. For them, the

---

bi ma anzal Allah (ruling according to Allah's revealed law), and *takfir* (accusing of apostasy). Corruption in this notion led to the "utter negligence and lack of recognition of the sanctity of human life". See Aref Ali Nayed *Building Peace: The Approach of Sheikh Abdullah bin Bayyah, Declaration Text* © 2010. Global Centre for Renewal and Guidance. See also article 5 of its Arabic version.

[604] Aref Ali Nayed. *Building Peace: The Approach of Sheikh Abdullah bin Bayyah, Declaration Text* © 2010. Global Centre for Renewal and Guidance.

truth and validity of one political system, religion and culture depends on the elimination or negation of its alternatives. Christians and Muslims through crusades and *jihad* in the names of their religions tried and failed to monopolize the governance of humankind. West and East also tried to impose their own culture and version of governance on certain parts of the world and failed. In national and international relations, diplomacy, negotiation, dialogue, gradual adoption and advancement of peace, propelling principles such as truth, justice, liberty, cooperation, active solidarity and the defense of human rights, as stated in *Pacem in Terris*, can help the world to get closer to the establishment of world peace.

3.8 Role and Nature of the States in International Relations: Positions from Christianity and Islam Doctrine and Practices

A State can be defined as a sovereign territory and a population that has the legitimate monopolization of the use of domestic force constitutionally authorized and conferred. The process of forming a state differs from epoch to epoch. The *terminus a quo* (point of origin) of the modern state formation process can be traced to the "centralized control over the means of violence and the means of revenue collection". Revenue collection, manifested in routine taxation of their populations, facilitates the acquisition of the means of violence such as the creation and maintenance of standing national armies and acquiring weaponry for control and expansion of their territory[605].

Peace and security are the dominant preoccupations of international relations and political systems. Thus, the threat to international relations is instability, negative crisis, insecurity, war and conflict. The role and nature of states in international relations is interest-seeking, manifested in security and power. Security is for self-preservation and power is for control over the territory. These interests provide the basis for state activities in international relations[606]. The concept of interest, defined in terms of power, security and survival, drives the actions of states in international relations[607]. In an anarchical, international, political world, states are collective actors that recognise no authority above them in their relations with one another. In international relations, politics are not a function of ethics, but ethics are a function of politics[608]. As such, any calculation that requires state self-preservation and protection is reasonable[609].

---

[605] Rae Heather, "Theories of state formation ". In *International Relations Theory for the Twenty-First Century*, edited by Martin Griffiths, published Routledge , USA and Canada, 2007 P. 123

[606] Waltz, 1979, p. 117. As cited by Jack Donnelly, 2000, *op.cit.*, 7-8.

[607] Mearsheimer, 1994/195:9-10, Gilpin, 1996:7-8, Keohane, 1986b:164-165. As cited by Jack Donnelly, op.cit. 2000, 7-8.

[608] Carr, 1946: 63-64, as cited Jack Donnelly, *op.cit.*

[609] Schwarzenberger, 1951, 13. See Jack Donnelly, *op.cit.* pages 7-8.

3.8.1 Positions from Christian and Islamic Doctrine and Practices on the Role and Nature of the States

Fifteenth century discoveries through exploration and navigation, coupled with commerce, colonization, evangelization and *islamization,* gave great impetus to international relations. Many temporary diplomatic missions and agents became permanent to tackle the nascent political, social, economic and religious needs of the changing era. The 17th century Treaty of Westphalia (1648) endorsed and recognized the legality of states. It also added conformity and uniformity to the international rules that were gradually adopted, applied, promoted and adjusted to by the states. Subsequent congresses, such as Vienna Congress (1815), Aix-la-Chapelle (1818) and the Conference of Vienna on Diplomatic Relations (1961), examined previous agreements, gave them international application, procedures and uniformity within an international cadre and order, and also established diplomatic immunities and privileges[610]. European states were the origin and home for all of the above mentioned treaties and congresses that helped shape the Westphalian concept of 'territorial states.' Thus they became a model in the operation of a state. Being a Christian majority zone, Christians, after some difficulties, were able to "give to Cesar what belongs to Cesar and to God what belongs to God"[611]. This became the basis for separation of state and religion.

---

[610] Hyginus Eugene Cardinale, the Holy See and the International Order Pub. Colin Smythe Gerrards Cross 1976, England, pages 60-63.

[611] Gospel, Mark 12:17

Pacem in Terris considered "that relations between States, as between individuals, must be regulated not by armed force, but in accordance with the principles of right reason: the principles, that is, of truth, justice and vigorous and sincere co-operation"[612]. In *Pacem in Terris,* human society is considered "as being primarily a spiritual reality.... It is these spiritual values which exert a guiding influence on culture, economics, social institutions, political movements and forms, laws, and all the other components which go to make up the external community of men and its continual development" [613.] *Pacem in Terris* appealed for international relations based on truth, justice, charity, willing cooperation and freedom[614]. For Pope John XXIII, "it is quite impossible for political leaders to lay aside their natural dignity while acting in their country's name and in its interests. They are still bound by the natural law, which is the rule that governs all moral conduct, and they have no authority to depart from its slightest precepts"[615]. *Pacem in Terris* did not distinguish required individual attitudes in non-state relations from the attitudes required in interstate relations: "The idea that men, by the fact of their appointment to public office, are compelled to lay aside their own humanity, is quite inconceivable [because] their very attainment to this high-ranking office was due to their exceptional gifts and intellectual qualities, which

---

[612] *Pacem in Terris* pp.114

[613] *Ibid.*, pp.36.

[614] See *Pacem in Terris.*

[615] *Ibid.*

earned for them their reputation as outstanding representatives of the body politic"[616]. This position is more doctrinal than the nature of the state in international relations that we presented above. Thus, it is not the practice of the state in their interstate relations.

Turning our attention to the position of Islam and Muslim doctrine on the Westphalian state model, one should first investigate the Qur'an, *Sunnah* and *Hadith*. Islam preceded the Westpalian state model that owes its existence to the signing of the 17th century Treaty of Westphalia (1648). The word used in the Qur'an, that is close to *dawlah,* the word used to denote state in Arabic today, is *dula[617]*, and this was used in connection with economic monopoly: that is the circuit of wealth among the wealthiest. However, the Qur'an disapproved of this circuit of wealth among the wealthiest[618]. Another Qur'anic word used to denote a

---

[616] *Ibid.*, pp. 81-82.

[617] Qur'an, Al-Hashr/Exile/59:7

[618] "And What God has bestowed on His Apostle (and taken away) from the people of the townships, - belongs to God, - to His Apostle and to kindred and orphans, the needy and the wayfarer; In order that it may not (merely) make a circuit/*dulatan* (going round and round) between the wealthy among you. So take what the Apostle assigns to you, and deny yourselves that which he withholds from you. And fear God; for God is strict in Punishment" Qur'an, Al-Hashr/ Exile/59:7. If the circuit of economic power or purchasing power between the wealthy is disapproved by the Qur'an, the circuit of political power between and among the members of a single family without the consent of the ruled is also disapproved by Islam. There are many *ahadith* to that regard : "Whoever delegates a position to someone whereas he sees someone else as more competent (for the position), verily he has cheated Allah and His Apostle and all the Muslims". See Ibn Taymiyya, Assiyasah Ash-Shar'iyya, 1996. What if you seek for it and know that there are better competent people than you? This *hadith* answers the question: "Do not ask for

state, could be *balad* singular and *bilad* plural[619]. All the English translations and commentaries we consulted for these verses translate *balad* to mean either city or land. None of these terms captures the full concept of Westaphalian state model.

The Qur'an give some of the following categories for natural social settings: *dhakar wa unthaa* (male and female), *shu'ub* (nations/races/people), *qaba'il* (tribes/ethnicities)[620], and *ummah* (nation, people, generation, community)[621]. In addition to these the Qur'an also mentions *qawm* (people)[622], *qariyah*

---

a position of authority, for if you are granted this position as a result of your asking for it, you will be left alone (without God's help to discharge the responsibilities involved in it), and if you are granted it without making any request for it, you will be helped (by God in the discharge of your duties)." See Sahih Muslim.

[619] For instance Qur'an states: "They were the people who perpetrated tyranny in *bilad/* countries or cities or lands," Qur'an, Al-Fajr/The Dawn/ 89;11. The next verse in singular form is read as: "I swear by this *balad/* city or land, this *balad/* land in which you are free to dwell " Qur'an, Al-Balad/ The City/ 90:1-2.

[620] Qur'an, Hujurat/The Private Apartments/49:13: "O men! Behold, We have created you all out of a male and a female, and have made you into nations and tribes, so that you might come to know one another. Verily, the noblest of you in the sight of God is the one who is most deeply conscious of Him. Behold, God is all-knowing, all-aware".

[621] *Ummah* nation, people; generation. (see Hans Wehr, A Dictionary of Modern Written Arabic, Third Edition, 1976, page 25). Qur'an/Al-Baqara/The Cow/2:143: "Thus, have We made of you an *Ummah* justly balanced, that ye might be witnesses over the nations, and the Apostle a witness over yourselves; and We appointed the Qibla to which thou was used, only to test those who followed the Apostle from those who would turn on their heels (From the Faith). Indeed it was (A change) momentous, except to those guided by God. And never would God Make your faith of no effect. For God is to all people Most surely full of kindness, Most Merciful".

[622] Qur'an, Ash-shu'ara/The Poets/26:160. *Qawm* can mean a basic social unit based on kinship,

(village)[623], *madinah* (city)[624], *hizb* (party)[625] and *firqah* (sect).[626] However, the Qur'an mentions no clear-cut *modus operandi* and *modus vivendi* for these social categories apart from the rule of justice, enjoining what is right and eschewing *zulm* and *'udwan* (oppression and injustice). Hence, we do not see the concept of the Westphalian model of a state in the Qur'an or in the prophetic tradition. Any social settings, institutions, governments or organizations that emanate from the public consensus of its people and base their foundations on the principles of justice and righteousness can be suitable for Muslims, whether it is called a caliphate or a state, nation or *ummah*, village or town federation or confederation of states.

What is true is that the post-colonial legacy, the states Muslims live with now, are not the "organic" outgrowth of their societies. It is a European idea of a state, and a European idea of law. "Muslims in these societies have not been through the process of negotiating these questions for themselves. The colonial period was an intrusion into what might have been an organic development of

---

Fellowship, tribesmen, kinsfolk, kin, kindred; tribe, race, people. Hans Wehr, *A Dictionary of Modern Written Arabic*, Third Edition, 1976, page 800.

[623] Qur'an, Yusuf,/Joseph/12:82 .

[624] Qur'an, Yusuf,/Joseph/12:30.

[625] Qur'an, Rome/30:32.

[626] Qur'an, Rome/30:32.

state institutions"[627]. What existed in pre-colonial Muslim lands was a concept or a theory of a common good or of a commonwealth of all the Muslims living as one community under the guidance and direction of a supreme executive head, called a Caliphate, kingdom, *immamate*, *ummahood*, *sultanate*, or empire.

Under the caliphate, Muslims have the right to live their lives according to the principles of Qur'an and *Sunnah* and non-Muslims also have the right to live their lives in accordance with the dictates of their religions. The object of such a caliphate is to protect people's religious freedom, their lives, their intellects, their progeny, dignity and property. This is at theoretical level. It has not always been the case at the practical level. Muslims, after the death of Uthman, the third caliph, never lived under one single central authority. However, there is no text, either from the Qur'an or *Sunnah*, on the detailed operation of those socio-political settings such as Caliphate, kingdom, *immamate*, *ummahood*, *sultanate* and empire. They were necessitated by the circumstances as happened at a certain moment to the Europeans with the Westphalian model.

The Qur'an talks about some of the monarchies and monarchical figures such as David and his kingdom[628], Solomon and his Kingdom[629], the queen of

---

[627] Abdullahi An-na`im, Celebration of Heresy: interview with *Emory in the World* accessible at www.law.emory.edu/aannaim/pdfiles/heresy.pd

[628] Qur'an, Al-Baqara/The Cow/ 2:251: "And God gave him David the dominion and wisdom, and taught him of what He wills".

[629] Qur'an, Sad/38:35-39.

Sheeba[630], Pharaoh of Egypt[631] and others[632]. A few of the rulers mentioned in the

Qur'an were good rulers and others were cruel[633]. Ibn Khaldun described kingship

as follows: as the nature of kingship is a social necessity for people its domain is

dominium and coercion, both of which are signs of anger and bestiality and they

(kings) rule mostly in a tyrannical manner[634]. However, kings and kingdoms are

not tyrants in themselves if they rule with justice and are appointed by the consent

of the people.

The Qur'an also talks about *khalifa* in the singular and it describes

individuals such as: Adam[635] and Dawud (David)[636] for instance, but it also uses a

---

[630] Qur'an, An-Naml/ The Ant/27:22-24.

[631] Qur'an, Al-Qasasa/The Story/ 28:4 "Truly Pharaoh had exalted himself in the land and reduced its people into sects, oppressing a group of them, slaughtering their sons, and sparing their women. Indeed he was of those who cause corruption".

[632] Qur'an, Yusuf/Joseph/12: 54.

[633] Such as Pharaoh, see Qur'an, Al-Fajr/The Dawn/ 89: 6-12.

[634] Ibn Khaldun, *Muqaddimah* Vol. I. P. 326.

[635] "And when your Lord said to the angels, 'I am appointing on earth a vicegerent', they said, 'will You appoint therein one who will do corruption therein and shed blood, while we glorify You with praise and sanctify You?' He said, 'Assuredly, I know what you know not'" Qur'an, Al-Baqra/The Cow/2:30.

[636] "O David! Behold, We have made you a vicegerent on earth: judge, then, between human beings with justice, and do not follow vain desire, lest it lead you astray from the path of God: verily, for those who go astray from the path of God there is suffering severe in store for having forgotten the Day of Reckoning!" Qur'an, Sad: 26. David as biblical figure is different from Dawud as a Qur'anic figure. In chapters xi and xii. of 2 Samuel, David is associated with adultery, fraudulent dealing with one of his own servants, and the contriving of his murder. chapter xiii,

plural form referring to the people[637]. In either single or plural the condition of being *khalifah* is based on faith and righteousness[638]. The Qur'anic concept of *khalifah* here is faith in God and righteousness. Every faithful and righteous person is *khalifa* and *khilafah* vice regency (caliphate) may not necessarily refer to a single universal centralized and uniform political government over all Muslims in the world. This, if it ever happened, was destroyed with the death of Uthman Ibn Afaan who reigned from 644 to 656, a few decades after the death of the Prophet. After this period, the Muslim political system was turned into a kingdom first by Mu'awiyah, or into a dynasty by those who followed him up to the time of the Ottoman Caliphate in 1924. These kingdoms also used the same

---

describes the story of rapes, incest, and fratricide in David's own household! The Qur'anic David is an upright just man, "endowed with all the virtues, in whom even the least thought of self-elation has to be washed off by repentance and forgiveness." See Yusuf Ali's commentary on Qur'an 38:26.

[637] "To those of you who believe and keep doing pious deeds Allah has given the promise (whose fulfilment and implementation is obligatory for the *Umma* [Community]): He will surely bestow upon them *khilafa* (the trust of right to rule) as He granted (the right to) rule to those who were before them. And (through dominance and rule) He will strengthen and stabilize their *Din* (Religion) for them which He has liked for them, and (by this strength and rule) He will for sure change their former state of fear (which was due to their political, economic and social handicap) to that of peace and security. They will worship Me (fearlessly and) will not associate any partner with Me (i.e., will follow and obey only My command and system). And after this, whoever adopts ingratitude (i.e., aversion to, and denial of, My commands) it is they who will be defiant (and disobedient)". Qur'an/An-Nur/The Light/ 24:55. Muhammad Tahir-ul- Qadari's translation/interpretation.

[638] Qur'an, An-Nur/ The Light/24:55.

political will, whims and methods as those of their contemporary empires and kingdoms in other cultures and/or religions. Those powers in Muslim culture sought to gain political power and to gain territorial expansion, economic aggrandizement and latifundianism (personal wealth).

Islam sees the role and nature of states in international relations as protecting people's religious freedom, their lives, their intellects, their progeny, dignity and property. However, what Islam says may be different from what Muslims actually do. In interstate relations, Muslim majority states have no different role and nature from Christian majority states. They all look to national interest, self-preservation and power. What Christian and Muslim doctrines expect from states in international relations, is not necessarily in tandem with the role and nature of Westphalian states.

However, Christianity has accepted that states do not need to choose any one religion, and Christianity no longer discusses the laity of the state. This is not the case with some Muslim perspectives. *Pacem in Terris* takes for granted the difference in the nature and role of religious and state institutions. Its quest for peace among peoples and states is rooted in a clear distinction existing between the nature and role of religion and that of the state.

Conclusion

Pacem in Terris is a religious document promulgated by the spiritual head of Roman Catholicism: "We do not find in John XXIII an academic or diplomatic abstraction of peace, nor vague and confused wishful thinking about it. He proposes instead a spiritual revolution with a solid rational foundation accompanied by a purified faith[639]. It exhorts Catholics to work for world peace in collaboration with other 'goodwill' peacemakers who might not be Catholics.

Pacem in Terris is also a universal document, addressed to "all men of goodwill". More importantly, it is universal because of the nature of its content, searching for the establishment of a world "order" that can recognize and protect human rights and restore peace for humankind. According to Cardinal Peter K.A. Turkson, "It is universal because it derives from the irreducible human essence, whether seen in terms...of the fundamentals of human nature (a consensus that suits secular thinkers), or...of the divine origin and eternal destiny of human existence (a spiritual or religious conviction)"[640.] It is universal because "it contained something truly new: a radical re-imagining of harmony in the world founded on human relationship and dignity–so radical, indeed, that human relationships on every scale, from worldwide and among regions and major States

---

[639] Cardinal Turkson K A Peter. *"Pacem in terris* as a living document"*, Trastevere, 29 May, 2012, p. 8.

[640] Turkson Peter K.A., *op.cit.*, p. 8.

265

down to the dyad of two people, are founded on the same principles of relationship and dignity and animated by the same virtues of truth, justice, love and freedom. And most fundamentally, this is all given a transcendental starting point in God's creation of man"[641]. Furthermore, its emphasis on the common origin of humankind, on their dignity, rights and duties; its appeal for the establishment of super-national authority in the advancement of human rights and welfare, give it an intensity of privilege and universal accommodation and criticisms which earlier such pronouncements hardly get.

Pacem in Terris is a living document: its first sections on human rights can be seen in tandem with United Nations' 1948 Universal Declaration of Human rights. *Pacem in Terris* calls for the need to observe equality among nations, and for the state to be the subject of the same rights and duties as individuals. Equality among states is not realized in international relations; what exists is equity among them. Better relationships and co-operation between nations as stated in *Pacem in Terris* is still a real need. Its exhortation to Catholics to work with non-Catholics for peace and development can be applied in many places in the world.

Negotiation, dialogue and diplomacy are the means to reach settlements of international disputes and conflicts, not the force of arms. The basis of international systems, as well as their legality, is their commitment to the rule of law in international relations. This needs constant negotiation, dialogue, debate

---

[641] Cardinal K.A. Turkson Peter, *op.cit.* page 8.

and education, which in turn can facilitate ever wider commitment and acceptance of international systems. The absence of these methods undermines the credibility and viability of international systems.

There is a tendency in both religious and secular sections of world society to see international systems as somehow pathological and malign. It is very important to study the sources of these destructive attitudes and to challenge them in their own languages through debate, dialogue and negotiation. Doctrine, ideology and theology, while not in themselves pathological and malignant, can be "like nuclear energy in potency": they can be used for peacemaking, peace-building and peacekeeping, but they can also be used destructively against the international system. Knowing how to use such energies constructively is crucial for the international community which must tackle this challenge in the interest of international peace.

Pacem in Terris proposes principles such as truth, justice, liberty and charity as the core of interstate relations. These have to be supported by active solidarity, collaboration, and cooperation in seeking the common good. To facilitate the realization of the common good, *Pacem in Terris* supported a world public political authority such as the United Nations.

These positions of *Pacem in Terris* are not, in principle, at loggerheads with an Islamic perspective about the establishment of world peace. However, because the nature and the role of states in international relations are sometimes different in Christian and Islamic religious perspectives, "The nature of international diplomacy, the embedded institutional rationality, is such that it may restrain and limit the possibility to express religious views on political issues or international negotiations"[642].

Catholicism, represented by Holy See at international organizations such as the UN, is involved in the promotion of peace through the defense of human rights and the promotion of development. The Holy See is involved in the Non Proliferation Treaty (NPT), the International Agency for Atomic Energy (IAEA), the Convention on Biological Weapons (BWC), the Convention on Chemical Weapons (CWC), and the Ottawa Convention on Anti-Personnel Mines. The Holy See has supported the 2008 Oslo Convention on Cluster Munitions. Besides being involved in the UN, the Holy See signed an "Agreement of Cooperation with the Organization of African Unity" (OAU) (19 October 2000). There are many international Catholic organizations and Catholic inspired NGOs (Non-Governmental Organizations) that contribute to peacemaking and peace building nationally and internationally[643].

Islam is not represented by the Muslim majority states at the United Nations. However, Muslim majority states are also involved in peacemaking and peace-building around the globe. Many Muslims, inspired by their religion, are

---

[642] The Caritas in Veritate Foundation Working Papers "The city of God in the Palace of Nations" International Catholic Organizations & Catholic Inspired NGOs Their Contribution to the Building of the International Community, Published by Mathias Nebel, FCIV, 16 chemin du Vengeron, CH-1292 Chambésy, 2012, Editorial.

[643] *Op.cit.*

actively involved in peace work. Important contributions can be recalled from the Muslim sector to the international system and peace building operations: Abdullah bin Bayyah, one of Islam's foremost living Sunni scholars, has been involved in the reconciliation process in Somalia in his "The Somalia Declaration". Abdullahi Ahmed An-Na'im has spent the past twenty years working towards revitalization of *Shari'a* and to give it a wider legitimacy for human rights.

Fifty years after *Pacem in Terris*, some contries are still aiming at wiping out one another or at least weaking one anothers' progress and prosperty. Diseases, poverty,tyranny and genocide are still visible around the globe. Thus, the two biggest religions of the world in synergy with political leaders should immensely contribute to the establishment of peace and justice and to influence, through their interreligious dialogue, the actions of states towards saving humanity from destruction.

Establishment of national and international peace and security has long been sought for by the people of the good-will and bonafide of the world. This unceasing and indefatigable seek for peace and security should be pursued in truth, justice, charity, liberty, solidarity, collaboration, cooperation, dialogue, synergy and constructive engagement of all the people on earth. There should be neither segregation nor supremacy; neither subterfuge nor hoodwink in this process. The quests for peace and security should be palpable and stupendous for just and inclusive peace and security -not peace and security for one nation, and destruction and war for others- the world need an inclusive and comprehensive peace and security for all its people, nations and states. In this interdependent and interconnected globalized world, peace, security, stability and the progress of one nation is intrinsically entangled with many. War in one country affects the smooth operations of the international systems. Thus, it is our responsibility and those of our decision and policy makers in both public and political office to make pursuance of peace, security and tranquility in the truth and justice as their main pivotal point around which decision and policies evolve and revolve. We should promote alliance of civilization and culture- rather than clash of civilization and culture- through engagement of heart and mind rather through humiliation, deprivation, subjugation, imposition, unilateralism, intimidation and destruction.

Political and religious leaders who provide us with resolution for peace, security and prosperity for all humankind are the best of the humanity.

Bibliography and References

Church documents

1. Catechism of the Catholic Church, Libreria Editrice Vaticana, 1993

2. Compendium of the Social Doctrine of the Church, 2005, Libreria Editrice Vaticana, 2004.

3. Dialogue and Proclamation 1991 AAS 84 (1992)

4. *Lumen Gentium* 1964, in AAS 57 (1965),

5. Benedict XVI, *Caritas In Veritate*, 2009, AAS 101 (2009)

6. Benedict XVI, Westminster Hall Speech, 17 September 2010

7. Benedict XVI, Papal Address to General Assembly of Italian Bishops, 24 May 2012.

8. Giovanni Paolo II, *Discorso di Giovanni Paolo II al corpo diplomatico accreditato presso la santa sede per lo scambio degli auguri per il nuovo anno, Sabato, 10 gennaio* 1987, *Libreria Editrice Vaticana, Vaticano* 1987.

9. Giovanni Paolo II, *Discorso di Giovanni Paolo II al corpo diplomatico accreditato presso la Santa Sede , 11 gennaio* 1986.

10. *Gaudium et Spes* Pastoral Constitution on the Church in the Modern World 1965

11. Gregory XVI, *Mirari Vos* 15 August 1868, ASS 4 (1868)

12. John XXIII, *Pacem in Terris*, 1963, AAS 55, (1963)

13. John XXIII, *Mater et Magistra*,1961, AAS 53 (1961)

14. John Paul II, *Sollicitudo rei socialis* 1987, AAS 79 (1987)

15. John Paul II, *Laborem exercens*, 1981, AAS 73 (1981)

16. John Paul II, "For a World Worthy of Man", Pub. United Nations Educational, Scientific and Cultural Organization, Beugnet S.A. Paris France, 1980.

17. John Paul II's Address to the 34th General Assembly of the United Nations, New York Tuesday, 2 October 1979.

18. John Paul II, Women: Teachers of Peace, Message for the XX VIII world day of peace 1 January 1995.

19. Leo XIII, *Rerum Novarum* 15 May 1891, AAS 23 (18901891)

20. Leo XIII, *Immortale Dei,* 1885, ASS 18 (1885)

21. Paul VI, Nostra Aetate 1965, AAS 58 (1966)
    Paul VI, *Populorum Progressio*, 1967, AAS 59 (1967)
22. Paul VI, E*ecclesiam Suam* August 6, 1964, AAS 56 (I964)

23. *Paul VI, Discours du Pape Paul VI à l'Organisation des Nations Unies à l'occasion du 20ème anniversaire de l'organisation 4 octobre 1965*

24. Paul VI's 1970 January Address to the Diplomatic Corps

25. Pius XI, *Quadragesimo Anno* 1931, AAS 23 (1931),

26. Pius XII, *Ad Apostolorum Principis* 29th June 1958, AAS 50 (1958)

27. Pius XI, Quadragesimo Anno 1931, AAS 23 (1931)

28. Pius XII, *Invicti Athletae* 16 May 1957

29. Pius IX, *Quanta Cura* 1864, ASS 3 (1867)

Sacred Books

1. Bible,The New Jerusalem Bible (NJB) published in 1985.

2. Bhagavad Gita, Divine Life Society Publication, 2000. Accessible at www site: http://www.SivanandaDlshq.org/. Last accessed 10/10/2012.

3. Qur'an, Ali Yusuf Abdullah,The Meaning of the Glorious, The Islamic Bulletin. Accessible at www.islamicbulletin.org. Last accessed 06/06/2012.

4. Qur'an, Asad Muhamamad, The Message of the Qur'an. Accessible at www. Altafsir.com. Last accessed 06092012.

Religious Books

1. Bukhari Abū 'Abd Allāh Muḥammad ibn Ismā'īl ibn Ibrāhīm ibn alMughīrah ibn Bardizbah alJu'fī, *Sahih Bukhari*, Complete digitized translation of Sahih alBukhari from Muhammad Muhsin Khan. Accessible at www.sunnah.com/bukhari. Last accessed 11102012.

2. Ibn Hanbal Ahmad, *Musnad*, Darul hadith, Cairo, Islamic Education.com 2008, accessible at www.islamieducation.com. Last accessed 10252012.

3. Ibn Anas Malik, *Muwatta*, accessible at www. sunnah.com/malik. Last accessed 0513 2012.

4. Ibn Mâjah Muḥammad ibn Yazīd, *Sunan* Ibn Mâjah, accssible at www.sunnah.com/ibnmajah. Last accessed 12252012

5. Nawawi Abu Zakaria Mohiuddin Yahya Ibn Sharaf, Fourty Hadith, (40 *Hadith*). Accessible at www.http://sunnah.com/nawawi40. Last accessed 04 162013.

6. Naysaburi Abū alḤusayn ʻAsākir adDīn Muslim ibn alHajjaj, *Sahih Muslim*, accessible at www.sunnah.com/bukhari. Last accessed 11102012.

7. Saabiq Sayyid, *FiqhusSunnah*, Accessible at www.islamfuture.wordpress.com/2009/09/04/fiqhussunnahfivevolumes/. Last accessed 03042013.

8. Sulaymān ibn alAshʻath alAzdi asSijistani Abū Dāwūd , *Sunan Abū Dāwūd* Translation: Ahmad Hasan. Accessible a thttp://www.usc.edu/org/cmje/religioustexts/hadith/abudawud. Last accessed 110512.

9. Tirmidhi Abu ʻIsa Muhammad, *Jami` atTirmidhi*, acessible at http://sunnah.com/tirmidhi. last accessed 12252012.

Other Books

1. Albright Madeline, The Mighty and the Almighty: Reflections on America, God, and World Affairs, HarperCollins, New York, USA, 2006.

2. AbuNimer Mohammed, Nonviolence and Peace Building in Islam: Theory and Practice, University Press Florida, Florida, USA, 2003.

3. Abu Zahra Muhammad, Concept of War in Islam, Ministry of Waqf, Cairo, Egypt, 1961.

4. AlButi Muhammad Sa'id R., Jihad in Islam, How to Understand and Practise It. Translated and abridged by Munzer Adel Absi, Dar AlFikr Publishing House, Damascus, Syria, 1995.

5. Almawardi Abū alHasan ʿAlī ibn Muhammad ibn Habīb alBasrī, *AlAhkaamalsultaniyya walwilayatualdiniyya*, 3rd edition, Maktabatu ibn Qutaiba, Kuwait, 1973.

6. AlTabarani Sulayman b. Ahmad, *AlMu'jam AlAwsat*, Dar alHaramayn, Cairo, Egypt, 1995.

7. Anderson Benedict, Imagined Communities: Reflections on the Origin and Spread of Nationalism (New Edition), Verso, UK, 2006.

8. AnNaʿīm Aḥmad Abd Allāh, Islam and the Secular State: Negotiating the Future of *Shariʿa,* Library of Congress, USA, 2008.

9. AnNa'im Ahmed Abdullahi, African Constitutionalism and the Contingent Role of Islam. Philadelphia, University of Pennsylvania Press, Pennsylvania, USA, 2006.

10. AnNa'im Ahmed Abdullahi, Toward an Islamic Reformation: Civil Liberties, Human Rights and International Law, Syracuse University Press, Syracuse, NewYork, USA, 1990.

11. Aquinas Thomas, Summa Theologiae, Black Friars, Ontario, Canada, 1975.

12. Arbor Ann, Edmund Burke, In The beauties of the late Right Hon. Edmund Burke, selected from the writings, Pub. Ann Arbor, University of Michigan Library, Michigan, 2011. Accessed at http://quod.lib.umich.edu/e/ecco/004795912.0001.002/1:12?rgn=div1;view=fulltext. Last accessed 532013.

13. Armitage David, The declaration of independence: a global history, Harvard University Press, Cambridge, USA, 2007.

14. Armstrong David, Lorna Lloyd, John Redmond From Versailles to Maastricht: International Organisation in the Twenty First Century, Palgrave, New York, USA, 1996.

15. Ansari Muhammad FazlurRahman, The Quranic Foundations and Structure of Muslim Society volume II, Indus educational foundation, karachi, Pakistan, 1977.

16. Asad Muhammad, The Principles of State and Government in Islam, Dar AlAndalus, Singapore, 1980.

17. Asamoah Kwame Botwe, Kwame Nkrumah's politicocultural thought and policies: an Africancentered Paradigm for the Second Phase of the African Revolution, Routledge, New York, USA, 2005.

18. Bashier Zakaria, War and Peace in the Life of the Prophet Muhammad, The Islamic Foundation, Markfield, UK, 2006.

19. Barston Ronald Peter, Modern Diplomacy, Third edition, Pearson Education, UK, 2006.

20. Charfi Mohamed et al, Islam and liberty: the historical misunderstanding, Zed Books, London UK, 2005.

21. Berkey P.Jonathan, The Formation of Islam: Religion and Society in the Near East, 6001800 Cambridge University Press, Cambridge, UK, 2003.

22. Bill A. James, The Eagle and the Lion: The Tragedy of AmericanIranian Relations, Yale University Press, New Haven, USA, 1988.

23. Boucher David, Political Theories of International Relations: From Thucydides to the Present, Oxford Clarendon Press, UK, 1998.

24. Boucher David, The Limits of Ethics in International Relations: Natural Law, Natural Rights and Human Rights in Transition, Cambridge University Press, Cambridge, UK, 2009.

25. Brown Chris, Terry Nardin, Nicholas J. Rengger, International relations in political thought: texts from the ancient Greeks to the First World War, Cambridge University Press, Cambridge, UK, 2002.

26. Brown Michael E., Theories of War and Peace: An International Security Reader, MIT Press, Cambridge Mass, UK, 1998.

27. Bueno de Mesquita Bruce, The war trap, Yale University Press, New Haven, USA, 1981.

28. Bukay David, The Truth About Muhammad, Founder of the World's Most Intolerant Religion, Regnery Press, Washington DC, USA, 2006.

29. Bull Hedley, The Anarchical Society. A Study of Order in World Politics, Second Edition Columbia University Press, New York, USA, 1977.

30. Burke Edmund, (17291797) Reflections on the Revolution in France: And on the Proceedings in Certain Societies in London Relative to that Event. Printed for J. Dodsley, in Pall Mall M.Dcc.XC .

31. Burke Edmund, The works of Edmund Burke: with a memoir, Volume 1, Harper and Brothers Publisher, New York, USA, 1860.

32. Burton John, The Sources of Islamic Law: Islamic Theories of Abrogation, Edinburgh University Press, UK, 1990.

33. Cathie Carmichael, Ethnic Cleansing in the Balkans: Nationalism and the Destruction of Tradition, Volume 8 of Routledge Advances in European Politics, London, UK, 2002.

34. Chicago Global Affairs Council, Engaging Religious Communities Abroad: A New Imperative for US Foreign Policy, The Chicago Global Affairs Council, Chicago, USA, 2010.

35. Cirincione Joseph, Bomb Scare: The History and Future of Nuclear Weapons, Colombia University Press, New York, USA, 2007.

36. Clausewitz von Carl, On War, edited and translated by Michael Eliot Howard and Peter Paret, Princeton University Press, Princeton, New Jersey, USA 1989.

37. Cook David, Understanding Jihad, University of California Press, California, USA, 2005.

38. Cox Harvey, Our religions, edited by Sharma Arvind,et al. Pub.Harper Collins, New York, USA, 1993.

39. Crozier Andrew J., Causes of the Second World War, Blackwell Publishers Ltd, Oxford, UK,1997.

40. Dabashi Hamid, Authority in Islam from the Rise of Muhammad to the Establishment of the Umayyad, Transaction Publishers, New Jersey, USA,1989.

41. Dalberg John Emerich Edward, 1st Baron Acton (1834–1902), British historian. Letter, April 3, 1887, to Bishop Mandell Creighton. The Life and Letters of Mandell Creighton, vol. 1, ch. 13, ed. Louise Creighton (1904).

42. Davies Peter, Human Rights, Routledge, London, UK, 1988.

43. Dembour MarieBénédicte, Who believes in human rights?: Reflections on the European Convention, Cambridge University Press, Cambridge, UK, 2006.

44. Dicey Venn Albert, Introduction to the Study of the Law of the Constitution (LF ed.) [1915, ed. Roger Michener E. , Liberty Fund, Indianapolis, USA, 1982.]

45. Donnelly Jack, Realism and International Relations, Cambridge University Press, Cambridge, UK, 2000.

46. Duncan William, The Orations of Marcus Tullius Cicero, Volume 4 trans. By William Duncan, Sidney's press 1811 Original from the University of California, Digitized Feb 26, 2008.

47. Dunn Dennis J., The Catholic Church and Russia: Popes, Patriarchs, Tsars, and Commissars, Ashgate Publishing, Burlington, USA, 2004.

48. Dunne Tim, Inventing International Society: A History of the English School, St Antony's Series, Macmillan, London, UK, 1998.

49. Dunne Tim, Milja Kurki, Steve Smith eds., International Relations Theories: Discipline and Diversity, 2nd edition, OxfordUniversty Press, Oxford, UK, 2010.

50. Dunne Tim, Steve Smith, Amelia Hadfield eds., Foreign Policy: Theories, Actors, Cases, Oxford Universty Press, Oxford, UK, 2008.

51. Dunne Tim and Booth Ken eds., Worlds in Collision: Terror and the Future of Global Order, PalgraveMacmillan, London, UK, 2002.

52. Dunne Tim and Wheeler Nicholas J., eds. Human Rights in Global Politics, Cambridge University Press, Cambridge, UK, 1999.

53. Dupuy André, Words that Matter: The Holy See in Multilateral Diplomacy: Anthology (19702000), The Path of Peace Foundation, New York, USA, 2003.

54. Forsythe David, Human Rights and Peace International and National Dimensions, The University of Nebraska Press, Nebraska, USA, 1993.

55. Frankel Benjamin, Realism: restatements and renewal, Frank Cass and Company LTD. London, UK, 1996.

56. Gardner N.Richard, Blue Print For Peace: Being the Proposals of Prominent Americans to the White House Conference on International Cooperation, McGrawHill Book Company New York, USA,1966.

57. Garthoff Raymond L., Reflections on the Cuban missile crisis, the Brookings Institution Washington DC, USA, 1998.

58. Gauhar Altaf, Challenge of Islam, Islamic Council of Europe, UK, 1978.

59. Ghazali Abu Hamid, Ihia'Uluom Adin, (Revival of Religious learnings) translated by FazlulKarim, DarulIshaat, Keighley, UK, 1993.

60. Giandurco Joseph Robert, The Holy See as Juridical Subject "Sui Ius" in International Law, Romae, 1994.

61. Gilbert Marc Jason, The Vietnam War on Campus: Other Voices, More Distant Drums, Praeger Publisher, USA, 2001.

62. Glendon MaryAnn, Rights talk: The impoverishment of political discourse, The Free Press, Macmillan Inc., New York, USA, 1991.

63. Griffiths Martin and O'Callaghan Terry, International Relations : The Key Concepts, Routledge, New York, USA, 2002.

64. Gopin Marc, Between Eden and Armageddon: The Future of World Religions, Violence, and Peacemaking, Oxford University Press, Oxford, UK, 2000.

65. Gullen M. Fethullah, Essays, Perspectives, Opinions, Light Inc., New Jersey, USA, 2005.

66. Hamidullah Muhammad, The Emergency of Islam Lectures on the Development of Islamic WorldView, Intellectual Tradition and Policy. Translated an edited by Afzal Iqbal, Adam Publishers & Distributors, Delhi, India, 1995.

67. Hanhimäki M. Jussi, United Nations: A very Short Introduction, Oxford University Press, New York, USA, 2008.

68. Hebblethwaite Peter, John XXIII: Pope of the Council, Geoffrey Chapman, London,UK, 1984.

69. Hobbes Thomas, The Leviathans, Chapter XIV 1660, Oregon State University, accessible at http://oregonstate.edu/instruct/phl302/texts/hobbes/leviathancontents.html. Last accessed 25102012.

70. Hoffman Stanely, The State of War: Essays on the Theory and Practice of International Politics, Praeger, Calinfonia,USA, 1965.

71. Hoffman Stanely, Duties beyond Borders: On the Limits and Possibilities of Ethical International Politics, Syracuse University Press, New York, USA,1981.

72. Hoffman Stanely, World Disorders: Troubled Peace in the PostCold War Era, Updated ed. Rowman & Littlefield, Maryland, USA, 2000.

73. Hoffman Stanely, Dead Ends: American Foreign Policy in the New Cold War, Ballinger Publishing, Florida, USA, 1983.

74. Hoffman Stanely, et al, The Ethics and Politics of Humanitarian Intervention, University of Notre Dame Press, Notre Dame, USA, 1996.

75. Hooker Matheson Virginia and Saikal Amin, Islamic perspectives on the new millennium, Institute of Southeast Asian Studies, Singapore, 2004.

76. Howard Eliot Michael and Paret Peter, Carl von Clausewitz On War, Edited and translated by Princeton University Press, New Jersey, USA, 1989

77. Hyginus Eugene, The Holy See and the International Order, Colin Smythe Gerrards Cross, Buckinghamshire, England, 1976.

78. Ibn Hisham, *Siratu annabawiya*,(the Biography of the Prophet) vol. 2, DarulJiel, Beirut, Lebanon, 1975.

79. International Commission on Intervention and State Sovereignty The responsibility to protect: research, bibliography, background: Supplementary Volume 2 (ICISS) 2001.

80. International Center For Transitional Justice,Transitional Justice in the Former Yugoslavia. accessible at http://ictj.org/sites/default/files/ICTJFormerYugoslaviaJusticeFacts2009English.pdf. Last accessed 03032013.

81. Izetbegović Alija, The Islamic Declaration, Sarajevo, Bosnia and Herzegovina, 1990.

82. Kadayifci S.Ayse, Standing on an Isthmus: Islamic Narratives on Peace and War And Peace In Palestine Territories, Lexinton Books, UK, 2007.

83. Kalin Ibrahim, Islam and Peace, The Royal Aal AlBayt Institute for Islamic Thought, Amman, Jordan, 2012.

84. Khadduri Majid, The Islamic Conception of Justice, Johns Hopkins University Press, Baltimore, Maryland, USA, 1984.

85. Khadduri Majid, The Islamic Law of Nations Shaybàni's Siyar, John Hokins University Press, Baltimore, Maryland, USA, 1966.

86. Khatami Mohammad, Islam, Dialogue and Civil Society, The Foundation for the Revival of Islamic Heritage, Karachi, Pakistan, 2000.

87. King Peter, Housing, Individuals and the State: The Morality of Government Intervention, Routledge, New York, USA, 1998.

88. Koylu Mustafa , Islam and its Quest for Peace: jihad, Justice and Education, The Council for Research in Values and philosophy, Washington DC, USA, 2003.

89. Langholtz Harvey J.and Chris Stout E.,The psychology of diplomacy, Praeger, Connecticut USA, 2004.

90. Leukel Schmidt Perry, War and Peace in World Religions, SCM Press, London, UK, 2004.

91. Lewis Bernard, From Babel to Dragomans: Interpreting the Middle East, Oxford University Press, New York, 2004.

92. Luis Lugo E., Sovereignty at the Crossroads?: Morality and International Politics in the PostCold War Era Rowman and Littlefield Publisher, Maryland, USA, 1996.

93. Ma'aroof Muhammad Khalid, Afghanistan in World Politics A Study in Afghan US relations, Gian Publishing House, Delhi , India, 1987.

94. Machiavelli Nicolo, The Prince, written c. 1505, , published 1515, Translated by W. K. Marriott, The Original Version of this Text was Rendered into HTML by Jon Rolandof the Constitution Society, accessible at http://www.constitution.org/mac/prince.pdf. Last accessed 10122012.

95. Riga Peter, Peace on Earth, A commentary on Pope John's encyclical, Herder and Herder, New York, USA, 1964.

96. Mahnken G.Thomas, Technology and the American way of war Since 1945, Colombia University Press, New York, USA, 2008.

97. Matlàry Haaland Janne, When Might Becomes Human Right Essays on Democracy and the Crisis of Responsibilty, Gracewing, UK, 2007.

98. Marchione Margherita, Pope Pius XII: Architect for Peace, Paulist Press, New Jersey, USA, 2000.

99. Mbiti S.John, African religions & philosophy, 2nd edition, Heinemann publishers, New Hampshire, USA,1990.

100. McBeth Leon H., ed., A Sourcebook for Baptist Heritage, Broadman Press, Nashville, USA, 1990.

101. Mixed Blessings: US Government Engagement with Religion in Conflict Prone Settings, Centre for Strategic Studies, Washington DC, USA, 2007.

102. Mohammad Mehdi ShamsuDin, The System of Ruling and Management in Islam, DarAlMaarefa, Beirut, Lebanon, 1985.

103. Montesquieu CharlesLouis de Secondat Baron de La Brède, The Spirit of Laws, Translated by Thomas Nugent, revised by J. V. Prichard. Based on edition published in 1914 by G. Bell & Sons, Ltd., London UK. Rendered into HTML and text by Jon Roland of the Constitution Society. http://www.constitution.org/cm/sol02.htm. last accessed 12062013

104. Morgenthau Hans J., Politics Among Nations: The Struggle for Power and Peace, Fifth Edition, Alfred A. Knopf, New York, USA, 1978.

105. Morse George P. et al, Official Catholic Teaching on Catholic Education, Catholic Committed to support the Pope, Washington DC, USA, 1996.

106. Mutahhari Morteza, Jihad The Holy War of Islam and Its Legitimacy in the Quran, Translated by: Mohammad Salman Tawhidi, The Islamic Propagation Organization, Tehran, Iran, 14051985.

107. Mutua Makau, Human Rights: A Political and Cultural Critique, University of Pennsylvania Press, Philadelphia, USA, 2002.

108. Najeebabadi Akbar Shah, The History of Islam, Vol. 1. Darussalam, Int'l Publishers & Distributors, New York, USA, 2000.

109. Niou Emersion M.S., et al, The Balance of Power Stability in International systems, Cambridge University Press, Cambridge, UK, 1989.

110. Pickthall Muhammad Marmaduke,The Cultural Side Of Islam, Publishers, The Commitee of Madras Lecture in Islam, Lahore, Pakistan, 1937.

111. Plato, Republic, Book IV, with introduction and notes, T.Herbert Warren, Macmillan and Co.,London, UK, 1892. Accessible at

http://archive.org/stream/republicofpla00plat#page/n7/mode/2up. Last accessed 10 062013.

112. Qaradawi Yusuf (Sheikh), State in Islam, third edition, AlFalah Foundation for Translation, Publications & Disrtibution, , Cairo, Egypt, 2004.

113. Raymond Aron, Peace and War: ATheory of International Relations, with a new introduction by Mahoney J.Daniel and Anderson C. Brian , Transaction Publisher, New Jersey, USA, 2003.

114. Raysūnī Aḥmad, Imam AlShatibi's Theory of the Higher Objectives and Intents of Islamic Law, The International Institute of Islamic Thought, Virginia, USA, 2005.

115. Roberts Ivor, (Sir) Satow's Diplomatic Practice, 6th Edition, Oxford University Press, NewYork, USA, 2009.

116. Rizvi Sayyid Muhammad, How did Islam Spread? By Sword or By Conversion Publ. North American Shia IthnaAsheri Muslim Communities (NASIMCO) Concord, Canada, 2006.

117. Robbins Keith, The Abolition of War: the Peace Movement in Britain, 19141919, University of Wales Press, 1976.

118. Royal Aal AlBayt Institute for Islamic Thought, Jihad and the Islamic Law of War, Amman, Jordan, 2007.

119. Sa'id Jawdat, NonViolence The Basis of Setting Disputes in Islam, first Edition, Translated by Munzer A.Absi H.Hilwàni.Revised by Anas anRifa'i .Dar al Fikr, Damascus, Syria, 2002.

120. Sachar Howard M., A History of Israel From The Rise Of Zionism To Our Time, 3rd Ed. Alfred A.Knopf INC, New York, USA, 2010 .

121. Schuck M.J.,That they be one: the Social Teaching of the Papal Encyclicals17401989, Georgetown University press, Georgetown, USA, 1991.

122. Senghor Leopold, On African Socialism, trans. Mercer Cook, Praeger, New York, USA, 1964.

123. Simon Gerhard, Church, State and Oppression in the U.S.S.R., trans. By Kathleen Matchett in collaboration with Center for Study of Religions and Communism, University of California Press, Berkeley and Los Angeles, USA, 1970.

124. Stuart Mill John, On Liberty, Batoche Books Limited Kitchener, Ontario, Canada, 2001.

125. Terje Aven and Ortwin Renn, Risk Management and Governance: Concepts, Guidelines and Applications, SpringerVerlag, Berlin Heidelberg Germany, Dordrecht Netherlands, London UK, New York USA, 2010.

126. Thompson Allan, The Media and the Rwanda Genocide, Pluto Press , London England, Fountain Publishers Kampala, Uganda, 2007.

127. Todd Peters Rebecca, In Search of the Good Life: The Ethics of Globalization, Continuum International Publishing Group, New York, USA, 2004.

128. Troiani Luigi, *Regionalismi Economici e Sicurezza*, Franco Angeli, Italia, 2000.

129. Tzu Sun, Art of War, Trans. From Chinese Lionel Giles with an Introduction and Critical Notes, Department of Oriental Printed Books and Manuscripts, British Museum, London, UK, 1910.

130. University of Adelaide, Discourses of Niccolo Machiavelli on the first ten (books) of Titus Livius to Zanobi Buondelmonti and Cosimo Rucellai Chapter III. web edition published by eBooks@Adelaide. Accessible at http://ebooks.adelaide.edu.au/m/machiavelli/niccolo/m149d/. see also http://www.constitution.org/mac/disclivy.txt. last accessed 04142012.

131. Wallensteen Peter, Understanding Conflict Resolution, War, Peace and Global system, SAGE Publications Ltd , London, UK, 2007

132. Walzer Michael, Just and Unjust Wars: A Moral Argument with Historical Illustrations, fourth edition, Basic Books, New York, USA, 1977.

133. Watt Montgomery W., Muhammad at Medina, Oxford University Press, Amen House, London UK, 1956.

134. Weisbord Robert G. and Sillanpoa Wallace P., The Chief Rabbi, the Pope, and the Holocaust: an era in VaticanJewish relations, Transaction Publisher, New Brunswick, New Jersey, USA, 1992.

135. White Charles, Three years in Constantinople: or, Domestic manners of the Turks in 1844, Henry Colburn, London, UK,1846.

136. Williams Bruce, Justice and Allied Virtues Based on the Summa Theologiae of St. Thomas Aquinastreaties on Justice, IIII,qq.57122supplemented with modern sources, third edition, Pontifical University of St. Thomas Aquinas, Angelicum Rome, Italy, 2009.

137. World Commission on Environment and Development's (the Brundtland Commission) report Our Common Future, Oxford University Press, Oxford, UK. 1987.

138. Wright Quincy, A Study of War, University of Chicago Press, Chicago, USA,1964.

139. Yu Xintian, Ed., Cultural Factors in International Relations. The Council for Research in Values and Philosophy, Washington, DC, USA, 2004.

140. Zlotowitz Meir (Translator and compiler),The ArtScroll Tanach Series,The Book of Ruth, Megillas Ruth /A new translation with commentary anthologised from Talmudic,Midrashic and Rabbinic sources, Fourth impression, Mesorah Publications Ltd. Brooklyn, New York, USA, 1979.

Articles

1. Alford Helen, *"The Holy See and the PostCommunist States"*. In Oikomia February 2010 issue also available at http://www.oikonomia.it/pages/2010/2010_febbraio/editoriale.htm. last accessed 1205 2011.

2. AnNa'im Ahmed Abdullahi, *"Human Rights in the Muslim World: Sociopolitical Conditions and Scriptural Imperatives A Preliminary Inquiry"*. In Harvard Human Rights Journal Volume Three, Spring 1990.

3. AnNa'im Ahmed Abdullahi, *"The Law Applied Contextualising the Islamic Shariah"*. In A Volume in Honor of Frank E. Vogel edit. Peri Bearman etal. Publ. I.B. Tauris & Co. Ltd. 2008.

4. AnNa'im Ahmed Abdullahi, *"Arab and American revolutions in history"*, 24th February, 2011. Accessible at http://blogs.ssrc.org/tif/2011/02/24/arabandamericanrevolutionsinhistory. Last accessed 06 162011.

5. Annan A.Kofi, Annual Report to the General Assembly, 20 September 1999 accessed at http://www.un.org on 4th May 2012. Last accessed 11112012.

6. Aquinas Thomas, Commentary on the Gospel of John , 14, lecture 7, n.1962

7. AnNa'im Ahmed Abdullahi, *"Islam and Human Rights"* accessible at http://www.alfikra.org/article. Last accessed 02022012.

8. Bemporad Jack,*"Norms of War in the Jewish Tradition"*. In World Religions and Norms of War, UN Press, 2009.

9. Bigo Didier, *"Globalized (in)Security: the Field and the Banopticon"* 2006. Accessible at www.people.fas.harvard.edu/~ces/conferences/muslims/Bigo.pdf. Last accessed 04142013.

10. Bin Ali Alwazir Ibrahim, *"The Relationship Between the Ruler and the Ruled: A Mutually Obligating Agreement"*, accessilble at www.alhewar.com. Last accessed 09102011.

11. Birks John W. and Sherry Tephens L., *"Possible Toxic Enviroment following a Nuclear War,"* In The Medical Implications of Nuclear War, National Academies Press, Pages 155166.

12. Bukay David, *"Peace or Jihad: Abrogation in Islam"*. In Middle East Quarterly, Fall 2007.

13. Caldicott Helen, *"Life confronting and overcoming Deat"* a paper presented at World Council of Churches, Vancouver, Canada, 1983.

14. Campbell Francis, *"The Crown's Oldest Diplomatic Relationship Is With the Papacy"* 14th October 2010. Accessed at http://www.sces.uk.com. Last accessed 04012011.

15. Chibli Mallat, *"Islam and Public Law, Introduction: On Islam and Democracy".* In SOAS/Institut du Monde Arabe, June 1990. Accesseble at www.soas.ac.uk/cimel/materials/public.html. Last accessed 06062012.

16. Cochran John K. et al. *"SelfRestraint: A Study on the Capacity and Desire for SelfControl".* In Western Criminology Review 7(3), 27–40 (2006).

17. Crane Robert Dickson, *"Human Rights in Traditionalist Islam: Legal, Political, Economic and Spiritual Perspectives".* In The American Journal of Islamic Social Sciences 25:1 2007.

18. Del Gaudio Donna, *"The Fight against Apartheid".* In Human Rights, ed. By Peter Davies, Routledge, London, Uk, 1988.

19. Duncan Mark, *"Theonomy: What It Is; What It Is Not"*, March 29, 2000. accessible at http://www.ipc.faithweb.com. Last accesed 05152012.

20. Eisenhower Dwight D., MilitaryIndustrial Complex Speech, 1961, accessible at www.http://coursesa.matrix.msu.edu/~hst306/documents/indust.html. Last accessed 06062012.

21. Einstein Albert's Letters to President Franklin Delano Roosevelt dated 2nd August 1939. Accessible at http://hypertextbook.com/eworld/einstein.shtm. Last accessed 05132012

22. Fadel Mohammad, *"International Law, Regional Developments: Islam"*. In Max Planck Encyclopedia of Public International Law www.mpepil.com also accessible at http://www.law.utoronto.ca/documents/Fadel/Max_Planck_Final.pdf. last accessed 10062012.

23. Fox Jonathan *"The Multiple Impacts of Religion on International Relations: Perceptions and Reality"*. Accessible at http://www.ifri.org/files/politique_etrangere/4_2006_Fox.pdf. Last accessed 04062012.

24. Frame John M., *"Penultimate Thoughts on Theonomy"*. In IIIM Magazine Online, Volume 3, Number 34, August 20 to August 26, 2001.

25. Gallup International, *"Voice of the People Religiosity Around the World"* 2005, accessible at http://www.gallup.co.kr/gallupdb/reportDownload.asp?seqNo=95. Last accessed 04062013.

26. Gyekye Kwame *"Person and community: Ghanaian philosophical studies I,"*. In Cultural Heritage and Contemporary Change Series II Africa Vol.I, published with support of CIPSH/UNESCO the Council for Research and Values and philosophy Washington, 1992.

27. Hinze Firer Christian *"Women, Families, and the Legacy of Laborem ExercensAn Unfinished Agenda"*. In Journal of Catholic Social Thought 6:1, 2009.

28. Hoffman Stanely, *"International Organization and the International System"*. In International Organization, Vol. 24 No. 3 Summer, 1970.

29. Huntington Samuel P.,"*The Clash of Civilizations?*". In foreign Affairs summer 1993, accessible at http://www.foreignaffairs.com. Last accessed 05062012.

30. Iannaccone L.R., "*Voodoo Economics? Reviewing the Rational Choice Approach to Religion*". In Journal for the Scientific Study of Religion, vol. 34, n° 1, 1995.

31. Jackson Sherman, "*Jihad and the Modern World*".In The Journal of Islamic Law and Culture, vol. 7 no. 1 (2002): 126.

32. Jackson Sherman, "*Legal Pluralism Between Islam and the NationState: Romantic Medievalism or Pragmatic Modernity?*". In Fordham International Law Journal, vol. 30 no. 1 (December, 2006): 15876.

33. Jackson Sherman, "*Shari'ah, Democracy and the Modern NationState: Some Reflections on Islam, Popular Rule and Pluralism*". In Fordham International Law Journal, vol. 27 no. 1 (2004): 88107.

34. Jackson Sherman, "*Islamic Law and Jurisprudence*". Ed. N. Heer (Seattle: University of Washington Press, 1990). In the Journal of Near Eastern Studies vol. 53, no. 2 (April 1994): 6869.

35. Jackson Sherman, "*Domestic Terrorism in the Islamic Legal Tradition*". In The Muslim World, vol. 91, no. 3 and 4 (Fall 2001): 293310.

36. Judy Benjamin A., "*Conflict, PostConflict, and HIV/AIDS — the Gender Connections Women, War and HIV/AIDS: West Africa and the Great Lakes*". Accessible at http://www.rhrc.org/resources/sti/benjamin.html. Last accessed 11212010.

37. Lima Manlio, " *English Common Law and Islam: A Sicilian Connection"*, accessible at at www.bestofsicily.com/mag/art283.htm. Last accessed 06112012.

38. Makdisi A.John, *"The Islamic Origins of the Common Law"*. In North Carolina Law Review, June 1999,v77, i5, pp. 16351739.

39. Mansingh Surjit, *"India and China Today and Tomorrow"*. In The International Spectator: Italian Journal of International Affairs Volume 46, Issue 2, 2011.

40. Manzone Gianni *'La pace Della "Famiglia Umana" nell' enciclica Pacem In Terris"* In *Costruire L'unità della Famiglia Umana, l' orizzonte Profettico del Cardinale Pietro Pavan* (1903 1994). *A cura di Lino Bosio e Fabio Cucculelli,* edizioni Studium, Roma, 2004.

41. Mawdud Abu al'A'la, *Human Rights in Islam*. In Tawhid Journal, vol. IV No. 3 RajabRamadhan, 1407.

42. Munir Muhammad, *"Refugee Law in Islam",* accessible at http://works.bepress.com. Last accessed 11192012.

43. Nye Joseph S., *"Soft Power, Hard Power and Leadership"* accessible http://www.hks.harvard.edu/netgov/files/talks/docs/11_06_06. Last accessed 03162013.

44. Ottaviani Alfredo, *"A Classic Text The future of offensive war"*. In Oikonomia, accessible at www.oikonomia.it/pages/febb/classica.htm. Last accessed 01172012.

45. Onah Godfrey Igwebuike, *"The Meaning of peace in African Traditional Religion and Culture"*. In Africa World, accessible at www.afrikaworld.net/afrel/goddionah.htm. Last accessed 06122012.

46. Pew Forum on Religion and Public Life, March 21, 2007 accessible at http://www.pewforum.org. Last accessed 06122013.

47. Philpot Daniel, *"On the Cusp of Sovereignty: Lessons from the Sixteen Century"*. In Sovereignty at the Crossroads?: Morality and International Politics in the PostCold War Era, Ed. Rowman and Littlefield Publisher, Maryland, 1996.

48. Philpot Daniel, *"The Challenge of September 11 to Secularism in International Relations"* In World Politics, vol. 55, n° 1, 2002. International Studies Quarterly, International Security, and World Politics.

49. Rayan Samuel,*"International models of peace making."* In Holy Land Hollow Jubilee, God Justice and the Palestinians, (eds) , Naim Ateek and Michael prior, Milisende, London, UK, 1991.

50. Roback Alan, *"New Models Confirm Nuclear Winter"* In Bulletin of the Atomic Scientists September 1989.

51. Silvano M.Tomasi, *"Historical introduction to the Multilateral Activities of the Holy See."* Accessible at http://www.holyseemissiongeneva.org. Last accessed 08042012

52. Simon Critchley, '*Politics and Original Sin*'. In The ends of history 89.09 From hope to fear: the long two decades Of democracy and illiberalism Of capitalism and crises, Aspenia, an Aspen Istitute Italia Review Year 14n.4546 2009.

53. Sodano Angelo: *"Per la libertà ed il progresso dei popoli La Santa Sede e gli Stati postcomunisti dell'Europa a vent'anni dalla caduta del Muro di Berlino (1989 – 2009)"*. In www.Oikonomia.it, accessible at

http://www.oikonomia.it/pages/2010/2010_febbraio/PDF/03_studi_sodano.pdf. Last accessed 09112012.

54. Steinfels Peter, *"Pacem In Terris A retrospective on the 40th anniversary of Pacem In Terris"* (2003), accessible at http://vincenter.org/content/pacemterrisretrospective. Last accessed 06062013.

55. Suro Roberto, *"Pope, On Latin Trip, Attacks Pinochet Regime"*. In New York Times
Published: April 01, 1987.

56. Troger KarlWolfgang, Islam and Christian Muslim Relations: peace and Islam in theory and Practice, 199091 Vol.III.

57. Troiani Luigi, *"The war, obsolete factor in international relations"*. In Oikonomia, June 2004. Accessible at http://www.oikonomia.it. Last acessed 04032013.

58. Waltz Kenneth, *"The Spread of Nuclear Weapons: More May Better,"* Adelphi Papers, Number 171 (London: International Institute for Strategic Studies, 1981) accessible at http://www.mtholyoke.edu/acad/intrel/waltz1.htm. last accessed 10052012.

59. Weissbrodt David, *"Human Right : An Historical Perspective"* In Human Rights ed. By Peter Davies, Routledge, London Uk, 1988.

About the Author

Omar Sillah, Ph.D. is an academician and multireligious scholar. Sillah is an expert in dealing with people and their issues in a sensitive, efficacious, empathetic and reasonable manner. His interest, training and involvement include international relations, multifaith and multicultural coexistence, spirituality, peace and justice, security and conflict resolution. He holds degrees and doctorate from the Pontifical University of St. Thomas commonly known as Angelicum University, Rome, Italy. Sillah received a Master of Arts graduate degree in Religious Studies from the Institute of Interdisciplinary Studies on Religions and Culture at Pontifical Gregorian University, Rome, Italy. He received a Diploma from the School of International Politics, Development, and Cooperation (SPICES), Rome, Italy. Between 1998 2003 Mr. Sillah acquired a Higher Diploma in Islamic Sciences and M.A. (*Ustathia*) in Islamic Civilization respectively from the Superior Institutes for Islamic Civilization, Ezzaituan University, Tunis, Tunisia.

Sillah has traveled the world extensively. Born in West Africa, he had the opportunity to visit and study in North Africa and Europe. He is a family man and a strong believer in his faith. He is wellread when it comes to social, intercultural, multi religious, political, peace and security related issues. He defends his opinion and is very tolerant when it comes to others' points of view.

Sillah also acquired a graduate certificate in Religious Pluralism from the Shalom Hartman Institute, Osher Department for Religious Pluralism, Jerusalem. He holds a certificate as a Graduate Fellow from the Russell Berrie Foundation for Interreligious Dialogue, Institute for International Education and Pope John Paul II Center for Interreligious Dialogue.

www.ingramcontent.com/pod-product-compliance
Lightning Source LLC
Chambersburg PA
CBHW081423090426
42740CB00017B/3160